MW00773656

CELEBRATING THE SAINTS

The Feasts, Festivals, and Commemorations of *Lutheran Service Book*

William C. Weedon

TO MY SISTER IN CHRIST,
MY COMPANION IN THE PILGRIMAGE,
MY BELOVED WIFE: CINDI DEVRIES WEEDON

Concordia
Publishing House

Published by Concordia Publishing House
3558 S. Jefferson Ave., St. Louis, MO 63118-3968
1-800-325-3040 • www.cph.org

Copyright © 2016 William C. Weedon

All rights reserved. No part of this publication may be reproduced, stored in a retrieval system, or transmitted, in any form or by any means, electronic, mechanical, photocopying, recording, or otherwise, without the prior written permission of Concordia Publishing House.

Scripture quotations are from the ESV® Bible(The Holy Bible, English Standard Version®), copyright © 2001 by Crossway, a division of Good News Publishers. Used by permission. All rights reserved.

The quotations from the Lutheran Confessions in this publication are from *Concordia: The Lutheran Confessions*, second edition; edited by Paul McCain et al., copyright © 2006 Concordia Publishing House. All rights reserved.

Hymn texts with the abbreviation *LSB* are from *Lutheran Service Book*, copyright © 2006 Concordia Publishing House. All rights reserved.

Manufactured in the United States of America

Library of Congress Cataloging-in-Publication Data

Names: Weedon, William, author.
Title: Celebrating the saints : the feasts, festivals, and commemorations of
    Lutheran service book / William C. Weedon.
Description: St. Louis : Concordia Pub. House, 2016. | Includes index.
Identifiers: LCCN 2015049739 (print) | LCCN 2016003410 (ebook) | ISBN
    9780758651808 | ISBN 9780758651815 ()
Subjects: LCSH: Church year meditations. | Lutheran Church—Prayers and
    devotions. | Lutheran Church—Missouri Synod. Commission on Worship.
    Lutheran service book.
Classification: LCC BV4812.A1 W44 2016 (print) | LCC BV4812.A1 (ebook) | DDC
    242/.3--dc23
LC record available at http://lccn.loc.gov/2015049739

3 4 5 6 7 8 9 10   25 24 23 22 21 20

Contents

The Movable Days and Seasons of the Christian Church Year 244

INTRODUCTION

"The memory of the righteous is a blessing." (Proverbs 10:7)

The first part of the Augsburg Confession starts with the Holy Trinity and concludes with the saints. It is surely remarkable that the cult of the saints was *not* included among the abuses needing correction, but simply as part of the universal faith that the Lutherans rejoiced to receive from the ancient Church. The Apology and the Smalcald Articles make it clear that this was no carte blanche approval of ancient or medieval excesses. There were manifest abuses that had crept in and required correction. Nowhere, for example, do the Sacred Scriptures provide a command to invoke the saints, a promise about this being pleasing to God, or an example of *anyone* ever invoking the saints. The idea that the Lord Jesus needs to be made propitious toward a believer by pleading the merits of His saints is worse than blasphemy. Still, despite the abuses, Lutheran Christians knew and confessed that there was a rightful place in the life of the congregation and of the individual Christian for the remembrance of the saints.

Luther was convinced of this. He once wrote:

> We rightly honor the saints when we recognize that they are held up before us as a mirror of the grace and mercy of God. For just as Peter, Paul, and other saints like us in body, blood, and infirmity, were made blessed by the grace of God through faith, so we are comforted by their example that God will look in mercy and grace on our infirmity. . . . Honoring the saints, also, consists in exercising ourselves and increasing in faith and good works in a manner similar to what we see and hear they have done.

Similarly, Urbanus Rhegius, confessor at Smalcald, wrote:

> We should nevertheless honor the saints just as the early church honored them by respectfully celebrating their memory. It gave thanks to God for setting them free, for the grace given to them, for their blessedness, and for the excellent gifts which God through the saints poured out on the church. . . . Are not the saints the brightest mirrors of divine grace in which we see what the grace of God can do?

The Saint, *the* Holy One, of course, is our Lord Jesus. From the start, Lutheran Christians delighted to keep the yearly cycle of feasts and festivals that celebrated the grace-filled events of our Lord's life: His annunciation, visitation, nativity, circumcision, epiphany, Baptism, transfiguration, Passion, resurrection, and ascension. The life of Jesus is a gift so huge that the Church simply cannot fit it all into one celebration. It spills out across a whole year. As we live through the cycle of the Church Year, we annually witness those great events by which Christ won our salvation through the Word that is read, sung, and preached.

Yet, intertwined with the Lord's story are the stories of those who are His. We think first of His apostles (each with his own day), who above all were the witnesses to His resurrection. We remember also His friends: His holy mother; St. John the Baptist; Mary, Martha, and Lazarus; Mary Magdalene; Joseph of

Arimathea, and so many others. Nor ought we forget His ancestors, the holy patriarchs, and the faithful of the Old Testament who waited in repentance and faith for His advent. Our calendar provides an opportunity to remember all of these so that we may contemplate God's grace in their lives, see examples of faith for our own, and offer God hearty thanks.

But there's even more. From Pentecost down to this day, the Lord has continued to raise up in His Church those whose lives proclaim the triumph of His grace. As we remember this or that person from different centuries in our commemorations, we know we are recalling but the smallest piece of the marvelous story of God's love for the human race that has unfolded in the Church. There are many more whose stories we won't know until the light of eternity.

This little volume, though, is offered with the intention of at least allowing the reader to come to know and love *these* saints of the Lord Jesus a little better. The calendar of *Lutheran Service Book* introduces us to a host of pilgrims who walked the way before us.

Their holiness was no personal achievement. Most of them delighted to sing even as we do: "Thou only art holy; Thou only art the Lord, Thou only, O Christ, with the Holy Ghost, art most high in the glory of God the Father!" (*LSB*, pp. 188–89). Their holiness was always and only the righteousness of *the* Saint, the Holy One, the Lord Jesus, whose perfect obedience to His Father even to the cross God credited to them by faith. They are holy because the blood of Calvary forgave their sins. They are holy because the Holy Spirit joined them to the Savior in living faith, and so His love shone through their lives. "We love because He first loved us."

None understood this better than the eccentric Lutheran pastor Berthold von Schenk. He wrote once: "It was a sad loss to the church, a grave mistake, when a few stupid people pushed the saints out of the picture. It was a sad mistake when they took them out of the life of the church, but it was an even greater mistake to place them in the niche of supernatural people" (*The Presence*, p. 124). Von Schenk adds:

> The one essential condition in the life of every saint which made it possible for the life of heaven to begin on earth was the one thing which we seek so madly to avoid, the one universal fact which faces every single soul on earth— suffering. Not a few angel-faced, spineless people. They were human, of flesh and blood. Very human at times, beaten, wounded, scarred, for saints always bear the stigmata of their Lord. When they were persecuted, what did they do? They returned love, invincible, divine love, purified of self, and in union with their crucified Lord they received their foretaste of Heaven. This is the mystery of the cross. The saints got their love on Calvary. That is where you and I must get it too. (*The Presence*, pp. 125–26)

What wise words! The more we learn to celebrate the stories of the saints, the more we realize that we are always and only celebrating the love that shone forth from our Lord's cross. That's the literal font of all holiness.

WILLIAM WEEDON
TUESDAY OF TRINITY XIX, 2015

"Our churches teach that the remembrance of the saints is to be commended in order that we may imitate their faith and good works according to our calling."
(Augsburg Confession 21)

The Lutheran reformers understood that there was great benefit in remembering the saints whom God has given to His Church. The Apology of the Augsburg Confession (Article 21) gives three reasons for such honor. First, we thank God for giving faithful servants to His Church. Second, through such remembrance our faith is strengthened as we see the mercy that God extended to His saints of old. Third, these saints are examples by which we may imitate both their faith and their holy living according to our calling in life.

The calendar of commemorations given below lists a number of men and women from both the Old and New Testaments and from the first nineteen centuries of the Church's life. Their defense of the fundamental beliefs of the Christian faith and/or their virtuous living has caused these individuals to stand out over time as persons worthy of recognition. In every case, the purpose of our remembrance is not that we honor these saints for their own sake, but as examples of those in whom the saving work of Jesus Christ has been made manifest to the glory of His holy name and to the praise of His grace and mercy.

"Therefore, since we are surrounded by so great a cloud of witnesses, let us also lay aside every weight, and sin which clings so closely, and let us run with endurance the race that is set before us." (Hebrews 12:1)

LUTHERAN SERVICE BOOK, P. XII

1
JANUARY

On this day, the Holy Church celebrates with great joy the Feast of the **Circumcision and Name of Jesus**.

The world wakes up groggy from an evening of wild partying, ostensibly to welcome in the civil New Year. In contrast, the Church wakes up and calls her children to come together to praise God for an odd gift: the circumcision of a baby Jewish boy two millennia ago. "What?" the world asks with bleary eyes. "Are you serious?"

We are indeed. Today marks the eighth day since Christians celebrated Jesus' birth. Eight days after He was born, Mary and Joseph brought their baby boy to receive circumcision (Luke 2:21). As part of the ceremony, the child was named Jesus, meaning "the Lord saves," the very name the angel had foretold to His parents.

Jews had been circumcising their male children ever since the days of Abraham. Circumcision brought that child into God's covenant promise with Abraham, marking him as one of God's own. This people eagerly waited for God to keep the biggest part of His promise to Abraham: the day that all the families of the earth would be blessed through one of Abraham's descendants. The sign of God's promise was put, one must say, in a logical spot. They bore on their bodies a constant reminder of the promised Seed, the Savior, the Blessed One.

When Mary and Joseph had Jesus circumcised, the circumcision to end all circumcisions took place. Christ's active and passive obedience are both confessed here. Actively, the Giver of the Law humbly stooped to stand under the Law in order to fulfill it perfectly for all people. No human born from Adam in the usual way could ever do this. With His circumcision,

Remember now the Son of God
And how He shed His infant blood.
Rejoice! Rejoice! With thanks embrace
Another year of grace!
This Jesus came to end sin's war;
This Name of names for us He bore.
Rejoice! Rejoice! With thanks embrace
Another year of grace! (LSB 896:2–3)

Jesus' unbroken "yes" to the will of His Father had begun. Passively, His infant bloodshed portended a greater bloodshed to come. It foreshadowed already the blood pressed from Him in the garden, running down His face from the cruel crown of thorns, staining the wood of the cross. This was why He came: to spill His blood. That's how He would provide the covering that blots out the sin of the world. All of it. That's how the blessing would come.

In the earliest days of the Church after Pentecost, some false teachers insisted that to be a Christian a man needed to be circumcised and told to keep the Law of Moses. In a way, Paul agreed, and yet more profoundly, he disagreed. He agreed that circumcision was important, but that it only benefited the person who kept the whole Law, and did so perfectly. The only person who could do this, of course, is Jesus. When you are baptized into Him, His circumcision and perfect obedience are counted as your very own. Everything that is His is signed over to you, put to your account in the water with God's Word.

What does the circumcision of a newborn Jewish boy two thousand years ago have to do with you today? Absolutely everything!

Lord God, You made Your beloved Son, our Savior, subject to the Law and caused Him to shed His blood on our behalf. Grant us the true circumcision of the Spirit that our hearts may be made pure from all sins; through Jesus Christ, our Lord, who lives and reigns with You and the Holy Spirit, one God, now and forever. Amen.

READINGS
NUMBERS 6:22–27 / GALATIANS 3:23–29 / LUKE 2:21

11

2
JANUARY

On this day, we remember a nineteenth-century Lutheran named **J. K. Wilhelm Loehe, Pastor**.

Born in 1808, Wilhelm Loehe came to maturity at a time when the theological "leadership" of the Lutheran Church in Germany was largely in the grip of Rationalism. To give a sense of how bad that could be, one of his contemporaries (C. F. W. Walther) described hearing sermons on such stirring topics as the profitableness of raising potatoes! And it only grew worse by the year.

Yet, in this barren wasteland, the Lord raised up faithful servants, among whom was Loehe. Though he never left his German homeland, Loehe, shaped by the mind of the Church, dreamed big. His heart turned to the plight of North America. He organized the sending of pastors to help gather the many Lutheran immigrants in the new land into congregations and to begin mission work among the Native Americans in Michigan. He helped found a practical seminary to meet the massive need for pastors (Concordia Theological Seminary of Fort Wayne, Indiana, is the result of his work). He organized deaconess houses and helped the sisters to undertake all kinds of charitable work, above all caring for orphans and the aged. For Loehe, the service of love flowed naturally and inevitably from the Divine Service.

He wrote an explanation to Luther's Catechism, revised the liturgy, and published a popular prayer book, *Seedgrains of Prayer.* Perhaps his greatest work is *Three Books on the Church.* In it, he provides a thoughtful meditation on the glory of the Bride of the Christ and the role of the Lutheran Church within the church catholic.

One thing's needful; Lord, this treasure
*   Teach me highly to regard.*
All else, though it first give pleasure,
*   Is a yoke that presses hard!*
Beneath it the heart is still fretting and striving,
No true, lasting happiness ever deriving.
*   This one thing is needful; all others are vain—*
*   I count all but loss that I Christ may obtain!* (LSB 536:1)

He died January 2, 1872, having served his beloved parish in Neuendettelsau for some thirty-five years. Today's prayer comes from his hand.

Most glorious Trinity, in Your mercy we commit to You this day our bodies and souls, all our ways and goings, all our deeds and purposes. We pray You, so open our hearts and mouths that we may praise Your name, which above all names is holy. And since You have created us for the praise of Your holy name, grant that our lives may be for Your honor and that we may serve You in love and fear; for You, O Father, Son, and Holy Spirit, live and reign, one God, now and forever. Amen.

6
JANUARY

With overflowing joy, the Church of Jesus Christ celebrates today the feast of His glorious **Epiphany**.

Epiphany is the feast of light. Originally, this feast celebrated all the ways that our Lord revealed His glory, showing that He was indeed "God of God, Light of light, very God of very God." Epiphany gathered into one celebration our Lord's birth, the visit of the Magi and the mysterious star, Jesus' Baptism, and the miracle at Cana. Gradually across the centuries, the other events spun off to their own feasts, leaving for this day just the Wise Men and the star.

Perceptively, Luther noted that the star didn't actually get the job done. It announced to those ancient stargazers *that* a king had been born to the Jews. But it didn't tell them *where* to find Him. Using human reason, they trotted off to the logical spot, Jerusalem, only to find business as usual and no one celebrating the birth of a king.

Nature, and even a miracle such as this star, only gets you so far. The Scriptures, however, can get you all the way to where the child may be found. King Herod asked the scribes about the ancient prophecy, and they answered from Micah: "In Bethlehem of Judea." That's where the promised king would be born when He came. With the prophecy tucked into their hearts, the Magi journeyed toward the city of David. And suddenly the star they had seen when it rose reappeared, and this time it led the way to the house where the child and His mother were found.

There the visitors from the east opened their gifts and gave the child gold, frankincense, and myrrh. Long has the Church seen in these presents a mysterious confession. Gold confesses the child to be a king. Frankincense

The eastern sages saw from far
And followed on His guiding star;
And, led by light, to light they trod
And by their gifts confessed their God. (LSB 399:2)

---

confesses Him to be God Himself in our flesh. And myrrh? That is the oddest gift, for it confesses His death: He came to be a sacrifice, to offer His life on our behalf.

The Church rejoices on Epiphany at the way God threw open the door of His grace to Gentiles, to non-Jews, as the Magi are traditionally regarded. For the Christ Child is King of all people, not just God's ancient people! He is God come in the flesh to battle the enemies of the entire human race. The sacrifice He will offer is in exchange for every human. When the Magi kneel before Him in worship, they are but the very first of countless non-Jews who will fall before Him century after century.

Did they have the experience so many have had in all those years? That while they offered Him gifts, the feeling that the gift exchange was all backward? He had come to offer them and us the true and lasting gifts: His embrace, His welcome, His forgiveness and love. Here is the light that shines more brightly than the miraculous star. Here is the light of divine love shining from the face of Mary's Son.

O God, by the leading of a star You made known Your only-begotten
Son to the Gentiles. Lead us, who know You by faith, to enjoy in heaven the
fullness of Your divine presence; through the same Jesus Christ, our Lord,
who lives and reigns with You and the Holy Spirit, one God, now and forever.
Amen.

READINGS
ISAIAH 60:1–6 / EPHESIANS 3:1–12 / MATTHEW 2:1–12

10
JANUARY

On this day, the Church remembers three great theologians from the fourth century AD: **Basil the Great of Caesarea, Gregory of Nazianzus,** and **Gregory of Nyssa, Pastors and Confessors.**

The three men commemorated this day are two brothers (Basil, bishop of Caesarea, and Gregory, bishop of Nyssa) and a close friend (Gregory, bishop of Nazianzus). They collectively are known as "the Cappadocian fathers" since they grew up together in Cappadocia (all born around AD 330) and were steadfastly and stubbornly united in their orthodox confession of the blessed Trinity.

Toward the end of his little work *De Spiritu Sancto* (*On the Holy Spirit*), in which he defended the true deity of the Third Person of the Trinity, St. Basil penned these words: "I was taught too by the children at Babylon, that, when there is no one to support the cause of true religion, we ought alone and all unaided to do our duty. They from out of the midst of the flame lifted up their voices in hymns and praise to God, reeking not of the host that set the truth at naught, but sufficient, three only that they were, with one another" (par. 79). Though they often felt quite lonely in their struggle, these three confessors of the blessed Trinity constantly called the faithful of the Church to join them in glorifying the Father, the Son, and the Holy Spirit, of one nature, equal in majesty, though three distinct persons. No wonder Basil saw in the three children a picture of himself, his brother, and their dear friend! As the Hebrew children would not bend the knee to idolatry, neither would they.

Gregory of Nazianzus, who ended up as the Patriarch of Constantinople, was famous in his own day for preaching the Word with eloquence. Gregory

Triune God, be Thou our stay;
*   O let us perish never!*
Cleanse us from our sins, we pray,
*   And grant us life forever.*
Keep us from the evil one;
*   Uphold our faith most holy,*
*   And let us trust Thee solely*
*   With humble hearts and lowly.*
Let us put God's armor on,
*   With all true Christians running*
*   Our heav'nly race and shunning*
*   The devil's wiles and cunning.*
Amen, amen! This be done;
*   So sing we, "Alleluia!"* **(LSB 505)**

---

of Nyssa, though in many ways the most speculative of the Cappadocians, almost sounds like Luther when he exhorts his adversaries: "Let the inspired Scripture, then, be our umpire, and the vote of truth will be given to those whose dogmas are found to agree with the Divine words."

Almighty God, You revealed to Your Church Your eternal being of glorious majesty and perfect love as one God in a Trinity of persons. May Your Church, with bishops like Basil of Caesarea, Gregory of Nazianzus, and Gregory of Nyssa, receive grace to continue steadfast in the confession of the true faith and constant in our worship of You, Father, Son, and Holy Spirit, who live and reign, one God, now and forever. Amen.

18
JANUARY

On this day, the Church celebrates what was anciently called the Chair of St. Peter, now called the **Confession of St. Peter**.

"But who do you say that I am?" Jesus asked the twelve disciples, and the question is put to every generation since.

Peter and the others had seen Jesus do ordinary human things. They saw Him eat and drink, grow tired and sleep, tell stories, and even pray. But they'd also seen Him do things that no other human being *could* do. He walked on water as though it were dry land! He commanded the winds and they obeyed! He multiplied a handful of food to feed vast multitudes. He spoke words of truth that cut to the heart like no one ever did. Who is this, then?

Peter spoke up for the Twelve and for all Christians across the ages: "You are the Christ, the Son of the living God." That is, You are the one for whom Your people have long waited. You are the promised King of Israel from David's line. You are one of us and yet You are so much more. You really are the Son of the living God. You are God and man together as one, come to save us.

Jesus responded, "Blessed are you, Simon Bar-Jonah! For flesh and blood did not reveal this to you, but My Father who is in heaven." This is the same as St. Paul's observation in 1 Corinthians 12: "No one can say 'Jesus is Lord' except in the Holy Spirit." No one figures out who Jesus is by exercising their own ingenuity. This conviction that Jesus is God's own Son, showing up in our human flesh, filled to the brim with divine life, always comes as revelation from the blessed Trinity.

This is the confession celebrated today, the confession on which Christ Himself builds His Church. Against it the gates of hell don't stand a chance.

Built on the Rock the Church shall stand
Even when steeples are falling.
Crumbled have spires in ev'ry land;
Bells still are chiming and calling,
Calling the young and old to rest,
But above all the souls distressed,
Longing for rest everlasting. (LSB 645:1)

Through this confession, the Holy Spirit still calls and gathers, enlightens and sanctifies believers. Through it, He binds hearts to their Savior and builds up the Church as the very temple of God upon earth.

The Church isn't founded, then, on the person of St. Peter or any of the other apostles. Good thing, too! Recall that right after making his confession, Peter tries to rebuke his Lord for saying He must go to Jerusalem to die. Jesus then rebukes Peter! No, the Church is founded upon the *truth* that the heavenly Father put into Peter's mouth that day in Caesarea Philippi: "You are the Christ, the Son of the living God." That confession saves the one who believes it. The ministry of that confession is indeed the very rock on which Christ continues to build His Church, and before that confession hell's gates still tremble!

Heavenly Father, You revealed to the apostle Peter the blessed truth that Your Son Jesus is the Christ. Strengthen us by the proclamation of this truth that we, too, may joyfully confess that there is salvation in no one else; through the same Jesus Christ, our Lord, who lives and reigns with You and the Holy Spirit, one God, now and forever. Amen.

READINGS
ACTS 4:8–13 / 2 PETER 1:1–15 / MARK 8:27–35 (36–9:1)

20
JANUARY

Today, we rejoice to remember the Lord's handmaiden **Sarah**, wife of Abraham and ancestress of the Messiah.

Just when some might be thinking about a bit of blissful retirement, Sarai's big adventure begins. She and her husband, Abram, had never been blessed with children. They doted a bit on Abraham's nephew, Lot. He was, Sarai must have thought, the nearest she'd ever come to having a son.

But then God speaks to her husband, and their entire life is turned upside down. She learns that she's moving. Where? God would let them know when they got there. She learns that God has promised that she and her husband would have children (though up until that time, Sarai was barren, unable to bear a child). She also learns that God intended to give to her offspring the land of Canaan, where a child born of her lineage would bring blessing to all the families of the earth. She even got a new name: Sarah.

It was all a bit much to swallow, but she followed her husband obediently. Walking together in faith, they learned that the living God takes delight in doing what seems to our minds to be utterly impossible. That is how He teaches His children to trust His promises, not their own wisdom, and receive from Him every good thing. But this walk is not a single, steady ascent. It's no victory march. It has its ups and downs. Sarah knew them all.

When famine sent them into foreign lands, her husband, in fear and doubt about God's protection, passed her off more than once as merely his sister. God intervened and Sarah's honor was protected. As the years passed and no child appeared, Sarah suggested that Abraham should take her maid and have a child with her. Abraham did so, but again God intervened and showed that this was not how He would keep His promise. It wasn't until every earthly avenue had been closed to them that the blessed Trinity

A noble army, men and boys,
  The matron and the maid,
Around the Savior's throne rejoice,
  In robes of light arrayed.
They climbed the steep ascent of heav'n
  Through peril, toil, and pain.
O God, to us may grace be giv'n
  To follow in their train! **(LSB 661:4)**

---

appeared and announced the fulfillment of the promise within the year. Sarah, hiding in the tent, couldn't keep from laughing upon hearing the announcement. She was old and saw no way she'd ever conceive.

God, though, had the last laugh as Sarah miraculously conceived in her old age and gave birth to a little boy. They named him Isaac, which means "laughter." God hadn't needed them to figure out for Him how to keep His promises after all! Sarah laughed again at how everyone would join her mirth at this most ridiculous situation. What is impossible for humans is never impossible for God. Nothing is more certain than His promises to us. Sarah learned this and laughed with delight. We remember and rejoice!

Lord and Father of all, You looked with favor upon Sarai in her advanced years, putting on her a new name, Sarah, and with it the promise of multitudinous blessings from her aged womb. Give us a youthful hope in the joy of our new name, being baptized into the promised Messiah, that we, too, might be fruitful in Your kingdom, abounding in the works of Your Spirit; through Jesus Christ, our Lord, who lives and reigns with You and the Holy Spirit, one God, now and forever. Amen.

24
JANUARY

Today, the Church delights to celebrate the companion of St. Paul, **St. Timothy, Pastor and Confessor**.

The Festivals of St. Timothy and St. Titus cluster around that of St. Paul's conversion. This is most fitting, since both were close companions of the great apostle to the Gentiles. They labored with him to preach the saving Gospel.

St. Paul first encountered Timothy on his second missionary journey. He soon took the young man under his wing as pastor and missionary in training (see Acts 16:1–3). St. Timothy had a Jewish mother, but his father was a Greek. In order to use him most efficiently for the ministry that St. Paul envisioned among the Jewish communities, he circumcised him.

Despite his previous lack of circumcision, his faithful mother, Lois, and grandmother Eunice raised Timothy in a faith-filled home. They loved the Word of God and had carefully nurtured the lad in the faith. They had taught him the promises and songs of the Holy Scriptures. He knew the story of God's people. Paul would later praise this godly heritage that shaped Timothy: "From childhood you have been acquainted with the sacred writings, which are able to make you wise for salvation through faith in Christ Jesus" (2 Timothy 3:15).

St. Paul's great love for Timothy, whom he called his son in the faith, resulted in the two letters in the New Testament that bear Timothy's name. These crucial writings provide us with invaluable information about the shape of church life during the later apostolic age. In them, we see that each local community had a pastor who worked with others to oversee the life of the congregation. These men above all labored in teaching and preaching, but they also administered a lively ministry of mercy together with deacons.

On what has now been sown
Thy blessing, Lord, bestow;
The pow'r is Thine alone
To make it sprout and grow.
Do Thou in grace the harvest raise,
And Thou alone shalt have the praise! (LSB 921:1)

They were, like St. Timothy, to devote themselves to the reading of the Word of God so that they could rebuke and comfort with full assurance.

The early tradition of the Church suggests that St. Timothy was with St. Paul in Rome when the great apostle was at last beheaded for his unwavering confession of Christ. Afterward, St. Timothy is said to have returned to Ephesus in Asia Minor, there serving as bishop until he also was granted a martyr's death toward the very end of the first century AD.

Lord Jesus Christ, You have always given to Your Church on earth faithful shepherds such as Timothy to guide and feed Your flock. Make all pastors diligent to preach Your Holy Word and administer Your Means of Grace, and grant Your people wisdom to follow in the way that leads to life eternal; for You live and reign with the Father and the Holy Spirit, one God, now and forever. Amen.

READINGS
ACTS 16:1–5 / 1 TIMOTHY 6:11–16 / MATTHEW 24:42–47

25
JANUARY

Today, we rejoice to remember the **Conversion of St. Paul**, when Christ brought him out of darkness and began to make him a witness to the Light.

He'd been so utterly convinced that it was a fraud, a dangerous fraud. He'd believed it was his calling and duty to stamp out the deception spread by those belonging to the Way wherever he found it. He'd already caused all kinds of suffering for the Christians in Jerusalem and the surrounding area. But in his zeal, it wasn't enough to stamp it out in Jerusalem. The supposed heresy was spreading like gangrene and, like gangrene, required desperate measures. With zeal for the truth and for upholding the honor of the God of Israel, Saul was riding toward Damascus with letters of authority in hand. He fully intended to arrest and haul back to Jerusalem any of these followers of Jesus that he found there.

Yet, in one swift encounter, all Saul's certainties crumbled to the ground. A bright light knocked him flat on his face and blinded his eyes. And he heard a voice. A voice of unspeakable tenderness and mercy addressed him: "Saul, Saul, why are you persecuting Me?" In terror, unable to see in the bright light who was speaking to him, yet no doubt with a sense of foreboding, he asked, "Who are You, Lord?" Then the One he dared to declare mere deception and fraud spoke. "I am Jesus, whom you are persecuting."

Conversion means turning. In that encounter with the risen Lord Jesus, Saul's life would begin to turn around. Instead of opposing and fighting Christians, this formerly persecuting and hate-filled man would become the Lord's chosen vessel to bring to all people the joy and light of Christian hope. "Jesus is Lord" would become his constant message. "Christ crucified,

Praise for the light from heaven
And for the voice of awe;
Praise for the glorious vision
The persecutor saw.
O Lord, for Paul's conversion,
We bless Your name today;
Come shine within our darkness
And guide us on our way. (LSB 517:12)

---

risen, returning in glory" would become his constant theme. Who would imagine such a thing? Only the God of grace!

Saul, turned to the great apostle Paul, would never cease to marvel at this grace of the Lord Jesus in welcoming even a servant such as he. If this "chief of sinners" can be the Lord's, so can any sinner. If He can turn around someone like Saul, then who is there that is beyond the hope of repentance? There is not one! For that, all glory to the Savior's grace, all glory to the love that turns and captures hearts to do His bidding!

Almighty God, You turned the heart of him who persecuted the Church and by his preaching caused the light of the Gospel to shine throughout the world. Grant us ever to rejoice in the saving light of Your Gospel and, following the example of the apostle Paul, to spread it to the ends of the earth; through Jesus Christ, Your Son, our Lord, who lives and reigns with You and the Holy Spirit, one God, now and forever. Amen.

READINGS
ACTS 9:1–22 / GALATIANS 1:11–24 / MATTHEW 19:27–30

26
JANUARY

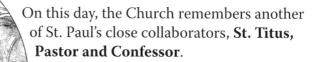

On this day, the Church remembers another of St. Paul's close collaborators, **St. Titus, Pastor and Confessor**.

Clustering around the Festival of St. Paul's conversion are two of his close companions: St. Timothy and St. Titus. Unlike Timothy's Jewish background (on his mother's side), Titus was a Gentile convert to Christianity. The little we know of him comes from almost incidental mentions in Acts and in Paul's Epistles.

From Galatians 2, we learn that Titus accompanied Paul and Barnabas on a trip up to Jerusalem and he became a famous case in point. The Gospel Paul proclaimed did not require that those turning to Christ from the Gentiles should first become Jews and accept circumcision. Rather, by Baptism they were given all that was Christ's and were adopted into the family of God. Paul pointed out that the apostles in Jerusalem so concurred with this approach that Titus was not compelled to receive circumcision "though he was a Greek" (a Gentile).

Though it is not clear from Acts if Titus came along on the earlier missionary journeys, he is mentioned by name as being part of the third great missionary journey. Paul used him to help in the gathering of the offering from the Corinthians and gave him high praise. "As for Titus, he is my partner and fellow worker for your benefit" (2 Corinthians 8:23). Paul rejoices that God had put into Titus's heart "the same earnest care I have for you" (2 Corinthians 8:16). Paul speaks of being distressed when he came to Troas because he didn't find Titus there (2 Corinthian 2:13) and how when Titus finally arrived he was comforted (2 Corinthians 7:6). In the letter that bears Titus's name, Paul affectionately calls him, "Titus, my true child in

Amen, Lord Jesus, grant our prayer;
Great Captain, now Thine arm make bare,
  Fight for us once again.
So shall Thy saints and martyrs raise
A mighty chorus to Thy praise,
  Forevermore. Amen. (LSB 666:4)

---

a common faith" (Titus 1:4). At the end of 2 Timothy, St. Paul longingly speaks of the absence of his dear friend who has gone to Dalmatia. In Titus 3:12, he begs Titus, who had been setting things in order in the Church on Crete, to do his best to rejoin Paul at Nicopolis, where he planned to spend the winter.

All in all, the portrait that emerges here is of an energetic young pastor and missionary. Titus was a true kindred spirit to St. Paul in zeal for spreading the Gospel and loving the people of God. According to early tradition, after the death of Paul, St. Titus returned to Crete. There he finished his ministry, serving as bishop of the Church where he had labored in earlier years. Like his great mentor, he is said to have sealed his ministry with his own martyr's death around AD 96.

Almighty God, You called Titus to the work of pastor and teacher. Make all shepherds of Your flock diligent in preaching Your Holy Word so that the whole world may know the immeasurable riches of our Savior, Jesus Christ, who lives and reigns with You and the Holy Spirit, one God, now and forever. Amen.

READINGS
ACTS 20:28–35 / TITUS 1:1–9 / LUKE 10:1–9

27
JANUARY

This day the Holy Church remembers **St. John Chrysostom, Preacher**.

St. John was born in Antioch sometime before AD 350 and was instructed in the faith early by his godly mother, Anthusa. After being ordained a presbyter of the church, he became famous for his sermons in his hometown. He preached with power from the Holy Spirit and had the gift of expressing the truth of God with both beauty and straightforwardness. He tended to preach without allegorical elaboration.

His famous preaching resulted in him being elected bishop of Constantinople in the fall of AD 397, where he continued to speak the Word of God with such sweetness that he won the name "Chrysostom" or "golden-mouth." To this day, his many sermons provide valuable insight into the Bible. Luther frequently cited him. One of the themes that John never tired of hammering home from Scripture was the privilege of loving the poor and providing their needs, constantly warning against the snare of riches.

As a faithful teacher of the Church, John preached the free salvation of Christ: "God was about to punish them, but He did not do it. They were about to perish, but in their stead He gave His own Son and sent us as the heralds to proclaim the cross" (*Treasury of Daily Prayer*, p. 1157). His confidence in the Scripture's truth shines in Sermon 33 on Acts: "No doubt: this is in our favor, for if we told you to be persuaded by arguments, you might be perplexed: but if we bid you believe the Scriptures, and these are simple and true, the decision is easy for you. If any agree with the Scriptures, he is the Christian."

John was not only an extraordinary preacher but also a gifted liturgist. The most common liturgy used to this day among the Eastern rite Christians

Glory be to Him who loved us,
Washed us from each spot and stain;
Glory be to Him who bought us,
Made us kings with Him to reign!
Glory, glory
To the Lamb that once was slain! **(LSB 506:2)**

---

is the Divine Service that he is said to have authored. The preface in that liturgy shows the golden-mouth at his very best: "You brought us into being out of nothingness and, when we had fallen, You raised us up again. You did not cease to do everything until You had brought us into heaven and given us Your kingdom which is to come. For all these things we thank You and Your only-begotten Son and Your Holy Spirit."

John's determination to reform the Church and the Byzantine court ran into no little opposition with the governing authorities. Finally, his preaching against the erection of a silver statue of the empress Eudoxia resulted in exile. He died in that exile at the town of Comana on September 14, 407. His final words reportedly were, "Glory to God for all things!" On January 27, 438, his bones were finally brought back to Constantinople, where he had served as bishop years earlier.

O God, You gave Your servant John Chrysostom grace to proclaim the Gospel with eloquence and power. As bishop of the great congregations of Antioch and Constantinople, he fearlessly bore reproach for the honor of Your name. Mercifully grant to all bishops and pastors such excellence in preaching and fidelity in ministering Your Word that Your people shall be partakers of the divine nature; through Jesus Christ, our Lord, who lives and reigns with You and the Holy Spirit, one God, now and forever. Amen.

2
FEBRUARY

Today, the Church remembers and thanks God for the
Purification of Mary and the Presentation of Our Lord.

They brought the offering of the poor. They could only afford the turtledoves. But it was an offering commanded in the Law—for the life of every firstborn Israelite belonged to Yahweh and had to be redeemed, ever since the firstborn of Egypt died in the exodus. Yet, even as they purchased the offering and entered the temple precincts, they knew that the real offering was not the birds, but the babe. He would be the Offering to end all offerings. In Him, the Law would be fulfilled. They thought that they and a handful of others were the only ones in the know.

But then they see him—according to tradition, an old man. He is not looking at them. He is looking at the babe in Mary's arms. And he is coming across the courtyard with the familiar look on his face. Mary had seen it before. It was on the face of Elizabeth when she had looked in awe at Mary's swelling womb. It was on the face of the shepherds when they knelt beside the manger. Now it is on the face of this old man as he hurries toward them, aged arms outstretched, reaching for the child.

Simeon holds the child, looks into His infant face, and he begins to pray. Not to any other, but to Him, to the child in his arms: "Now, Lord! Now You can let your servant go in peace. I've seen Your salvation. A light for the Gentiles. Glory for your people Israel."

Which is all to say, "I can just die now." Now that I know that the Death of death lives and breathes on earth, I have no fear. How could I fear the displeasure of God when I see the irrefutable testimony of His love right here in my arms? God so loved the world that He gave His only-begotten Son. Gave Him into the flesh.

In the arms of her who bore Him,
Virgin pure, behold Him lie
While His aged saints adore Him
Ere in perfect faith they die.
Alleluia, alleluia!
Lo, the incarnate God Most High! (LSB 519:2)

It was surely a stroke of genius when some long-forgotten Lutheran suggested that the words of Simeon were the perfect words to sing when we come back from partaking of the Eucharist. Having received the body and blood of Him whom Simeon held all those centuries ago, we pray with him, "It's okay, Lord. I can just die now. Take me home! I've seen Your salvation. I've tasted Your life. My sins are forgiven. My death is destroyed. I have nothing to fear because You have given yourself to me entirely. I can go home right now."

Almighty and ever-living God, as Your only-begotten Son was this day presented in the temple in the substance of our flesh, grant that we may be presented to You with pure and clean hearts; through Jesus Christ, our Lord, who lives and reigns with You and the Holy Spirit, one God, now and forever. Amen.

READINGS
1 SAMUEL 1:21–28 / HEBREWS 2:14–18 / LUKE 2:22–32 (33–40)

5
FEBRUARY

Today, the Church remembers the ancestor of Christ, the holy patriarch **Jacob (Israel)**.

Jacob was a quiet man. He was the sort who enjoyed staying home and fixing food, rather than ranging about and hunting. It must have been terrifying when he had to leave that home to escape his brother's murderous plans. But God comforted him with a remarkable vision. In a dream he saw a ladder or stairway from heaven to earth, angels ascending and descending on it. Above it stood the promising God. The God of his fathers, Abraham and Isaac. God promised the frightened Jacob that He would be with him, never forsaking him, until he is brought safely home.

Jacob woke from the dream and promptly missed the whole point. He was lying down and looking up with his head on the stone. He thought the ground he slept on must be holy at that spot, where he saw the ladder reach up into heaven. What's holy, though, is not so much the ground as the man who was lying on the ground. Jacob is one of the rungs in the ladder by which the God of Abraham would step down from heaven to earth in human flesh to truly be with us, Immanuel. He's one of the rungs by which God would enter history to bring His own safely home. Jacob, not the ground, is holy. His holiness is not due to any of Jacob's own actions, but solely due to his Lord's choosing. He is holy, that is, set apart for the Lord's great purpose for salvation. Angels go up and down those stairs, accompanying the whole glorious condescension, the story of Israel!

Some people think the Church is "holy ground," "the house of God," "the gate of heaven." They are right, of course. But it is such not because of any given location on the earth, but because of the Person about whom we

O Father, light from heaven send;
As morning dew, O Son, descend.
Drop down, you clouds, the life of spring:
To Jacob's line rain down the King. (LSB 355:2)

---

gather there. That Person is the God of Abraham, Isaac, and Jacob. He took the final step off the last rung, the blessed Virgin, and stepped out upon this earth, the God who will not leave us or forsake us until He has brought us home again. Our Lord Jesus Christ is the promised offspring through whom all the families of the earth will be blessed. He is the union of heaven and earth. He is both God and man in one person, and by His holy cross and Passion He has flung open wide the kingdom of heaven to all believers.

Not the place, then, Jacob, but you. *You.* Your flesh and blood—one of the ancestors of the long-expected Christ; one of the precious rungs by which the eternal Word stepped down into human flesh. Glory to You, O Christ, the God of Jacob and yet his descendant! Glory to Your condescension!

O Lord Jesus, Your ancestor Jacob wrestled with God and would not let Him go until he had been blessed, thus winning the name Israel. Give to all who have been baptized into You a faith like Jacob that holds tightly to You and Your promises in all adversity, obtains great blessings, and finally looks upon the face of God and lives. Amen.

10
FEBRUARY

On this day, the Church remembers **Silas, Fellow Worker of St. Peter and St. Paul**.

Silas (or Silvanus, in its Latin form) was a companion of St. Paul from the inception of Paul's second missionary journey and later became a secretary for St. Peter as well (see 1 Peter 5:12). The young man shared in the various hardships of the Gospel. He learned early and well from the apostles that through many tribulations we enter the kingdom of God.

Acts 16 records one of the most stirring scenes in the New Testament. Paul and Silas, in answer to the famous Macedonian summons, had crossed for the first time with the Good News into the continent of Europe. They made their way to the Roman colony of Macedonia, where the Lord opened Lydia's heart to hear and believe the Gospel. They proceeded to anger some local businessmen by driving out a demon from a slave girl, who as a fortuneteller had been a source of revenue for them. Now she was, in their eyes, worthless. They demanded the arrest of Paul and Silas and a thorough beating by the magistrates. "These men are Jews, and they are disturbing our city. They advocate customs that are not lawful for us as Romans to accept or practice" (Acts 16:20–21). The crowd joined in the fray, and Silas and Paul were finally hauled off for further punishment by beating with rods and handed over to the town jailer. They were locked in stocks in the deepest and darkest part of the prison.

What they proceeded to do shows how serious Paul was when he wrote, "Rejoice always!" About midnight, Silas and Paul were awake, keeping vigil in prayer and song. They sang their hymns to God, and God answered. A mighty earthquake shook the prison, and miraculously all the doors were opened and every man's bonds loosed. Afraid that his charges had gotten away, the jailer was prepared to kill himself. Paul called out from inside that all were accounted for and he had no reason to fear.

When life's troubles rise to meet me,
  Though their weight
    May be great,
They will not defeat me.
God, my loving Savior, sends them;
  He who knows
    All my woes
Knows how best to end them. (LSB 756:2)

The jailer called for lights and prostrated himself before Silas and Paul: "Sirs, what must I do to be saved?" Then came their beautiful answer, "Believe in the Lord Jesus, and you will be saved, you and your household." Luke records that Silas and Paul spoke the Word to the jailer and in great joy the man received Holy Baptism.

Silas, then, was not merely a man to keep Paul company. He was truly a co-worker in the apostolic endeavor, a fellow speaker of God's gracious promises in Christ to any who would hear and give heed. And for his service in bringing the Gospel to foreign lands, we give God thanks and praise.

Almighty and everlasting God, Your servant Silas preached the Gospel alongside the apostles Peter and Paul to the peoples of Asia Minor, Greece, and Macedonia. We give You thanks for raising up in this and every land evangelists and heralds of Your kingdom, that the Church may continue to proclaim the unsearchable riches of our Savior, Jesus Christ, who lives and reigns with You and the Holy Spirit, one God, now and forever. Amen.

13
FEBRUARY

This day, the Holy Church remembers the companions and co-workers of St. Paul **Aquila, Priscilla, and Apollos**.

The first mention of Aquila and Priscilla is in Acts 18. St. Paul had journeyed from Athens to Corinth. There in that bustling seaport, he happened upon these two devout Jews, who opened their home to him. Emperor Claudius had just recently driven all the Jews out of the empire's capital with the result that these two landed in Corinth about the same time as Paul. As newcomers to Corinth, fellow Jews, and people of the same trade, it proved an ideal situation. The apostle stayed in their home and joined them in plying the trade of tentmaker, but his chief occupation was witnessing to the Gospel.

Some time after Paul left Corinth to return to Antioch, another disciple, Apollos, made his way to the city. He was a Jew also, but a native of Alexandria in Egypt. Luke tells us that he was both eloquent in his speaking and competent in his knowledge of Scripture. What he didn't have was a complete grasp on how Jesus of Nazareth had fulfilled the entirety of the Scriptures by His innocent suffering, death, and resurrection. "He knew only the baptism of John" is how Luke describes it.

After Apollos spoke with boldness in the synagogue, Aquila and Priscilla took him aside and gently instructed him more fully in "the way of God." They didn't embarrass him by correcting him publicly. In private, they opened up to him more than he had ever yet dared to believe. His vast knowledge of the Scripture and his eloquence would henceforth be used to spread the saving name of Jesus.

After a time, Apollos left Aquila and Priscilla behind in Corinth and went on to preach the Good News in Achaia. He proved to be a huge help to the believers there by his solid apologetic efforts. He opened the Old Testament Scriptures to show that the Messiah they were waiting for had already come: Jesus of Nazareth.

God's Word is our great heritage
And shall be ours forever;
To spread its light from age to age
Shall be our chief endeavor.
Through life it guides our way,
In death it is our stay.
Lord, grant, while worlds endure,
We keep its teachings pure
Throughout all generations. (LSB 582)

The final mention we have of the three is in the last chapter of 1 Corinthians. Paul had urged Apollos to visit the Corinthian congregation again, where Apollos first had learned the fullness of the Gospel, but for the present he wasn't inclined to return. "He will come when he has opportunity" (1 Corinthians 16:12). Aquila and Priscilla had apparently moved on to the Roman province of Asia and met up again with Paul. He sent greetings to the congregation at Corinth from them and the congregation that met in their house. Through His faithful servants Aquila, Priscilla and Apollos, the Word of the Lord continued to grow.

Glorious and most blessed Trinity, we give You thanks for Aquila, Priscilla, Apollos, and all the men and women across the ages who have taught Your Word and helped Your people to a stronger rejoicing in Your love and grace. Fill us with a love for Your Scriptures, the humility to be taught by others, and zeal to share the Gospel with others to the glory of Your name. Amen.

14
FEBRUARY

On this day, the Church remembers the holy **martyr St. Valentine**.

The story of the man commemorated this day is in large part unknown. Some centuries after Valentine's death, Pope Gelasius would write that Valentine is among those "whose names are justly reverenced among men, but whose acts are known only to God." What is known is that Valentine ended life confessing Christ to the last, dying a martyr's death in Rome under Emperor Claudius II around AD 270.

Although we cannot know with any kind of certainty, later tradition has suggested that he was both a doctor and priest. He was thus a man marked by his kindness and tender care of others in body and in soul. In this, he mirrored our Lord Jesus Christ, who healed the ailments of the body and yet more wondrously brought peace to the soul with His words of promise and hope.

The very day that Valentine was to face his martyrdom, he is said to have brought consolation to the daughter of his jailer by writing to her a small note of encouragement. The young girl had reportedly come to love this godly man and was grieved at the thought of his death. But Valentine knew that death was a defeated enemy because of Christ's death and resurrection. So he comforted the young lady. Hence, the custom of St. Valentine's day notes arose, which has spread far and wide.

From the relative obscurity of his life, we may learn a valuable lesson: God remembers what people forget. Baptized into Christ, marked with the holy cross as the Lord's own, fed with the body and blood of the Savior, Valentine lived and served, loved and died a witness to the invincible love of God in Christ Jesus. God remembers His saints across the ages, even the multitude of His own who never end up with a commemoration in the

Love in Christ is strong and living,
Binding faithful hearts in one;
Love in Christ is true and giving.
May His will in us be done.
Love is patient and forbearing,
Clothed in Christ's humility,
Gentle, selfless, kind, and caring,
Reaching out in charity.
Love in Christ abides forever,
Fainting not when ills attend;
Love, forgiving and forgiven,
Shall endure until life's end. (LSB 706)

Church's calendar (other than All Saints' Day). Not one is forgotten. This will be apparent on the Last Day when Christ will call the dead to life and remember the deeds of all, crowning His grace in the lives of His own. Among the saints gathered before Him that day will be faithful Valentine, whose trust in Christ's promises was not in vain.

For your holy martyr St. Valentine, all glory to You, Lord Jesus Christ!

Almighty and everlasting God, You kindled the flame of Your love in the heart of Your holy martyr Valentine. Grant to us, Your humble servants, a like faith and the power of love, that we who rejoice in Christ's triumph may embody His love in our lives; through Jesus Christ, Your Son, our Lord, who lives and reigns with You and the Holy Spirit, one God, now and forever. Amen.

15
FEBRUARY

Today, we remember two friends of St. Paul, **Philemon and Onesimus**.

Did Martin Luther have in mind the two saints we commemorate today when he wrote these oft-quoted lines in *Freedom of the Christian*? "A Christian is the freest lord of all, subject to none. A Christian is the most dutiful servant of all, subject to all." To the world, this will always seem nonsensical. But think of Philemon and Onesimus.

Philemon was the master of Onesimus, but at some point Onesimus fled his master and thus became an escaped slave. St. Paul's preaching had already won Philemon and his household to the faith. But on his missionary journeys, the Lord providentially granted Paul to come across Onesimus and bring to him the Gospel too. He believed and was baptized.

What happens when the saving faith in Jesus Christ comes between two humans who are at enmity with each other—one who was slave and one free?

In the letter that bears the name of the man to whom it was addressed, Philemon, St. Paul opens up a whole new way of thinking. To be a perfectly free lord of all and subject to none *is* to be so utterly free that one can become a perfectly dutiful servant of all, subject to all. Paul sends Onesimus (whose name rather unfortunately means "useless") back to his master to be a dutiful servant. Yet, he urges that master to receive his one-time wayward servant as Paul's own child (Philemon 10), indeed "my very heart" (v. 12). Paul confesses that he would gladly have kept Onesimus, but would not consider doing so without Philemon's consent.

How should Philemon look upon Onesimus now? "For this perhaps is why he was parted from you for a while, that you might have him back forever,

Son of God, eternal Savior,
  Source of life and truth and grace,
Word made flesh, whose birth among us
  Hallows all our human race:
By Your praying, by Your willing
  That Your people should be one,
Grant, O grant our hope's fruition:
  Here on earth Your will be done. **(LSB 842:4)**

---

no longer as a bondservant but more than a bondservant, as a beloved brother" (Philemon 15). Onesimus returned to Philemon as a brother in Christ. Yet, precisely because he came as his spiritual equal, baptized into the same Lord and Master, he humbly returned joyfully to Philemon's service. How would Philemon receive him? St. Paul acts out the Gospel by offering to be the Christlike substitute who pays for the (financial) sins of Onesimus: "If he has wronged you at all, or owes you anything, charge that to my account. I, Paul, write this with my own hand: I will repay it—to say nothing of your owing me even your own self" (Philemon 18–19).

Behold the mystery of the Church! Before the Lamb of God who has taken away the sin of the world, we stand as brothers and sisters. Since our Master dons a towel to wash feet, we see it as an honor to be a servant to others.

Lord God, heavenly Father, You sent Onesimus back to Philemon as a brother in Christ, freeing him from his slavery to sin through the preaching of the apostle Paul. Cleanse the depths of sin within our souls and bid resentment cease for past offenses, that, by Your mercy, we may be reconciled to our brothers and sisters and our lives reflect Your peace; through Jesus Christ, our Lord. Amen.

16
FEBRUARY

On this day, the Holy Church rejoices to remember the birth of **Philipp Melanchthon, Confessor**, friend and co-worker of blessed Martin Luther.

Born this day in 1497, Philipp Melanchthon was an outstanding layman, a teacher whose brilliance was soon noted. At the young age of 21, he was called to Wittenberg University to become a professor of Greek. Thus he was drawn into the circle of Luther and thrown into the maelstrom of the Reformation. The two men began a long career of teaching side by side. Luther regarded Melanchthon's book *Loci Communes* (a comprehensive study of Christian doctrine, following the outline of Romans) as so well written that he felt it might well be appended to the Scriptures!

Melanchthon is especially remembered as the man who crafted the foundational Lutheran symbol: the Augsburg Confession. Luther, having been declared an outlaw in 1521, was not able to be present in Augsburg at the great Diet that Emperor Charles V summoned in order to solve with finality the religious problems that were fraying his empire. So Melanchthon was the primary theologian to represent the Lutherans. He arrived in town with a document in hand that showed the changes that the Lutherans had made in ceremonies and explained their biblical basis for doing so. But when he arrived, the opponents of the Lutherans had already spread vicious and false rumors about how Lutherans embraced nearly every heresy of the ancient Church. Melanchthon had to compose the response the princes would give to these calumnious charges. His gentle and irenic spirit shaped a response that breathes an eagerness "to maintain the unity of the Spirit in the bond of peace."

Shocked by the arguments used to refute the Augsburg Confession, Melanchthon set to work writing an Apology, or Defense, of the Confession. This was also included in the Book of Concord. The Diet of Augsburg

Lord Jesus Christ, with us abide,
For round us falls the eventide.
O let Your Word, that saving light,
Shine forth undimmed into the night. (LSB 585:1)

---

sadly did not bring an end to the conflict. When Rome finally acquiesced to the Emperor's demand for a General Council to address the issue, the Lutherans undertook to prepare a response. For this, Luther wrote the Smalcald Articles and Melanchthon wrote the Treatise on the Power and Primacy of the Pope, addressing what many (including Luther) thought to be a gaping hole in the original Augsburg Confession. These documents also were included in the Book of Concord.

Melanchthon's great interest in humanism and the study of language and ancient literature led him to reform the entire system of education that he found in Germany. To this day he is given the title of the Preceptor or Teacher of Germany. His desire for peace at times led him to choices that put him in conflict with other Reformers. Yet, Luther remained his loyal friend until Luther's death. Even his critics readily acknowledged the profound piety and reverence with which he approached the tasks laid on him. He was a man of humility and prayer, a faithful servant of God in his day.

Almighty God, we praise You for the service of Philipp Melanchthon to the one holy catholic and apostolic Church in the renewal of its life of fidelity to Your Word and promise. Raise up in these gray and latter days faithful teachers and pastors, inspired by Your Spirit, whose voices will give strength to Your Church and proclaim the ongoing reality of Your kingdom; through Your Son, Jesus Christ, our Lord. Amen.

18
FEBRUARY

Today, the Church rejoices to remember the blessed **Martin Luther, Doctor and Confessor**.

Odd the ways of God. He brought His servant Martin full circle. He had been born in Eisleben in 1483, and it was there he spent his final days on this earth in February of 1546. The local princes were squabbling and sought help from the great Reformer in settling matters in a Christian and godly way. Luther was loath to turn away such a request, though his health had been steadily deteriorating for some time. "Blessed are the peacemakers," our Lord had said, and it was in the service of peace that Luther died. He had thought early on that he would be martyred for his bold confession and sometimes sounded wistful that the Lord had not granted him this grace.

Luther had worn himself out with teaching, preaching, and assisting in the Reformation of the churches. After he came to understand that the righteousness God requires in the Law is a righteousness He freely gives as a gift for faith to receive, Luther was unstoppable. From his pen flowed a veritable stream of words nonstop: his translation of the Scriptures from the original languages into German, numerous hymns, various revisions of the Church's liturgies, collections of sermons, and commentaries on the Scriptures. His advice was sought far and wide. Yet, his earlier monastic life had taken its toll. His zeal for asceticism had wrecked his health early on. He never did anything by half measures when it came to the faith— either before the joy of the Gospel was revealed or after. So it was already a compromised body that undertook the tremendous strain of Reformation. Yet, to see his vitality spent in the service of God was truly to Martin Luther the only life worth the living.

Lord, help us ever to retain
The Catechism's doctrine plain
   As Luther taught the Word of truth
   In simple style to tender youth. (LSB 865:1)

He made his confession to Justas Jonas as he lay dying and was absolved. Before the end, Jonas asked him if he intended to die in the faith he had confessed, and he spoke his loud "Ja!" ("Yes!"). He repeated some of the promises of Scripture to himself as he lay on his deathbed. When Luther finally breathed his last, he left this age in the confidence both of sins forgiven through the blood of Christ and death destroyed by the Savior's death and resurrection. He departed knowing that though he was a poor sinner, he had a mighty Savior. His Savior would not forget him, but raise him from death in a glorified body.

It was after his death that his friends found the very last words that the great man had ever written. "We are all beggars; that is true." Beggars, indeed, but beggars before a God who delights in dishing out His rich bounties upon unworthy sinners. He died knowing that he had helped many in his own day and time see and know that the "just shall live by faith," and he was grateful for the privilege.

O God, our refuge and our strength, You raised up Your servant Martin Luther to reform and renew Your Church in the light of Your living Word, Jesus Christ, our Lord. Defend and purify the Church in our own day, and grant that we may boldly proclaim Christ's faithfulness unto death and His vindicating resurrection, which You made known to Your servant Martin through Jesus Christ, our Savior, who lives and reigns with You and the Holy Spirit, one God, now and forever. Amen.

23
FEBRUARY

Today, the Church delights to remember **St. Polycarp of Smyrna, Pastor and Martyr**.

Polycarp was born sometime around AD 69. He was a disciple of St. John, the apostle and evangelist. Eventually, Polycarp was made bishop of Smyrna in Asia Minor. We have from his hand a letter he wrote to the Philippian Church. This writing portrays a man who had devoted himself to the Scriptures and who sought to build up and encourage others by the use of the Word of God. It is a veritable patchwork of quotations from the Old and New Testaments! It also shows him to be a man of gentle and kind spirit, who would not presume to command, but exhorted his believers from the fullness of the Gospel: "These things, brethren, I write to you concerning righteousness, not because I take anything upon myself, but because you have invited me to do so. For neither I, nor any other such one, can come up to the wisdom of the blessed and glorified Paul. He, when among you, accurately and steadfastly taught the word of truth in the presence of those who were then alive. And when absent from you, he wrote you a letter, which, if you carefully study, you will find to be the means of building you up in that faith which has been given you" (*Epistle of Polycarp* 3). He was a man of the Word!

The account of his martyrdom on this day in AD 155 is a particularly beautiful treasure bequeathed us from the ancient Church. When urged to consider his advanced age and to offer the incense to the emperor, Polycarp answered: "Eighty and six years have I served Him, and He never did me any injury: how then can I blaspheme my King and my Savior?" (*Martyrdom of Polycarp*, 9). The great saint was then burned at the stake, stabbed with a spear, his body mutilated. His remains were denied to his followers for burial.

The Early Church was heartened by the faithful and bold witness this old man gave to his Savior in life and in death. The witnesses of his execution wrote

These saints of old received God's commendation;
They lived as pilgrim-heirs of His salvation.
Through faith they conquered flame and sword and gallows,
God's name to hallow.
They call to us, "Your timid footsteps lengthen;
Throw off sin's weight, your halting weakness strengthen.
We kept the faith, we shed our blood, were martyred;
Our lives we bartered." (LSB 667:2–3)

---

triumphantly, "Now, the blessed Polycarp suffered martyrdom on the second day of the month Xanthicus just begun, the seventh day before the Kalends of March, on the great Sabbath, at the eighth hour. He was taken by Herod, Philip the Trallian being high priest, Statius Quadratus being proconsul, but Jesus Christ being King for ever, to whom be glory, honor, majesty, and an everlasting throne, from generation to generation. Amen" (*Martyrdom of Polycarp*, 21). They knew that none of the circumstances of their lives were out of the control of Him who governs all things for their good.

O God, the maker of heaven and earth, You gave boldness to confess Jesus Christ as King and Savior and steadfastness to die for the faith to Your venerable servant, the holy and gentle Polycarp. Grant us grace to follow his example in sharing the cup of Christ's sufferings so that we may also share in His glorious resurrection; through Jesus Christ, Your Son, our Lord, who lives and reigns with You and the Holy Spirit, one God, now and forever. Amen.

24
FEBRUARY

Today, the Holy Church remembers and thanks God for
St. Matthias, Apostle.

We know little about the man himself, but we know more about the circumstances of Matthias's call to be an apostle. In the in-between period of the Ascension and Pentecost, after Judas's tragic suicide, the apostles, St. Mary, and the brothers of the Lord were devoted to a time of prayer. About 120 believers comprised the nascent Church. In the context of prayer and waiting for the outpouring of the Spirit, Peter was moved to fill the place vacated by Judas Iscariot among the apostles. Pointing to the Psalms (69 and 109), he showed that another was to take the office vacated by the man who had betrayed the Lord.

But not just any one of the believers would do. He laid down specific qualifications: "So one of the men who have accompanied us during all the time that the Lord Jesus went in and out among us, beginning from the baptism of John until the day when he was taken up from us—one of these men must become with us a witness to His resurrection" (Acts 1:21–22).

So the primary concern was that the man would have witnessed the ministry of Christ and seen with his own eyes the Lord Jesus risen from the dead. This qualified him to be a true apostle, a witness to the Resurrected One.

Two candidates were put forward, one of whom was Matthias. Prayer was offered for God to show His will and lots were then cast (the phrase can also mean votes cast). Thus the Eleven received and welcomed Matthias as one of their fellow apostles, and the Church has ever since honored him so.

Traditions about the location of his ministry vary. Some suggest he labored in Ethiopia, while another account links him to bringing the faith to Armenia, the first nation to accept Christianity. He is said to have been martyred at Colchis in Asia Minor, around AD 50. The great Cathedral at

For one in place of Judas,
      The apostles sought God's choice;
The lot fell to Matthias
      For whom we now rejoice.
May we like true apostles
      Your holy Church defend,
And not betray our calling
      But serve You to the end. (LSB 517:13)

Trier claims to be his final resting place, the only one of the Twelve (if the tradition is correct) who was buried north of the Alps. What is certain is that Matthias was a co-laborer with his fellow apostles. After the dispersion of the apostles, he brought his witness of Christ's resurrection to those who still "sat in darkness and the shadow of death" that they, too, might enter into the great joy of forgiveness and everlasting life.

When we gather in the New Jerusalem, one of whose foundation stones will bear the name Matthias, we shall perhaps be blessed to learn of his labors with certainty and celebrate with those brought to faith by his preaching of the saving Gospel. Until then, for Your servant Matthias, O Lord, receive our thanks and praise!

Almighty God, You chose Your servant Matthias to be numbered among the Twelve. Grant that Your Church, ever preserved from false teachers, may be taught and guided by faithful and true pastors; through Jesus Christ, Your Son, our Lord, who lives and reigns with You and the Holy Spirit, one God, now and forever. Amen.

READINGS
ISAIAH 66:1-2 / ACTS 1:15-26 / MATTHEW 11:25-30

7
MARCH

On this day, we remember two early Christian women, **Perpetua and Felicitas, Martyrs.**

The Roman Empire's persecution of the Christian Church was not a constant, but an on-again, off-again affair, sometimes worse here, sometimes there. At the beginning of the third century, Emperor Septimus Severus felt the threat of the Church anew and decreed that no one would be allowed to convert to Christianity. But the threat of the civil authorities never did slow down much the growing swell of those who called Jesus Lord and would not worship the emperor or the old gods.

In those years, about AD 203, a noblewoman, Perpetua, and her servant, Felicitas, were catechumens who received Baptism into the name of Christ and confessed Him, and this over the objection of Perpetua's father, who realized the danger this put his beloved daughter in. Perpetua and her servant were eventually denounced and jailed at Carthage in Northern Africa and held with three other Christians. Perpetua's father visited her in the jail to beg her to recant so that he would not be deprived of a dear daughter or his grandchild of a mother. Yet, even in jail they continued confessing Christ with such strong conviction that their jailer, with the grace of the Holy Spirit, was brought to faith in the Savior.

Though both were mothers and had little ones to tend, they made provision for their children's well-being with near relatives and bravely went to meet their torture and death on this day, March 7. According to an ancient account, the prisoners first endured scourging by gladiators, then were savaged by wild beasts. Before they were finally slain with the sword, Perpetua and Felicitas, bleeding and dying, gave to each other the kiss of peace. They died together as they had lived together, in the peace of Christ.

The account of their unswerving devotion to Christ above the claims of family and blood, their love for each other, and their scorn of death and

A noble army, men and boys,
    The matron and the maid,
Around the Savior's throne rejoice,
    In robes of light arrayed.
They climbed the steep ascent of heav'n
    Through peril, toil, and pain.
O God, to us may grace be giv'n
    To follow in their train! **(LSB 661:4)**

---

pain has lived on in the Church for century upon century. Their example and witness have served to bless and strengthen all those who face similar persecution and death across the ages and, sadly, even to this day.

"The matron and maid" indeed now around the Savior's throne rejoice "in robes of light arrayed." Well do we sing, "O God, to us may grace be given to follow in their train."

O God and Ruler over all our foes of body and soul, You strengthened Your servants Perpetua and Felicitas, giving them a confident and clear confession in the face of roaring beasts. Grant that we who remember their faithful martyrdom may share in their blessed assurance of victory over all earthly and spiritual enemies and hold fast to the promise of everlasting life, secured for us through Jesus Christ, our Lord, who lives and reigns with You and the Holy Spirit, one God, now and forever. Amen.

17
MARCH

Today, we remember and thank the blessed Trinity for **St. Patrick, Missionary to Ireland.**

Patrick was born into a Christian family in Roman Britain about AD 389. The borders of the empire were fraying fast. Raiders from Ireland pillaged the coast and carried Patrick back with them as a slave. Sent to herd pigs, Patrick served six years and pondered his fate and his faith. Led by a dream, he escaped his captivity and headed toward the sea. Since he had no money to pay for a voyage and would not submit to the sailors' lewd suggestions, he almost despaired. The sailors relented and let the young man cross back with them.

He finally made his way to France, where he became a monk and a priest. Elevated to be bishop, he returned to the land of his captivity about 433 to set his captors free from their slavery to idolatry. In this labor he spent the rest of his days. He preached throughout the land, founded communities, and imparted to the Irish Church of his day a true zeal for missions. In his great *Confession*, he wrote, "This is how we can repay such blessings, when our lives change and we come to know God, to praise and bear witness to his great wonders before every nation under heaven."

An ardent and orthodox confessor of the doctrine of the Holy Trinity, Patrick brought the joy of confessing the "Three in One and One in Three" through the length and breadth of the Island. His episcopal seat was said to be at Armagh. March 17 is generally regarded as the day of his death. Did he die singing his hymn? "I bind unto myself the name, The strong name of the Trinity By invocation of the same, the Three in One and One in Three. Of whom all nature hath creation, Eternal Father, Spirit, Word. Praise to the Lord of my salvation; Salvation is of Christ, the Lord!" (*LSB* 604:5).

I bind unto myself today
    The pow'r of God to hold and lead,
His eye to watch, His might to stay,
    His ear to hearken to my need,
The wisdom of my God to teach,
    His hand to guide, His shield to ward,
The Word of God to give me speech,
    His heav'nly host to be my guard.
Against the demon snares of sin,
    The vice that gives temptation force,
The natural lusts that war within,
    The hostile foes that mar my course;
Or few or many, far or nigh,
    In ev'ry place and in all hours,
Against their fierce hostility
    I bind to me those holy pow'rs. **(LSB 604:3–4)**

Faithful God, You never cease to give to Your Church those who delight to carry the Gospel to foreign lands. Receive our thanks this day for Your servant, Patrick, who carried the saving name of Jesus to Ireland and summoned its people to abandon idolatry and worship You, the only true God, the blessed Trinity. Strengthen today all missionaries, that they may fearlessly bear Your name and summon all sinners into the joy of forgiveness and the promise of resurrection through Jesus Christ, our Lord, who lives and reigns with You and the Holy Spirit, one God, now and forever. Amen.

19 MARCH

Today, the Church celebrates the Festival of
St. Joseph, Guardian of Jesus.

God promised to build King David a house. Centuries later, a carpenter, a son of David, welcomed into his home a woman pregnant with a child. The child was not of his own body, but still was the child of his heart. He welcomed the little carpenter, God in the flesh, who had come to build a true temple for God in human flesh and blood. Jesus was the name the angel gave, "for He will save His people from their sins." As Mary came nearer to term and the child grew in her womb, would Joseph place his hand on her tummy and feel the baby kick? Would he say to himself, "This is my Savior. This is the one we have prayed for and hoped for all our lives. He comes to set us free!"

Old Joseph didn't live to see how that redemption would take place. Scripture last mentions him in the temple with Mary and Jesus when the lad was twelve. Sometime between then and Jesus' Baptism at the age of 30, Joseph died. He didn't live to see the shame of the cross, when only Mary and her friends had the courage to stand by the Lord. He didn't live to see the triumph of the empty tomb when Jesus would begin spreading the joy of death's defeat into all the world. He probably never saw Jesus work a miracle, but that didn't matter.

Joseph died still full of faith and hope because he knew that God had come to be with us. He came to save us in that child, learning to walk and talk, embracing him, eating at his table and sleeping under his roof, playing with abandon and praying with glee. And so Joseph closed his eyes in peace and opened them in heaven's light only to be embraced by his child, his Jesus.

We sing our thanks for Joseph,
The guardian of our Lord,
Who faithfully taught Jesus
Through craft and deed and word.
Grant wisdom, Lord, and patience
To parents ev'rywhere
Who guide and teach the children
Entrusted to their care. (LSB 517:14)

While on earth, Joseph had cared and provided for the child and now in heaven the child of Mary would forever care and provide for him—the child, his Jesus, had built a lasting home for his foster father, indeed for all who welcome Him into their lives.

Joseph lurks in the background. But how our Lord loved his earthly protector and provider! You probably know what Joseph felt like. We're background people too, for the most part. Maybe often overlooked and forgotten, just doing the tasks the Lord has given us to do. That's okay. There's One who doesn't overlook or forget, who loves us and is waiting to welcome us home. The child who was born of Mary, nurtured by Joseph; the child who by His cross and resurrection has built and opened wide for all who trust Him—great and small alike—an eternal home. There's a reason He was the carpenter's son.

Almighty God, from the house of Your servant David You raised up Joseph to be the guardian of Your incarnate Son and the husband of His mother, Mary. Grant us grace to follow the example of this faithful workman in heeding Your counsel and obeying Your commands; through Jesus Christ, our Lord, who lives and reigns with You and the Holy Spirit, one God, now and forever. Amen.

READINGS
2 SAMUEL 7:4–16 / ROMANS 4:13–18 / MATTHEW 2:13–15, 19–23

25
MARCH

Today, the Church celebrates with great joy the Feast of the **Annunciation of Our Lord**.

The angel stands amazed before the maiden, and she looks in amazement at him. But his amazement is greater than hers. She is amazed at his appearing, but he is amazed at the tidings he brings. For she shall be a mother, though she knows not a man. She shall conceive in her womb and bring forth a son, though she is a virgin. But it is who her son will be that fills the angel with greatest awe. For this child that shall be born of her shall truly be hers. A creature of flesh and blood that grows from childhood to adulthood. A creature that eats and sleeps and breathes. Such a creature will her son be.

And that is why Gabriel stares at her in awe. For the little child that shall soon be conceived in her womb and that she shall feed at her breast is none other than the Son of the Highest, God the Son, the eternal Word of the Father through whom he—the angel—was made, through whom she—a human—was made, through whom all things are made. She shall be mother of the Maker. She shall be mother of the Eternal One who was before the stars began their shining. She shall be mother of Him whom it is our delight to serve and worship and praise world without end.

The child she bears shall reign over David's house forever. The promise of the Kingdom that has no end is fulfilled in Him. A forever Kingdom!

O Lady, do you know what that means? He will reign through endless days, and those over whom He reigns will live in endless life. Lady, do you know that you will carry in your womb Him through whom death itself will be destroyed? Lady, do you know that through the deeds of your Son the sin that separates the human race from the all-holy Father will be covered, atoned, pardoned? Lady, do

"For know a blessèd mother thou shalt be,
All generations laud and honor thee;
Thy son shall be Emmanuel, by seers foretold,
Most highly favored lady."
    Gloria! (LSB 356:2)

---

you know how He will do it? No. I can see that you do not know. That is best for now. The day will come when you stand on a darkened hill and see a sight of love so grievous that it will tear your soul in two. But it will be His love for you and for your fallen race that drives Him to it, Lady. So rejoice!

And do not worry yourself over how this promise I bring you will be fulfilled. God knows that you are a virgin. But His Holy Spirit will overshadow you and fill you and change you and inside of you life Himself will begin to grow, and so the Holy One born of you will indeed be my Master, my Lord, my God. It is impossible for any word of God to fail. His promises are more certain than heaven and earth. He said it and so, Lady, rejoice and be glad. It shall be so.

Meekly he sees her bow her head and utter the words, "Behold, the maidservant of the Lord. Let it be to me as you have said."

And so the moment has come and the great time of God's keeping all His promises has begun. Begun in Mary. Begun in her womb, which He shall make His holy temple and His home for the next nine months during which His tiny infant heart will beat beneath her own, till that moment when the Lord blesses us and keeps us and makes His face shine upon us and gives us peace.

Farewell, then, Lady until we meet once more, until together we bow before the child you will bear and worship at His feet and give Him eternal praise in the Kingdom He comes to prepare, in the presence of all who have trusted in Your Son for forgiveness and salvation, in the life that has no end, where the joys are eternal and where the sorrows are forgotten. Farewell, vessel of His grace! Farewell, temple of the Presence! Farewell, Mary, child of David, child of Abraham, mother of God! Farewell.

O Lord, as we have known the incarnation of Your Son, Jesus Christ, by the message of the angel to the Virgin Mary, so by the message of His cross and Passion bring us to the glory of His resurrection; through the same Jesus Christ, our Lord, who lives and reigns with You and the Holy Spirit, one God, now and forever. Amen.

READINGS
ISAIAH 7:10–14 / HEBREWS 10:4–10 / LUKE 1:26–38

57

31
MARCH

Today, we remember and thank
God for **Joseph, Patriarch**.

The story of the patriarch Joseph, beloved child of
Jacob, is one of the most stirring pieces of literature
in the Bible. It is also an amazing typological prophecy
of our Lord Jesus Christ. As the son of Jacob's favorite
wife, Rachel, Joseph had a special relationship with his
father that his brothers resented. God spoke to Joseph in
dreams. He foretold that Joseph's father and mother and all
his brothers would bow down to him. This only increased his
brothers' resentment of him.

When they had opportunity, they betrayed him. They sold him as
a slave to some passing traders. Joseph began a life of captivity in Egypt.
Meanwhile, his brothers took the beautiful robe that had belonged to Joseph
and marked him as the favored son, dipped it in the blood of an animal, and
led their father to believe that his beloved Joseph was dead.

In Egypt, God blessed the young man, and Joseph soon rose to
prominence with his master. But when his master's wife falsely accused
him of rape because Joseph would not consent to commit adultery with
her, he was put in prison. There God was with him and granted him favor
in the sight of the prison warden. When he interpreted dreams to Pharaoh's
cupbearer and baker, each came to pass as Joseph had foretold. He begged
the cupbearer to remember him to Pharaoh, but the cupbearer forgot
until Pharaoh had a dream that no one could interpret. The cupbearer
mentioned Joseph to Pharaoh. He was taken from prison and by God's
wisdom interpreted Pharaoh's dream and advised him what to do. Seeing

Be still, my soul; the Lord is on your side;
Bear patiently the cross of grief or pain;
Leave to your God to order and provide;
In ev'ry change He faithful will remain.
Be still, my soul; your best, your heav'nly Friend
Through thorny ways leads to a joyful end. (LSB 752:1)

---

the wisdom of the young man, Pharaoh made him to be the prime minister of all Egypt.

As famine ravaged Palestine, Joseph's brothers came to Egypt to buy grain. There they encountered Joseph, but now grown up and dressed as an Egyptian. He knew them, but they did not know him. He tested them and found they were indeed remorseful over their sin against him years before. He finally revealed himself, to their shock and then fear. He comforted them: "You meant evil against me, but God meant it for good, to bring it about that many people should be kept alive."

The Church cannot read the story of Joseph without thinking of our Lord. He, too, was rejected by His brothers, sold, handed over to arrest and even to death. Yet, the Father has raised Him, exalted Him, and all so that He could bring blessing, could save many lives. The biblical account of Joseph is a powerful prophecy of our Lord and His salvation. His story is the Old Testament explication of the promise from Romans 8:28: "And we know that for those who love God all things work together for good."

Glorious and blessed Trinity, how beyond all human wisdom is Your kind providence and plan! You graciously fulfilled Your promises to Joseph the patriarch in a wondrous way. Through the path of humiliation and suffering, You lifted him to glory and honor, prefiguring the Passion and resurrection of our Lord. Fill us with the confidence that You can and do work all things together to bring us blessing; through the same Jesus Christ, our Lord. Amen.

6
APRIL

Today, we rejoice to remember two gifted men from the sixteenth century, **Lucas Cranach and Albrecht Dürer, Artists**.

It is perhaps one of the more startling statements that can be found in Lutheran dogmatics: "Furthermore, the Gospel is such a means of grace in every form in which it reaches man, whether it is preached (Mark 16:15–16; Luke 24:47), or printed (John 20:31; 1 John 1:3–4), or expressed as a formal absolution (John 20:23), or *pictured in symbols or types* (John 3:14–15), or pondered in the heart (Romans 10:8)" (*Christian Dogmatics* 3:106; emphasis added). The footnote to the italicized words adds: "E.g., by a crucifix or some picture."

The Gospel itself, the Good News of our salvation, can be painted or drawn, and as such it remains "the power of God for salvation." How well the two men commemorated this day lived out this truth!

Lucas Cranach the Elder (1472–1557) served as court painter for the Electors of Saxony, and this naturally brought him into the sphere of the Reformation, which he heartily embraced. He became a dear friend of Luther and sought in his art to give expression to the Reformation insights into the Word of God. Among his famous portraits are the major figures of the Lutheran Reformation, including many of Luther. His woodcuts grace the pages of Luther's German translation of the Sacred Scriptures. His altarpieces are particularly known for showing not merely salvation's history but also the manner in which the salvation won by Christ reaches us today through Baptism, preaching, absolution, and the Sacrament of the Altar.

Albrecht Dürer (1471–1528) had a more tangential relationship with the

All people that on earth do dwell,
  Sing to the Lord with cheerful voice.
Him serve with mirth, His praise forthtell;
  Come ye before Him and rejoice. (LSB 791:1)

---

reformers. It was impossible at the time to be a man of letters and learning and not be impacted by what Luther was writing. In 1520, in a letter to a friend, Dürer shared that he desired to make a portrait of Luther as a lasting memorial, for he had been comforted by Luther's words. Significant here is the expression "lasting memorial," for this is what the Christian artist does in whatever medium he or she works. Through their artistic skill they participate in the great relay race: "One generation shall commend Your works to another, and shall declare Your mighty acts" (Psalm 145:4). Dürer used his vocation as artist to proclaim the Good News in a variety of mediums. Dürer's careful woodcuts in celebration of God's creation and salvation are treasured to this day. Perhaps his most famous drawing is the classic "Praying Hands."

O God, You pour out Your Spirit upon artists, giving them skill to reflect through the work of their hands the beauty of Your creation and the story of Your salvation. Receive our thanks this day for Your servants Lucas Cranach and Albrecht Dürer. We rejoice in the way their work celebrates to this day Your creation and the joys of our redemption. Continue to raise up artists to be a blessing to Your Church and a witness to the world; through Jesus Christ, Your Son, our Lord. Amen.

20
APRIL

Today, we remember and thank God for the great
reformer of the Church **Johannes Bugenhagen, Pastor**
to blessed Martin Luther.

Johannes Bugenhagen was one of the great reformers of the Lutheran
Reformation. Dr. Pomeranus (as Luther liked to call him) was born in 1485.
Having been ordained a priest and serving as a lecturer at Belbuck Abby,
Bugenhagen first encountered Luther's work through the famous 1520
treatise, *The Babylonian Captivity*. Bugenhagen initially was not persuaded.
The more he read of Luther, however, the more he came to agree with him.
He eventually relocated to Wittenberg and in 1523 was appointed the parish
pastor at St. Mary's, thus becoming Martin Luther's own pastor and his
confessor. These he remained to the end of his days, and in 1558 he was
buried at the church where he had labored so long.

He was not only a pastor but also a scholar. He earned a doctorate of
theology in 1533, awarded by the University of Wittenberg. He rendered
Luther's High German Bible into Middle Low German. In 1539, he was
additionally appointed superintendent of the church in Saxony.

His particular gift was in the practical reform of both church and
school. This was not a strong suit of Luther. Luther expected the world's end
to come any day and thus lacked the patience necessary to think through
the best way to reform the liturgy, church courts, and school life. Luther's
writings on these topics provided some fundamental directions, but giving
detailed concrete shape to the Reformation in such areas was in large part
the work of the man commemorated this day.

Bugenhagen carried out visitations in order to know for himself the
spiritual condition of the people for whom he was to create the Church
Order. Luther more than once complained about Bugenhagen's lengthy
absences from St. Mary's that left Luther to fill the pulpit! Those long

Preserve Your Word, O Savior,
To us this latter day,
And let Your kingdom flourish;
Enlarge Your Church, we pray.
O keep our faith from failing;
Keep hope's bright star aglow.
Let nothing from truth turn us
While living here below. (LSB 658:1)

---

absences were due precisely to the careful, methodical, and pastorally sensitive reforms he was undertaking. The orders that come from his hand (Denmark-Norway, Braunschweig, Hamburg, Pomerania, and a number of others) are all marked by their common sense and sobriety. They invariably walk a pastorally sensitive middle road when it comes to ceremonies, and they are intensely concerned with catechesis, passing on the faith. His work in this area was so extensive and so lasting and well received that he has sometimes been called "the Second Apostle of the North."

Bugenhagen, as Luther's pastor, preached his funeral sermon in tears. He extolled God for the extraordinary gifts He had showered on the Church through his colleague and prayed for the preservation of the work that had been begun. He seemed to have little idea of how much his own work was an answer to that prayer of preserving the Reformation.

Glory to You, blessed Trinity! You raise up in the Church faithful pastors to recall Your people to the richness of Your Word and to turn them away from the vain wisdom of this age. We give you thanks for the life and ministry of Your servant Johannes Bugenhagen. Through his example, inspire in all pastors a zeal to preach Your Word in all truth and purity and to work for the preservation of Your Church; through Jesus Christ, Your Son, our Lord. Amen.

21
APRIL

Today, the Church delights to remember the life and witness of **Anselm of Canterbury, Theologian**.

Anselm was born in Italy around the year 1033. Although he desired at age 15 to enter a monastery, he was refused because he lacked his father's permission. Some years after his father's death, at age 27, he was finally accepted as a novice and began living under the Rule of St. Benedict.

In 1078, he was elected abbot of Bec. Under his capable leadership, the abbey became famous for its scholarship welded to a solid piety of humility and charity. In 1093, he was forcibly made the Bishop of the Canterbury and thus primate of the Church in England. There he fought to maintain the church's own internal authority against the intrigues and plans of the Norman king.

Among his greatest works were *Cur Deus Homo*, or *Why Did God Become Man?* In this writing, Anselm lays out with remarkable clarity the teaching of the vicarious satisfaction. This doctrine—that Christ rendered satisfaction to the Father (who was offended by our sins) through His life and sufferings and was then vindicated by His resurrection—was *not* original to Anselm. Earlier Church Fathers had grasped and taught this scriptural doctrine as well. But Anselm expressed it with such clarity and force that his explication of it became a universal heritage throughout the Western Church.

In philosophy, Anselm is remembered as the man who invented the so-called ontological proof for the existence of God. If God is that than which none greater can be conceived, such a God truly existing would be greater than a God only so imagined. Thus by very definition of being, God is.

My guilt, O Father, You have laid
*   On Christ, Your Son, my Savior.*
Lord Jesus, You my debt have paid
*   And gained for me God's favor.*
O Holy Spirit, Fount of grace,
The good in me to You I trace;
*   In faith and hope preserve me.* (**LSB 568:5**)

Anselm's many prayers and meditations continue to be a source of blessing and encouragement for Christians. Even on his deathbed, his fertile mind was at work. He was contemplating writing a treatise on the origin of the soul. He died this day in 1109, and that year it happened to fall on Holy Wednesday.

Holy Father, the depths of Your Word are unsearchable. We give thanks to You this day for Your servant Anselm of Canterbury. Continue to raise up theologians in Your Church who will invite Your people to ponder ever more deeply the mystery of our redemption in the bright light of the Scriptures; through Jesus Christ, Your Son, our Lord, who lives and reigns with You and the Holy Spirit, one God, now and forever. Amen.

24
APRIL

Today, we remember and thank God for the life and music of **Johann Walter, Kantor** and co-worker of blessed Martin Luther.

Isaiah foretold that when God brought His people home from their exile it would be accompanied with song: "And the ransomed of the LORD shall return and come to Zion *with singing*; everlasting joy shall be upon their heads; they shall obtain gladness and joy, and sorrow and sighing shall flee away" (Isaiah 35:10; emphasis added). In fulfillment of that, the Church's life in this age has always been filled with music, and music requires musicians.

Martin Luther himself was a man of musical ability. He realized, though, that he didn't know enough on his own to tackle the challenges that were before the Church. He needed help in setting the office hymns and liturgy of the Church into the vernacular and in creating a body of hymnody in the language of the people. He needed the help of professional musicians. He turned, above all, to the man commemorated this day, Johann Walter.

Johann Walter was Luther's junior (born in 1496 in present-day Thuringia). He studied music and at the relatively young age of 21 began to serve as composer and bass kantor in Frederick the Wise's chapel. He rapidly became persuaded of the truth of the Lutheran cause and devoted his considerable talents toward furthering the joy of the Gospel through music that paired beautiful melody and harmony with the Word of God. In fact, he published the very first Lutheran hymnal in 1524, titled *Eyn geystlich Gesangk Buchleyn*, for which Luther himself provided the preface. In it he wrote, "I would like to see all the arts, especially music, used in the service of Him who gave and made them."

Johann Walter certainly agreed and gave his whole life to composing

There God shall from all evil
Forever make us free,
From sin and from the devil,
From all adversity,
From sickness, pain, and sadness,
From troubles, cares, and fears,
And grant us heav'nly gladness
And wipe away our tears.
In that fair home shall never
Be silent music's voice;
With hearts and lips forever
We shall in God rejoice,
While angel hosts are raising
With saints from great to least
A mighty hymn for praising
The Giver of the feast. (LSB 514:3–4)

---

and making music for the Church. For most of his ministry, he served as kantor in the city of Torgau. The Church still sings his settings and hymns today. He wrote the hymn from which the stanzas above were taken, "The Bridegroom Soon Will Call Us." For Johann Walter and all those who assist the Church in singing, ringing, sounding forth the praises of God, telling of His great salvation in Jesus Christ: glory to You, O Lord!

Lover of the human race, we glorify Your name for Johann Walter and all those through whom You give Your people the joy of blessing Your name with music. Strengthen the song of Your people that they may ever sing boldly and without fear of the great salvation which our Lord Jesus has won for us and for all; through the same Jesus Christ, Your Son, our Lord, who lives and reigns with You and the Holy Spirit, one God, now and forever. Amen.

25

APRIL

Today, the Holy Church celebrates the Festival of **St. Mark, Evangelist**, author of the second Gospel and companion of St. Peter and St. Paul.

John Mark was cousin to the apostle Barnabas. His mother's home in Jerusalem was a meeting place for the Early Church. "The weak by grace made strong" in the hymn stanza refers to the famous incident recorded in Acts 15. Though John Mark had begun the first missionary journey with Paul and Barnabas, he did not finish it. We're not told exactly why he returned, but it was clearly without Paul's blessing. Barnabas, the true son of encouragement, was all for giving the young man a second chance when he and Paul determined to begin a second journey. Paul adamantly refused. The disagreement became so sharp that they ended up splitting ways. Paul took Silas and went to Asia Minor; Barnabas took Mark and went to Cyprus.

If that were the end of the story it would be sad indeed. What a comfort, then, to read in St. Paul's final letter, 2 Timothy 4:11: "Luke alone is with me. Get Mark and bring him with you, for he is very useful to me for ministry." Though a veil of silence remains over the details of how it happened, the two were reconciled before Paul's death and the Church's ministry strengthened all the more.

Additionally, Peter, writing from Rome, would say, "She who is at Babylon [code name for Rome, as in Revelation], who is likewise chosen, sends you greetings, and so does Mark, my son." Thus Mark ministered not only with the apostles Barnabas and Paul but with Peter too. Very early and nearly unanimous tradition states that Mark's Gospel itself is actually a summary of the account of our Lord's life that Mark learned from Peter before the apostle's martyrdom in Rome. Scholars have pointed out that

For Mark, O Lord, we praise You,
  The weak by grace made strong,
Whose labors and whose Gospel
  Enrich our triumph song.
May we, in all our weakness,
  Reflect Your servant life
And follow in Your footsteps,
  Enduring cross and strife. (LSB 518:15)

Peter's sermon in Acts 10:34–43 provides a strikingly precise outline of Mark's Gospel.

Mark's is the shortest of the four canonical Gospels and the fastest paced ("immediately" is its watchword). It provides a beautiful picture of Christ as the conquering King, who battles and drives out the enemies of the human race (the demons) just as Joshua drove out the inhabitants of Canaan, a battle that culminates at the cross. The symbol associated with St. Mark is the lion, king of the beasts. Mark's Gospel contains some teaching sections from our Lord, but it is overwhelmingly a fast-paced action account, right up to the disproportionately long narrative of the Lord's Passion. In fact, it has been called a Passion narrative with a preface.

Mark is said to have finished his service to Christ by serving as bishop in the great city of Alexandria in Egypt, ultimately dying there a martyr's death.

Almighty God, You have enriched Your Church with the proclamation of the Gospel through the evangelist Mark. Grant that we may firmly believe these glad tidings and daily walk according to Your Word; through Jesus Christ, our Lord, who lives and reigns with You and the Holy Spirit, one God, now and forever. Amen.

READINGS
ISAIAH 52:7–10 / 2 TIMOTHY 4:5–18 / MARK 16:14–20

1
MAY

Today, the Church celebrates the Festival of **St. Philip and St. James, Apostles**.

St. Philip was from Bethsaida in Galilee, the same town on the shores of Lake Gennesaret that Peter and Andrew, James and John were from. We learn most about this disciple and apostle of Christ from John's Gospel. After Christ found Philip and called to him, "Follow me!" Philip, in turn, found Nathanael: "We have found Him of whom Moses in the Law and also the prophets wrote, Jesus of Nazareth." Nathanael was skeptical of our Lord's apparent Galilean origins, but Philip pressed him with the invitation: "Come and see!" The Church has echoed that invitation throughout the ages to any who are curious but doubtful.

Before the Feast of Passover at which our Lord was crucified and raised, some Greeks approached Philip because he was from Galilee and said, "Sir, we wish to see Jesus." When Andrew and Philip together brought the request to our Lord, He promised, "I, when I am lifted up from the earth, will draw all people to Myself." At the Last Supper, Philip, hearing Christ speak of the Father, begged to see the Father. Christ replied, "Have I been with you so long, and you still do not know Me, Philip? Whoever has seen Me has seen the Father."

After witnessing the Lord's resurrection and the dispersion of the apostles, tradition suggests Philip journeyed to Scythia and Phrygia. He is reported to have met his death by crucifixion in Hieropolis. His symbol is therefore a simple Latin cross.

The James commemorated today is not to be confused with the brother of John and son of Zebedee. To distinguish the two, the epitaph "the elder" is usually attached to John's brother, and "the less" (which may be taken as "the younger" or "the shorter") attached to this James. He was the son of

We praise You, Lord, for Philip,
Blest guide to Greek and Jew,
And for young James the faithful,
Who heard and followed You.
O grant us grace to know You,
The way, the truth, the life,
To wrestle with temptation,
To triumph in the strife. (LSB 518:16)

Alphaeus. Presumably it was his mother, Mary, who was among the women mentioned at the cross and the tomb. He had a brother Joseph (or Joses). Tradition suggests that he was martyred in Ostrakine in lower Egypt. His apostolic shield sports a fuller's club, for he was reportedly beaten to death with one.

In the Preface from the Divine Service for this day we pray, "It is truly good, right, and salutary that we should at all times and in all places give thanks to You, holy Lord, almighty Father, everlasting God: for You have mightily governed and protected Your Holy Church, in which the blessed apostles and evangelists proclaimed Your divine and saving Gospel. Therefore with patriarchs and prophets, apostles and evangelists, with Your servants Saints Philip and James, and with all the company of heaven we laud and magnify Your glorious name. . . ."

Almighty God, Your Son revealed Himself to Philip and James and gave them the knowledge of everlasting life. Grant us perfectly to know Your Son, Jesus Christ, to be the way, the truth, and the life, and steadfastly to walk in the way that leads to eternal life; through Jesus Christ, Your Son, our Lord, who lives and reigns with You and the Holy Spirit, one God, now and forever. Amen.

READINGS
ISAIAH 30:18–21 / EPHESIANS 2:19–22 / JOHN 14:1–14

2
MAY

Today, we remember and thank God for **St. Athanasius of Alexandria, Pastor and Confessor**.

Athanasius (likely born around AD 295) was serving as a deacon in the Church of Alexandria in Egypt when he first encountered the presbyter Arius. Arius preached that the Son of the Father was not eternal, but rather the first, highest, and noblest creature. Arius's watchword was "there was when He wasn't." Against this heresy (which still thrives today among Jehovah's Witnesses), Athanasius became a valiant defender. In AD 325, he attended the First Council of Nicaea with his bishop, Alexander. Here Arianism was flatly condemned. Our Lord was confessed to be "of one substance with the Father," as we still say today in the Creed that originated from this Council.

The Arian party did not readily give up. After Alexander died, Athanasius was appointed his successor. The new bishop, however, met bitter and lasting opposition. He was exiled to the West, and even though vindicated by a Synod in Rome, he continued to be out of favor with the Emperor and in the East.

After some years, he was allowed to return to Alexandria and resume his work. Yet, after ten years mostly devoid of conflict in which the great man wrote, visited, and cared for his large flock, trouble stirred again. Forced to flee, Athanasius spent time in Libya. Restored again for a while, exiled again for a while became the pattern of his life. He died this day in 373, having been exiled five times. He spent no less than seventeen years of his long episcopate in disfavor, forced from his church. Yet, he would not yield to anyone in the confession of our Lord's true and full divinity. It is no wonder, then, that he is remembered by the moniker *"Athanasius contra mundum."* Athanasius against the world!

His theological acumen was already apparent in his little treatise *On the Incarnation of the Word*, written as a young man: "By His death has salvation

Of the Father's love begotten
Ere the worlds began to be,
He is Alpha and Omega,
He the source, the ending He,
Of the things that are, that have been,
And that future years shall see
Evermore and evermore. (LSB 384:1)

---

come to all, and all creation been ransomed. He is the Life of all, and He it is that as a sheep yielded His body to death as a substitute, for the salvation of all, even though the Jews believe it not" (Par. 37). His depth of insight only grew during the years of suffering and struggle. Athanasius recorded the history of the Arian controversies; wrote a biography of his dear friend and mentor, St. Anthony; and provided us in his Easter letter of 367 one of the very first attempts we know of to list the authoritative books that compose the biblical canon. He says of them, "These are fountains of salvation, that they who thirst may be satisfied with the living words they contain. In these alone is proclaimed the doctrine of godliness. Let no man add to these, neither let him take [aught] from these" (Letter 39:6).

O God of truth and mercy, You upheld Your servant Athanasius to
confess with boldness the catholic faith against all hostility and resistance.
Uphold Your Church that trusts solely in the grace of Your eternal Word, who
took upon Himself our humanity that we might share His divinity; who lives
and reigns with You and the Holy Spirit, one God, now and forever. Amen.

4
MAY

On this day, we remember and thank God for
Friedrich Wyneken, Pastor and Missionary.

Born in Hannover in 1810, Friedrich Wyneken was the son of a Lutheran pastor. Like many before him, he followed in his father's footsteps. The evangelical preaching he heard as a young man planted firmly in his heart a desire to bring the saving Gospel to those who had never heard it. He arrived in Baltimore in 1838 and was eventually sent by the mission society of the old Pennsylvania Ministerium to labor in the "west."

His health began to fail somewhat due to the primitive conditions and the enormity of what he was facing. He returned to Germany and literally begged for help in this task. Wilhelm Loehe was among those who heard and heeded the call to support his mission. When Wyneken came back to America, he did not come alone. He brought a number of pastors with him, and they in turn brought others. Not only was work begun in reaching the many Germans who were already living in the new land and continued to flood in, but the Gospel also was brought to the Native Americans in Michigan.

Through Wyneken's efforts and with support from Loehe, a practical seminary was established in Fort Wayne, Indiana, to supply the "emergency preachers" that the frontier conditions so desperately required. In 1845, Wyneken returned to Baltimore as the pastor of St. Paul's Lutheran Church. His strong confessional convictions led to a rupture with the General Synod, and he sought union with a fledgling body that became The Lutheran Church—Missouri Synod. He joined the Synod at its second convention and was eventually elected its second president in 1850, after he had been called to serve Trinity Lutheran Church (Old Trinity) in St. Louis, Missouri.

Hark, the voice of Jesus calling,
"Who will go and work today?
Fields are white and harvests waiting—
Who will bear the sheaves away?"
Loud and long the Master calleth;
Rich reward He offers thee.
Who will answer, gladly saying,
"Here am I, send me, send me"? (LSB 826:1)

Health issues eventually caused him to be given a leave of absence from his congregation. He returned to the scene of his old labor in Fort Wayne and devoted himself full time to His work as Synod president. He discharged that office faithfully and with zeal, carrying out the required visitations of congregations and pastors under difficult conditions. He stressed the importance of maintaining doctrinal purity, catechizing the young, and living a holy life. He knew how easily Christians could be conformed to the sinful world. His increasing age and ongoing health issues eventually led to his being unable to fulfill the stringent demands of the presidency, which he left in 1864 in the midst of the Civil War. His final work in the Church was as pastor at Trinity Lutheran Church in Cleveland. He died this day in 1876.

Lord Jesus Christ, You want all to be saved and to come to the knowledge of the truth. We give You thanks for sending Friedrich Wyneken as missionary and pastor in Indiana, Ohio, and Michigan to evangelize the Native Americans in these states, to be a founder of Concordia Theological Seminary in Fort Wayne, and to serve as second president of The Lutheran Church—Missouri Synod. Protect and encourage all missionaries who confess the true faith among the nations by proclaiming Christ crucified; for You live and reign with the Father and Holy Spirit, one God, now and forever. Amen.

5
MAY

Today, the Holy Church rejoices to remember **Frederick the Wise, Christian Ruler**.

Frederick the Wise (1463–1525) was the Elector of Saxony from 1486 until his death. The term *Elector*, meaning the prince of this portion of Saxony, indicated that when the German states met to elect the next emperor of the Holy Roman Empire, the prince of Electoral Saxony was entitled to cast a vote.

In 1502, Frederick founded a brand-new university in the town of Wittenberg. In that same town he worked to amass an impressive quantity of holy relics (various body parts and possessions said to have belonged to the saints of the Church). By 1520, his relic collection numbered over nineteen thousand items. Guarantees of many years out of purgatory were promised to those who revered the sacred items. The contributions given by those who came to see and pray before the relics was a steady source of income for the fledgling university.

To this university came professors Martin Luther and Philipp Melanchthon. Frederick was delighted when Luther began to achieve some notoriety as a scholar to be reckoned with; it put his university on the map, as it were. As Frederick came to properly understand and believe the Gospel, he grasped Luther's growing critiques of the entire system of purgatory, the veneration of relics, and his rejection of indulgences. True, it meant less income from the veneration of the relics, but Frederick was a man who was concerned with truth and piously venerated the Sacred Scriptures above all. Luther was opening them up and bringing comfort and joy to him and many.

Frederick was actually the pope's choice for Holy Roman Emperor at the death of Maximillian. Yet, he ended up supporting his nephew, who then became Charles V. Charles was not in a position to deny his uncle

May ev'ry mountain height,
Each vale and forest green,
Shine in Your Word's pure light,
And its rich fruits be seen!
May ev'ry tongue
Be tuned to praise
And join to raise
A grateful song. (LSB 966:3)

---

his request for Luther's presence at the Diet of Worms in 1521, where the monk would speak for himself. After the Diet declared Luther an outlaw, it was Frederick who kept him safe by a friendly act of kidnapping. Luther disappeared from public view and was safely stowed at Wartburg Castle for some months. There he occupied himself with the translation of the New Testament into German, began his collection of sermons for the Church Year, and grew daily more miserable. Things at Wittenberg were in danger of taking a radical turn! Luther defied his prince's order to stay put and returned.

Though Luther's action endangered Frederick himself, Luther's relationship with the great man was not harmed. The Elector determined to give full scope for Luther to continue writing, preaching, and teaching. Frederick died a bachelor on this day in 1525. His brother John the Steadfast was his heir.

Heavenly Father, You provided wisdom and skill to Frederick the Wise as elector of Saxony during the early years of the Reformation, using His rule and authority to protect Martin Luther and preserve the preaching of the Gospel. Graciously regard all Your servants who make, administer, and judge the laws of this nation, and look with favor upon all the rulers of the earth. Grant them wisdom and understanding that they might provide sanctuary for Your Church to continue to proclaim the true faith; for You live and reign with the Son and the Holy Spirit, one God, now and forever. Amen.

7
MAY

Today, we remember and thank God for **C. F. W. Walther, Theologian**.

Carl Ferdinand Wilhelm Walther was born in 1811 in Saxony. His father, grandfather, and great-grandfather were pastors in the Lutheran Church. Both he and his brother ended up serving as pastors as well. He was educated at the University of Leipzig when Rationalism was in full bloom. He fell in with a group of students and others who took seriously the Sacred Scriptures and the Lutheran Confessions, and here he met the influential pastor Martin Stephan.

Walther was ordained in 1837. By that time, the staunchly confessional Lutherans in Saxony were convinced that the only safe course for the future was to emigrate to the United States. Walther joined Stephan's colony and left for the United States in 1839.

Stephan had himself declared bishop of the new colony before arriving in St. Louis. All the colonists swore an oath of obedience to their new bishop in matters both temporal and spiritual. When Stephan had to be removed from office amidst scandal, it was C. F. W. Walther who was sent to attend to this unpleasantness.

Without their bishop, the colony entered a great crisis. Were they a church? Did the pastors sin by leaving their calls in Germany? Did they have calls now? Ought the whole thing be abandoned and all return? Through this very difficult time, in which Walther fully participated in the angst of the colony, he was driven back to the Scriptures and to major writings of Luther. There he found comfort and conviction based solidly on the promises of God's Word. From this conviction he became the leading theologian of what would become The Lutheran Church—Missouri Synod.

His work at planting in the United States a Lutheran Church committed to the Lutheran Confessions, ruled by the Word of God, was tireless. He

O, where is your sting, death? We fear you no more;
Christ rose, and now open is fair Eden's door.
For all our transgressions His blood does atone;
Redeemed and forgiven, we now are His own. (LSB 480:4)

---

founded a seminary (Concordia Seminary, St. Louis), started a magazine called *Lehre und Wehre* that promoted confessional Lutheranism, served as a professor, and twice was the president of The Lutheran Church—Missouri Synod, all the while pastoring large congregations in St. Louis.

He guided the Synod through various controversies and difficulties. In all this he sought to be a faithful steward of the "faith once delivered to the saints" rather than a theological innovator. His great work on *The Proper Distinction between Law and Gospel* continues to be a guiding light for Lutheran pastors in how to preach. He tirelessly proclaimed Christ's universal atonement, rejoiced in the universal priesthood of all the baptized, and sought to ground faith solidly upon the promises of God's Word.

Walther was a hymnwriter (he wrote the hymn that began this devotion) and a liturgiologist. He gave great priority to publishing an Agenda (service book) and hymnal for the German-speaking churches. He encouraged the production of an English version of both for the growing number of English-speaking Lutheran churches. Through much of his ministry, he battled serious depression and anxiety, yet in his weakness the Lord's strength shone brightly.

Almighty God, through Your servant C. F. W. Walther You brought Lutheran pilgrims from Germany to confess the true faith. May the priesthood of Your saints now receive the Gospel of a crucified and risen Savior in faith as they offer back to You in love sacrifices of praise and thanksgiving, for You live and reign with the Son and the Holy Spirit, one God, now and forever. Amen.

9
MAY

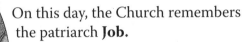

On this day, the Church remembers
the patriarch **Job.**

"**Consider the patience** of Job," James invites (cf.
James 5:11). In the book that bears his name, Job is
first revealed as a man "blameless and upright." The
Lord brags on this man to Satan, who insists that Job
only serves God out of self-interest. God permits Satan
to attack Job's possessions and family. In a single day,
Job's ten children die and he loses all his wealth. Truly, "the
thief comes only to steal and kill and destroy" (John 10:10).

Job responds to this horrid loss by faithful worship. He tears his
robe, shaves his head, and falls to the ground before the Lord. He confesses,
"Naked I came from my mother's womb, and naked shall I return. The LORD
gave, and the LORD has taken away; blessed be the name of the LORD" (Job
1:21).

God again boasts to Satan of Job's faithfulness in the face of disaster he
could not understand. Satan, however, insists that Job will cave and curse
God if God were to allow him to afflict Job's body. "Stretch out your hand
and touch his bone and his flesh, and he will curse you to your face" (Job
2:5). God then allows Satan to afflict Job physically, but not to kill him.

Yet, once again, patient, faithful Job does not disappoint. When even his
wife urges him to simply curse God and be done with it, Job dismisses her
words. He says, "Shall we receive good from God, and shall we not receive
evil?" (Job 2:10).

Job's friends come to comfort him. The bulk of the story is devoted to
the long back-and-forth between them. Job insists on his innocence; his
friends, one after the other, urge him to repent of whatever hidden sin led

I know that my Redeemer lives;
What comfort this sweet sentence gives!
He lives, He lives, who once was dead;
He lives, my ever-living head. (LSB 461:1)

---

to this great disaster. Does disaster come upon a person because of their unfaithfulness to God? Satan would always whisper that in the ears of suffering people: "You must have done something dreadful! Look at how you are being punished. The Lord must truly hate you."

Against this lie, Job serves as a bulwark. He had not been faithless to God. He knew he was a sinner from birth and he depended entirely on God's mercy and forgiveness. He didn't know why God allowed the horrible events to overtake him, but he was confident: "Though He slay me, I will hope in Him" (Job 13:15). His longing for a mediator was finally answered in our Lord. Here indeed is the "Redeemer" that Job knew lived and would stand upon the earth, the One who would raise him from death. God reveals Himself to Job at the end. Job confesses that God's actions are beyond human comprehension. Job prays for his friends, and God restores to him more children and great wealth.

Lord God, heavenly Father, You sanctified Your suffering prophet Job, showing him forth as blameless, true, God-fearing, just, and righteous. Through his valiant endurance and long-suffering patience, You taught us how to live in a broken world under Your great mercy as You set us free from our sins and rescued us from the punishments we deserve, through the all-sufficient sacrifice of Your only-begotten Son, who with You and the Holy Spirit lives and reigns, one God, now and forever. Amen.

11
MAY

Today, we remember and thank God for the brothers **Cyril and Methodius, Missionaries to the Slavs**.

How dear to the saints of God are those who first preach to them the joyous news of the death and resurrection of Christ for our salvation, the saving Gospel! The Slavic peoples have long remembered the labors of the two brothers we commemorate this day: Cyril and Methodius.

The brothers were born in Thessalonica, part of the Byzantine Empire, in the first half of the 800s. At the time, Macedonia was receiving an influx of Slavic people (and their own mother *may* have been a Slav). They labored to share with them the Christian faith.

In 862, at the invitation of a Moravian prince, they were dispatched from Constantinople to nurture and strengthen the Christian Church that had been begun by Roman missionaries in the area. As has happened so often, the need to put the Word of God into the native language led the brothers first to create an alphabet that suited the Slavonic tongue (often called Cyrillic, after Cyril). They then used this to write the Sacred Scriptures and translate the liturgy into the Slavs' native language. The use of Old Church Slavonic persists in parts of the Eastern Church to this day.

The brothers were summoned to Rome in 867, where their work was acknowledged and given papal blessing. They were ordained priests. Pope Adrian II also authorized the use of their liturgy in those Slavic territories.

Cyril, sensing his health failing, became a monk. He died a mere fifty days later. His brother then continued their great work alone. The pope had named him archbishop over the territory where he had labored. This put him in conflict with the claims of the Archbishop of Salzburg, and strife resulted. Methodius experienced deposition, arrest, and imprisonment, but at last vindication. The pope insisted he be restored to office.

Make songs of joy to Christ, our head;
Alleluia!
He lives again who once was dead!
Alleluia!
Our life was purchased by His loss;
Alleluia!
He died our death upon the cross.
Alleluia! (LSB 484:1–2)

Significantly, part of the conflict that persisted for a long time after Methodius's death was the Eastern freedom to use the language of the people in the Divine Service in contrast to the Western practice of imposing Latin everywhere. The endeavors of Saints Cyril and Methodius to provide Scripture and liturgy in the vernacular would not have a counterpart in the Western lands for many centuries. One day, though, a German monk named Luther would dare to render the Scriptures into German and provide a Divine Service for the first time for the German people in their own tongue.

The hymn used in the commemoration today comes from the Slovak Lutheran tradition.

Almighty and everlasting God, by the power of Your Holy Spirit You moved Your servant Cyril and his brother Methodius to bring the light of the Gospel to the Slavs, a people broken by hostility and division. By the love of Christ, overcome all bitterness and strife among us, and form us into one united family who live under the mercies of the Prince of Peace, who lives and reigns with You and the Holy Spirit, one God, now and forever. Amen.

21
MAY

Today, the Holy Church remembers and thanks God for
Emperor Constantine, Christian Ruler, and **Helena,
Mother of Constantine.**

Constantine was the emperor of the Roman Empire from AD 306 to 337.
He was born about AD 272 in present-day Serbia. His mother, Helena, was
not of noble birth and may have been only the concubine of his father.
Constantine entered the Roman army and became part of the bodyguard
for the emperor. Under Diocletian, the empire was divided into fourths,
and Constantine's father was given charge of one part. At his father's death,
Constantine assumed this office, and from it he gradually and with much
conflict fought his way clear to becoming the sole ruler of the empire.

In the process of acquiring the empire, Constantine had to fight many
a battle. Eusebius relates that on one occasion when his troops were clearly
outnumbered, a vision was granted him and Constantine heard the words,
"In this sign conquer." The sign referred to was the Greek letters Chi and Rho
combined: the first two letters of the name of Christ. Constantine supposedly
marked his soldiers' shields with this sign and proceeded to victory.

In AD 314, he issued the famous Edict of Milan. For the first time, being
a Christian was no longer a crime against the state. Christians' lives were
safe and their properties could not be seized. Church buildings for the first
time could be public edifices.

Helena had enthusiastically embraced the faith before her son. However,
once Constantine lent his support to Christianity, mother and son financially
supported the construction of church buildings throughout the empire.
Helena particularly was concerned with building churches connected with
the events recorded in the Gospels in Palestine. She is responsible for the
construction of the Church of the Holy Sepulchre in Jerusalem. Constantine
also saw to the building of what became known as Old Saint Peter's, the

We give Thee but Thine own,
Whate'er the gift may be;
All that we have is Thine alone,
A trust, O Lord, from Thee.
May we Thy bounties thus
As stewards true receive
And gladly, as Thou blessest us,
To Thee our firstfruits give! (LSB 781:1–2)

---

church that stood over the graves of Peter and Paul in the Vatican from the fourth century until its replacement by the present Basilica.

Constantine is remembered also as the man who convoked the Council of Nicaea in 325 that rejected Arianism, the teaching that Christ was not true God. Constantine was baptized on his deathbed in 337, not uncommon at the time. His mother had died only a few years earlier in 330. Together they are celebrated as worldly rulers who sought to strengthen and support the mission of Christ's Church on earth.

Almighty and everlasting God, by Your Spirit You brought Emperor Constantine to believe and confess the victory of the cross and moved his mother to help in the building of many churches where Your people could gather to receive Your gifts and praise Your name. Receive our thanks for them and for all benefactors who give generously of their wealth to further the work of Your Church in spreading the saving Gospel; through Jesus Christ, our Lord, who lives and reigns with You and the Holy Spirit, one God, now and forever. Amen.

24
MAY

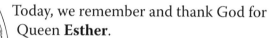

Today, we remember and thank God for Queen **Esther**.

Esther, or Hadassah as she was originally named, is the central figure in the biblical book that bears her name. She was an orphan raised by her relative Mordecai. When King Ahasuerus (Xerxes, who reigned 486–465 BC) became displeased with his queen, a search was made for a suitable replacement among the beautiful women of the kingdom. Esther was chosen.

Mordecai became a chief minister of the king and lived in the Persian capital Susa. He overheard a plot to kill the king and informed on the would-be assassins. This was recorded in the royal archives. When the high official Haman the Agagite commanded Mordecai to kneel before him, Mordecai refused. This convinced Haman that Mordecai and his people were rebellious and needed to be purged from the empire. If the king promised him the power to do this, he promised to pay ten thousand silver talents into the treasury. The king then issued a proclamation that the Jewish people be wiped out and their property taken. He did not realize that his wife was among those affected by the decree.

When Mordecai heard of the decree, he sought to get a message to Queen Esther. He reminded her that she would not escape just because she was in the king's harem. He said, "Who knows whether you have not come to the kingdom for such a time as this?" (Esther 4:14). Though the name of God does not appear in the Hebrew version of the book, Mordecai was clearly referring to God arranging for the queen at this time to be the instrument of salvation for His people.

Who trusts in God
A strong abode
In heav'n and earth possesses;
Who looks in love
To Christ above,
No fear that heart oppresses.
In You alone,
Dear Lord, we own
Sweet hope and consolation,
Our shield from foes,
Our balm for woes,
Our great and sure salvation. (LSB 714:1)

Esther took her life in hand; it was forbidden for anyone to approach the king without his leave and bore the death penalty if he did not graciously extend his scepter. He did extend the scepter to his beloved queen. She finally obtained the exact reversal of Haman's decree of destruction. Instead of the Jewish people being slain and their property confiscated, they were given a period of time to do this to their enemies. And in a great ironic twist, Haman was actually hanged on the very gallows that he himself had readied for hanging Mordecai. This astonishing reversal of fortunes for the Jewish people is still celebrated in their yearly Feast of Purim.

Queen Esther is remembered as a brave and faithful intercessor and ruler who risked her life to save her people.

Almighty and everlasting God, through the intercession of Queen Esther You worked a great salvation for Your ancient people, thwarting the plans of their enemies to destroy them. Continue to grant wisdom and courage to all Christian rulers, that they may provide a safe haven for the work of Your Church in bringing the message of salvation to people of every land; through Jesus Christ, our Lord, who lives and reigns with You and the Holy Spirit, one God, now and forever. Amen.

25
MAY

Today, the Holy Church rejoices to remember **Bede the Venerable, Theologian**.

The Venerable Bede was born in Northumberland, England, around AD 672. He never traveled more than 100 miles from his place of birth, yet this monk's reputation as theologian and historian spread throughout Europe and the world.

His parents sent him to the monastery at Monkwearmouth at age 7. When a sister monastery was founded in present day Jarrow, Bede was transferred there. In 686, plague swept through that monastery and for a time only two monks survived to carry on the round of singing together the Daily Office. One of them was Cleofrith, the abbot, the other a young boy of fourteen. That would be Bede.

He was made a deacon in 692 and at age 30 he was ordained a priest. He labored in the monastery in preaching, teaching, and above all, writing. His commentaries on Scripture proved popular throughout the Middle Ages and remain a source of inspiration and insight to this day. He excelled in music and poetry, particularly working in his native English. Perhaps his most famous writing is the thorough and careful *History of the English Church*. The man's piety shines in his observation (at least in the northern hemisphere) that the Church observes the Feast of St. John's Nativity in the days when the sun's light begins to diminish and our Lord's Nativity in the days when the light grows, since "I must decrease but He must increase!"

The account of the Venerable Bede's death on the Feast of the Ascension, May 26, AD 735, shows nearly everything one needs to know about this great man. He was still at work on an English translation of John's Gospel, with a

Be now our joy on earth, O Lord,
And be our future great reward.
   Alleluia, alleluia!
Then, throned with You forever, we
Shall praise Your name eternally.
   Alleluia, alleluia!
   Alleluia, alleluia, alleluia!
O risen Christ, ascended Lord,
All praise to You let earth accord:
   Alleluia, alleluia!
You are, while endless ages run,
With Father and with Spirit one.
   Alleluia, alleluia!
   Alleluia, alleluia, alleluia! (**LSB 493:5–6**)

---

young lad acting as his scribe. His strength was waning fast. He finished it, then fell to the floor of his cell singing the Gloria Patri, and that is how he died. He was buried in Jarrow; however, his remains were later moved to the great Cathedral in Durham.

Fitting, since he died upon the Feast of the Ascension, that our hymnal includes his Ascension Day hymn, "A Hymn of Glory Let Us Sing." The opening stanzas for today were taken from this hymn. Bede's life and ministry are an invitation for us and all people to join this humble monk, who delighted in the Word of God and in singing unending Glorias to Father, Son, and Holy Spirit.

Almighty and everlasting God, receive this day our thanks for Your servant, the Venerable Bede. Even as he took great delight in Your Word and sought to teach Your ways with zeal, so may Your people today follow His example and to our dying breath proclaim the great things You have done; through Jesus Christ, our risen and ascended Lord, who lives and reigns with You and the Holy Spirit, one God, now and forever. Amen.

31
MAY

On this day, we celebrate with great joy the Feast of **the Visitation of Our Lord** (three-year lectionary).

St. Luke's Gospel records in chapter 1 the visit of Mary to her kinswoman Elizabeth, when Mary was newly with child and Elizabeth in her sixth month. It would be the first meeting of John the Baptist and the Lord whom he was to serve.

From within the house, Elizabeth hears the greeting of her kinswoman and a miracle happens. The child within her leaps for joy. Elizabeth is herself filled with the Spirit and speaks, as she greets Mary.

It was a fearful secret Mary had been carrying. But she knows from the look of astonishment on Elizabeth's face that she, too, was in the know. God had let Elizabeth in on the great secret of the ages. She cries out, "Blessed are you among women, and blessed is the fruit of your womb! And why is this granted to me that the mother of my Lord should come to me? For behold, when the sound of your greeting came to my ears, the baby in my womb leaped for joy."

Perhaps she gave a knowing glance over at Zechariah, sitting silently in his corner—silent since he had doubted the words of Gabriel. Her next words seemed aimed at him: "And blessed is she who believed that there would be a fulfillment of what was spoken to her from the Lord." You can almost see Zechariah laughing silently in agreement.

The young Mary melts into a song of praise that is reminiscent of Hannah's hymn in 1 Samuel 2. We call Mary's song her Magnificat, from the first words of the song in Latin. In it, she praises God for His kind regard of her, a lowly and despised person. She praises His upside-down way of

Praise, all you people, the name so holy
Of Him who does such wondrous things!
All that has being, to praise Him solely,
With happy heart its amen sings.
Children of God, with angel host
Praise Father, Son, and Holy Ghost!
Alleluia, alleluia! (LSB 797:5)

---

working where He fills the hungry with good and sends the rich away empty, lifts up the lowly and tumbles the mighty from their thrones. Above all, she rejoices in how the fruit of her womb, the child whose heart now beats beneath her own, is the fulfillment of God's great promise to Abraham about the Seed who would come to bring blessing to all.

Mary's song of praise is the traditional canticle the Church delights to sing at Vespers or Evening Prayer, even as Zechariah's canticle is sung in the morning. By singing it with her, we confess that we, too, are among those for whom the Lord has done great things, and what is greater than the Son of God becoming flesh for us in Mary's womb to bring us all the blessing of eternal life?

Almighty God, You chose the Virgin Mary to be the mother of Your Son and made known through her Your gracious regard for the poor and lowly and despised. Grant that we may receive Your Word in humility and faith, and so be made one with Jesus Christ, Your Son, our Lord, who lives and reigns with You and the Holy Spirit, one God, now and forever. Amen.

READINGS
ISAIAH 11:1–5 / ROMANS 12:9–16 / LUKE 1:39–45 (46–56)

1

JUNE

Today, we remember the second-century Christian apologist, **St. Justin, Martyr**.

Though born in Judea, Justin was by his own acknowledgment raised in a pagan family and environment. As an eager student, he went in search of the truth. He sampled the various Greek schools of thought, all of which left him unsatisfied, spiritually hungry and thirsty. One day, an old man happened to witness to him, telling him the Good News about Jesus. He explained that in the writings of the apostles and prophets, Justin could find what he was looking for so unsuccessfully in philosophy. There he would come to know the true God and His Son, as the men who wrote these books were full of the Holy Spirit of God.

Justin began devoting his life to these writings, and through them the Spirit worked faith in the young man. He found in the strictly disciplined life of the early Christians everything he was looking for. He was particularly moved by their willingness to die, letting go of everything that is seen, in the sure confidence of what is not seen.

Justin immediately began defending his newfound faith. He wrote extensive apologies (defenses) to the Roman Emperor, arguing that Christians were not the immoral beasts their enemies made them out to be. Because he needed to defend Christians against the charges that swirled around their private worship services, Justin provided accounts about how the early Christians worshiped. These are among the earliest witnesses we have to the liturgy of the Early Church. He wrote of a gathering of all in one place on the Lord's Day, where the writings of prophets and apostles were read as long as time permitted. Then the president delivered the homily, inviting everyone there into the pattern of these good things. Prayer was offered for all. Bread, wine, and water were taken and blessed with a "pattern

Lord, 'tis not that I did choose Thee;
That, I know, could never be;
For this heart would still refuse Thee
Had Thy grace not chosen me.
Thou hast from the sin that stained me
Washed and cleansed and set me free
And unto this end ordained me,
That I ever live to Thee. (LSB 573:1)

---

of prayer from Him" and then a distribution was made of the Eucharist, which he confessed to be the body and blood of the eternal Word. (See Justin's *First Apology*, pars. 66–67.)

Justin and some of his disciples were martyred under the Prefect Rusticus around AD 165. The Roman account of their martyrdom survives. Commanded to sacrifice to the gods or to face terrible torture without mercy, Justin replied, "That is our desire, to be tortured for our Lord, Jesus Christ, and so to be saved, for that will give us salvation and firm confidence at the more terrible universal tribunal of our Lord and Savior." All the others said the same. They were, then, first scourged and finally beheaded, entering into the noble army of martyrs who sing praises to the Lamb without end.

Almighty and everlasting God, You found Your martyr Justin wandering from teacher to teacher, searching for the true God. Grant that all who seek for a deeper knowledge of the sublime wisdom of Your eternal Word may be found by You, who sent Your Son to seek and to save the lost; through Jesus Christ, our Lord, who lives and reigns with You and the Holy Spirit, one God, now and forever. Amen.

5
JUNE

Today, we remember and give thanks to God for His holy martyr
St. Boniface of Mainz, Missionary to the Germans.

Boniface was born in the English kingdom of Wessex around AD 675 to
a prosperous family. Against his father's wishes, Boniface became a monk
and at age 30, a priest. In 716, he joined a missionary foray into the land of
Frisia, working with Willibrord. War disrupted their efforts, and Boniface
returned home for a short time. The next year, he went to Rome, where the
pope appointed him bishop of a diocese not then in existence: Germania.

Boniface bravely headed into this new territory to plant the faith of
Christ and uproot the old idolatry. The Germans at the time worshiped
trees. In the northern part of present day Hesse, Boniface felled the Donar
Oak to show that it was no true god at all. The people were amazed that
the little man could fell the great oak without the gods bringing judgment
on him. With the wood of the old tree he built on the very site a chapel
dedicated to St. Peter. Many of the natives were converted.

In 732, the pope elevated Boniface to archbishop of all Germania.
Throughout the German-speaking lands, Boniface planted monasteries that
became centers of worship, learning, and further outreach. The missionary
spirit continued to burn in Boniface, and in 754 he returned to his first
mission field, Frisia, to continue work there.

He baptized many people on this mission and arranged to meet those
baptized for confirmation near Dokkum. But instead of his beloved newly
baptized, he encountered a hostile crowd of robbers and murderers. When
some of his followers wished to fight to protect the aged archbishop, Boniface
ordered them to lay down their weapons. He reminded them of the words of
St. Paul that we must "not be overcome by evil, but overcome evil with good"
(Romans 12:21). The old man and his companions were martyred and their

Lord, gather all Your children,
Wherever they may be,
And lead them on to heaven
To live eternally
With You, our loving Father,
And Christ, our brother dear,
Whose Spirit guards and gives us
The joy to persevere. (LSB 835:6)

---

possessions rifled. But instead of the hoped for treasure, they found only old books. Boniface supposedly held one of the books up when he was attacked. This book that bears the marks of violence (long a treasured memento of the great saint) is still found at Fulda, in Hesse, where the remains of Boniface at last were laid to rest.

As Willibrord is remembered as the "apostle" to the Frisians, so Boniface, the Englishman, has long been remembered as the "apostle" to the German-speaking peoples. Glory to You, kind Savior, for Your tireless witness Boniface of Mainz!

Almighty God, You called Boniface to be a witness and martyr in Ger-
many, and by his labor and suffering You raised up a people for Your own
possession. Pour out Your Holy Spirit upon Your Church in every land, that
by the service and sacrifice of many Your holy name may be glorified and
Your kingdom enlarged; through Jesus Christ, our Lord, who lives and reigns
with You and the Holy Spirit, one God, now and forever. Amen.

11
JUNE

On this day, the Church remembers and gives thanks to God for **St. Barnabas, Apostle**.

A Jewish Levite who originally hailed from the island of Cyprus, Barnabas steps into history in the account Luke provides in Acts 4. Originally named Joseph, this godly man sold some of his temporal possessions and laid the proceeds at the feet of the Twelve. This was to aid the poor in Jerusalem and support the Church's mission. The apostles gave him the name Barnabas, which means "Son of Encouragement." We also learn from Acts that Barnabas was cousin to the young John Mark, who would be the author of the second Gospel.

After Paul's conversion and initial ministry in Damascus, he visited Jerusalem but found the Church as a whole leery of this former persecutor. Barnabas, however, took Paul under his wing and introduced him to the apostles. He told them the story of what had happened to their erstwhile opponent.

When word reached the apostles that something was stirring in Antioch, where Gentiles were beginning to call on the name of Jesus, they dispatched Barnabas to investigate. Barnabas was overjoyed at the Spirit's work. He immediately headed to Tarsus to fetch Paul and bring him into the work. There they labored in the teaching, and their work was greatly prospered. Worshiping together in Antioch, the Spirit foretold a famine to afflict Judea. The two were sent to bring relief to the Jerusalem Church. Later, the Spirit instructed that Barnabas and Saul be set aside for the work to which He had called them. They were then dispatched on the first great missionary journey, spreading the saving name of Jesus to Jew and Gentile throughout Asia Minor.

For Barnabas we praise You,
  Who kept Your law of love
And, leaving earthly treasures,
  Sought riches from above.
O Christ, our Lord and Savior,
  Let gifts of grace descend,
That Your true consolation
  May through the world extend. (LSB 518:17)

Accompanying them on that journey at first was John Mark, but he did not complete the work and returned home. When the traveling companions contemplated a second journey, Barnabas was willing to give John Mark a second chance. Paul, at the time, thought it inadvisable. The two ended up sharply contending and dividing. Barnabas and Mark headed to Cyprus while Paul and Silas traveled first to Asia Minor and then into Europe.

From 1 Corinthians 9:6, it is apparent that Barnabas followed the same pattern as Paul in not making use of his right as a minister of the Gospel to receive pay. He was clearly known to the Church there, and he is also mentioned in Galatians 2:13. He is not mentioned again in the pages of the New Testament. A document survives from the Early Church known as *The Epistle of Barnabas*, but scholarly consensus is that it is not authentic. Tradition suggests that Barnabas died a martyr's death in Cyprus, continuing to preach the Good News to his native land, being stoned to death after first being tortured.

Almighty God, Your faithful servant Barnabas sought not his own renown but gave generously of his life and substance for the encouragement of the apostles and their ministry. Grant that we may follow his example in lives given to charity and the proclamation of the Gospel; through Jesus Christ, our Lord, who lives and reigns with You and the Holy Spirit, one God, now and forever. Amen.

READINGS
ISAIAH 42:5–12 / ACTS 11:19–30; 13:1–3 / MARK 6:7–13

12

JUNE

Today, the Church remembers and gives thanks to God for the great **Ecumenical Council of Nicaea, AD 325**.

Emperor Constantine summoned this first ecumenical council, which convened this day in the year AD 325 in the city of Nicaea (located in present-day Turkey). He invited the entire number of about 1,800 bishops of the Church, of which approximately 300 actually attended. The exact number varies in the accounts we have, though 318 is often the number given.

The council was convoked primarily to deal with the troublesome teaching of the Alexandrian priest Arius. Arius taught that the Son was not fully divine as the Father was. Arius's watchword was "there was when He wasn't." The overwhelming majority of the bishops gathered regarded this teaching as a great heresy, endangering the salvation of any who held it.

The council addressed the pressing issue before it by writing a statement of what the Church believed, basing it solidly on the teaching received from the apostles, and condemning the contrary doctrine. The statement of faith was the original form of our Nicene Creed (its third article was as yet undeveloped beyond the bare "and we believe in the Holy Spirit"). The Creed boldly asserted that the Son was "homoousious" (that is, of the same substance or essence) as the Father. Originally, heretics had used this term to teach a form of modalism. The council, however, retooled the term to confess the unity of essence between Father and Son, without equating their persons. Appended to the statements of faith was an explicit "anathema" (from the Aramaic for "condemned"), stating that the catholic and apostolic Church condemns against any who taught that "there was when He wasn't" and thus denied the full and true deity of the Son of God.

The council also took time to address a series of practical matters that had become contentious, dealing with the Church's ministry and congregations.

O God of God, O Light of Light,
*   O Prince of Peace and King of kings:*
To You in heaven's glory bright
*   The song of praise forever rings.*
To Him who sits upon the throne,
*   The Lamb once slain but raised again,*
Be all the glory He has won,
*   All thanks and praise! Amen, amen. (LSB 810:1)*

For these, "canons" (or rules) were composed. These form the beginning of the collection of what would become over the years the Code of Canon Law. Because they address situations in a specific historic context, the Church recognizes that these canons do not always apply to situations far removed from the ones in which they were first formulated.

The pattern of Church leaders meeting to confess doctrine, reject error, and offer guidance for the practical questions of the day became well established. Such councils or synods still characterize the Church's life today and have through the ages. Those councils that were widely received and upheld throughout the Church came to be recognized as "ecumenical," or worldwide.

Among the famous participants gathered at Nicaea were Bishop Alexander of Alexandria with his faithful deacon, St. Athanasius. St. Nicholas of Myra was also said to be among the participants, though the story of him striking Arius was a late addition and probably did not occur.

Lord God, heavenly Father, at the first ecumenical Council of Nicaea, Your Church boldly confessed that it believed in one Lord Jesus Christ as being of one substance with the Father. Grant us courage to confess this saving faith with Your Church through all the ages; through Jesus Christ, our Lord. Amen.

14
JUNE

Today, we remember the holy prophet **Elisha.**

Elisha, whose name means "my God is salvation," was a prophet sent to minister in the Northern Kingdom around the years 849–786 BC. He came from the small tribe of Issachar. When the prophet Elijah feared that his years of ministry among the northern tribes had been useless, God told him not to despair. The Lord retained a remnant even among the idolatrous northern tribes numbering seven thousand. Additionally, God still had tasks for Elijah to fulfill. Among those was this: "Elisha the son of Shaphat of Abel-meholah you shall anoint to be prophet in your place" (1 Kings 19:16).

Elijah, strengthened by the Lord's promises, happened upon Elisha, who was plowing in the field. Elijah threw over him his cloak. Elisha understood that he was being summoned to follow the great prophet. He bid his family farewell, sacrificed the oxen and gave them to the people, and thus turned his back on farming to become a disciple of Elijah.

When the Lord was preparing to take Elijah "up to heaven by a whirlwind" (2 Kings 2:1), Elijah repeatedly asked his servant Elisha to stay behind. Elisha refused to be separated from his master. The great power of God at work in Elijah was revealed once again when his rolled up cloak parted the Jordan and the two crossed on dry ground. Before his departure, Elijah asked if there was anything he could do for Elisha. Elisha boldly asked for a double portion of Elijah's spirit. Elijah said this would be granted if Elisha saw him when he is taken. Chariots and horses of fire separated the two and Elijah was carried to heaven. His cloak or mantel fell to the earth. Elisha took it up and struck the Jordan, asking, "Where is the Lord, the God of Elijah?" and the waters also parted for him. People immediately recognized that the same Spirit that had worked so many miracles through Elijah was now resting upon his disciple.

God of the prophets, bless the prophets' sons;
  Elijah's mantle over Elisha cast.
Each age its solemn task may claim but once;
  Make each one nobler, stronger than the last. (LSB 682:1)

The account of Elisha's life and ministry continued to overflow and abound with the miraculous. In this he portended the ministry of our Lord Jesus Christ. In answer to Elisha's prayer, God raised the dead, made iron to float (showing that grace is more powerful than the laws of nature), and healed the leper Naaman in the waters of the Jordan. Elisha saw into the unseen world with clarity and knew himself to be surrounded by the angels of the Lord, the chariots and horsemen of Israel. Even after he died, the Spirit so filled his remains that a dead man was restored to life when the corpse merely touched the prophet's bones. Luther loved to point out that this great prophet prophesied when a musician was brought to him and music filled his ears.

Lord God, heavenly Father, through the prophet Elisha, You continued the prophetic pattern of teaching Your people the true faith and demonstrating through miracles Your presence in creation to heal it of its brokenness. Grant that Your Church may see in Your Son, our Lord Jesus Christ, the final end-times prophet whose teaching and miracles continue in Your Church through the healing medicine of the Gospel and Sacraments; through Jesus Christ, our Lord. Amen.

24
JUNE

Today, the Holy Church rejoices to celebrate the Feast of **the Nativity of St. John the Baptist**.

Nine months of silence, of listening without talking. Nine months to reflect on what it all meant. "Your prayer has been heard"—and surely Zechariah thought, "But that prayer was ages ago! He's going to answer it now?" Most of all, the old man thought about the angel's words: "He will go *before the Lord* to prepare his way . . . in the power and spirit of Elijah . . . to make ready for the Lord a people prepared." He will go before the Lord. The great time of the fulfillment of all God's promises was at hand. And what a fine how-de-do! Nine months wordless when his heart was bursting with good news.

Then the child was born as the angel promised, yet silence still reigned. The eighth day came and the time for the child to be brought into the covenant of the God of Abraham. There's confusion over the name. Zechariah motions for the writing tablet and pens, "His name is John." No sooner had he finished writing than the dam burst and the joy pent up inside for nine months broke forth in praise.

"His mouth was opened and his tongue loosed, and he spoke, blessing God." The text of the Benedictus, Zechariah's hymn of praise, occurs a few verses later. Still, they are likely the actual words with which old Zechariah broke out of his silent prison.

They show us where Zechariah's heart has been these silent months. In his old father's heart, his beloved little John doesn't get the top billing. John's birth itself isn't what has been occupying his mind. Rather this: blessed be the Lord, the God of Israel! *He* has visited and redeemed His people. Zechariah remembered when Mary walked in and heard the words of Elizabeth, "Why is it granted that the mother of my Lord should come to me?" He has raised up salvation in the house of David, just like He promised

When all the world was cursed
  By Moses' condemnation,
Saint John the Baptist came
  With words of consolation.
With true forerunner's zeal
  The greater One he named,
And Him, as yet unknown,
  As Savior he proclaimed.
Before he yet was born,
  He leaped in joyful meeting,
Confessing Him as Lord
  Whose mother he was greeting.
By Jordan's rolling stream,
  A new Elijah bold,
He testified of Him
  Of whom the prophets told. (LSB 346:1–2)

He would through all the prophets. The little one in Mary's womb might even still have been a guest in his house at the moment. The God who had come among us at long last to rescue us from the hand of all who hate us. The God who promised long ago that through the promised Seed blessing would come upon all the families of the earth. What is that blessing? That we might serve Him without fear. That we might stand before Him clothed in a holiness so perfect, wrapped in a righteousness so complete, that fear has no room. It is a gift of perfect love that drives fear out forever. It was worth the long and silent wait to be able to sing the praises of such a great Lord who comes bearing so great a gift.

Almighty God, through John the Baptist, the forerunner of Christ, You once proclaimed salvation. Now grant that we know this salvation and serve You in holiness and righteousness all the days of our life; through our Lord Jesus Christ, Your Son, who lives and reigns with You and the Holy Spirit, one God, now and forever. Amen.

READINGS
ISAIAH 40:1–5 / ACTS 13:13–26 / LUKE 1:57–80

25
JUNE

Today, the Church delights to remember and give thanks to God for the **Presentation of the Augsburg Confession** to Emperor Charles V on this day in 1530.

In 1521, called to account for his faith, an Augustinian monk stood alone before the emperor at Worms. Nine tumultuous years later, a crowd of princes and representatives of free cities, with their theologians, stood before the same emperor in Augsburg to account for the faith they had now come to share with that erstwhile monk, Martin Luther. The document they presented and insisted upon reading in its entirety before Charles V that day in 1530 is the foundational confession of the Lutheran Church.

The responsibility for drawing it up fell to Philipp Melanchthon, since Luther was outlawed and not allowed to stand before the emperor. Melanchthon came to Augsburg with a series of articles already in hand that explained the changes that the Lutheran territories had made in a number of ceremonies and laid out the scriptural reasons for these. However, on arriving in the city, the Lutheran party was astounded at the misinformation spread abroad about them. They were being accused of nearly every ancient heresy. Clearly, they needed more than an explanation of abuses that had been corrected. They needed to show that they were actually not heretical and held to the same catholic and apostolic faith that the Church had always confessed.

So Melanchthon, under enormous pressure and in a very short time, drafted the first part of the Augsburg Confession to which he appended the second section on various corrected abuses. The conviction of the Augsburg Confessors is seen clearly here: "This then is nearly a complete summary of our teaching. As can be seen, there is nothing that varies from the Scriptures, or from the Church universal, or from the Church of Rome, as known from its writers. Since this is the case, those who insist that our teachers are to be regarded as heretics are judging harshly" (Augsburg Confession, Article

O Lord, let this Your little flock,
Your name alone confessing,
Continue in Your loving care,
True unity possessing.
Your sacraments, O Lord,
And Your saving Word
To us, Lord, pure retain.
Grant that they may remain
Our only strength and comfort. (LSB 647:2)

XXI, paragraph 1). The entire confession concludes with this assertion: "In doctrine and ceremonies we have received nothing contrary to the Scriptures or the Church universal. It is clear that we have been very careful to make sure no new ungodly doctrine creeps into our churches."

A pervasively irenic spirit and a careful and clear statement of doctrine characterize the Augsburg Confession. It aligns the Lutheran Church solidly with the ancient Church's teaching of Scripture and shows that the various abuses corrected in Lutheran territories on the basis of the Word of God were mostly medieval innovations, unknown in the first centuries. To be a Lutheran Christian remains to this day to be a confessor of the Augsburg Confession.

Lord God, heavenly Father, You preserved the teaching of the apostolic Church through the confession of the true faith at Augsburg. Continue to cast the bright beams of Your light upon Your Church that we, being instructed by the doctrine of the blessed apostles, may walk in the light of Your truth and finally attain to the light of everlasting life; through Jesus Christ, our Lord, who lives and reigns with You and the Holy Spirit, one God, now and forever. Amen.

26
JUNE

Today, we remember and thank God
for the holy prophet **Jeremiah**.

Serving as God's spokesman to the Southern
Kingdom of Judah in its sad twilight years, Jeremiah
is justly called "the weeping prophet." He came from
a priestly family in Anathoth of Benjamin, perhaps
descended from the priest Abiathar, whom Solomon
had exiled to that city. He was called as a youth to the
prophetic office. Like Moses before him, Jeremiah begged
to be excused from the call. God refused and commanded, "To
all whom I send you, you shall go, and whatever I command you, you
shall speak. Do not be afraid of them, for I am with you to deliver you"
(Jeremiah 1:7–8).

Thus began a long and exceedingly frustrating ministry. The people
of Judah, the kings and nobles, the priests and prophets, refused to
hear the Word of the Lord in Jeremiah's mouth. He spoke clearly and in
prophetic signs to them of the doom that was bearing down relentlessly: the
destruction of their city and temple by the Babylonians, the seventy-year-
long exile of the population in Babylon, and its eventual restoration.

In his extreme frustration at Judah's stubborn refusal to repent and her
blind determination to destroy herself, Jeremiah cried out, "Woe is me, my
mother, that you bore me, a man of strife and contention to the whole land"
(Jeremiah 15:10). In the course of his ministry, he was beaten, imprisoned,
starved. He was denounced as a traitor and falsely accused of being in the
service of the Babylonians. He saw his prophecies of destruction come true
before his very eyes, and he shared in the intense suffering of his people
during the final siege. He constantly warned against the false hope that

Preserve in wave and tempest
Your storm-tossed little flock;
Assailed by wind and weather,
May it endure each shock.
Stand at the helm, our pilot,
And set the course aright;
Then we will reach the harbor
In Your eternal light. (LSB 658:5)

---

lying prophets continued to give the people, even in the days after the city was taken.

Amid all the suffering and gloom that fill his writings, there shine also rays of sweet hope and comfort. He predicted the coming of One who would be a righteous branch, indeed whose name is the Lord our Righteousness. He told of a day when mourning would turn to joy, when God would give His people gladness for all their sorrow. He foretold the cutting of a new covenant that would be unlike the old covenant that Israel had broken. This would be a covenant of forgiveness: "For I will forgive their iniquity, and I will remember their sin no more" (Jeremiah 31:34). Above all, Jeremiah proclaimed to the broken people left in a destroyed city, who despaired that God would ever forgive their great sin, that God's steadfast love does not fail and is new every morning. Great is His faithfulness. Jeremiah is last heard of as a captive to those fleeing to Egypt. He is believed to have died on the way there, perhaps as a martyr.

Lord God, heavenly Father, through the prophet Jeremiah You continued the prophetic pattern of teaching people the true faith and demonstrating through miracles Your presence in creation to heal it of its brokenness. Grant that Your Church may see in Your Son, our Lord Jesus Christ, the final end-times prophet whose teaching and miracles continue in Your Church through the healing medicine of the Gospel and the Sacraments; through Jesus Christ, our Lord. Amen.

27
JUNE

Today, we remember **St. Cyril of Alexandria, Pastor and Confessor**.

Cyril was the patriarch of the Egyptian Church in Alexandria from AD 412 to 444. He was prolific writer, and his commentaries on Scripture continue to be studied and learned from to this day. This is apparent from a small section of Homily 40 on St. Luke: "Don't be troubled when you recall the greatness of your former sins. Know, instead, that much greater is the grace that justifies the sinner and absolves the wicked. Faith in Christ is a pledge to us of these great blessings. It is the way that leads us to life, it bids us go to the mansions above, it raises us to the inheritance of the saints, and makes us members of the kingdom of Christ."

Cyril is, however, mostly remembered as the champion of the true and orthodox teaching of the relations of the two natures in Christ against his opponent, Nestorius. Nestorius, the Patriarch of Constantinople, began to assert that it was wrong to call the blessed Virgin Mary anything more than "bearer of Christ." Cyril led the opposition affirming that to deny that the blessed Virgin was truly "bearer of God" fundamentally falsified the nature of the incarnation itself. Cyril knew he stood on solid ground. The Sacred Scriptures clearly reveal Mary's child to be Emmanuel, the God who is with us. Mary is the bearer of God-with-us. She is not merely mother of a part of Jesus, but mother of Him who was eternally Son of the Father and who assumed into the unity of His person a human nature in her womb. Her child is thus both God and man.

As ever, when faced with intractable doctrinal differences, the bishops convoked a council to decide the matter. It was held at Ephesus in AD 431. The view of Cyril prevailed and Nestorius was declared heretic and deposed. The bishops who confessed with Nestorius characterized Cyril as a monster intent on tearing apart the Church. It was, in fact, the preservation of the

Beautiful Savior,
King of creation,
Son of God and Son of Man!
Truly I'd love Thee,
Truly I'd serve Thee,
Light of my soul, my joy, my crown. (LSB 537:1)

Church that Cyril fought for. To teach falsely about the Lord Jesus Christ endangered the whole edifice of the Church catholic. The Church as a whole received the Council and its decision: it is regarded as an ecumenical council.

Cyril is cited a number of times in the Lutheran Book of Concord and is relied on quite heavily in the appended Catalog of Testimonies. The decision of the First Council of Ephesus is explicitly affirmed in the Formula of Concord:

> On account of the personal union and communion of the natures, Mary, the most blessed Virgin, did not bear a mere man. But, as the angel ‹Gabriel› testifies, she bore a man who is truly the Son of the most high God [Luke 1:35]. . . . Therefore, she is truly the mother of God and yet has remained a virgin. (Solid Declaration, Article VIII, paragraph 24)

Heavenly Father, Your servant Cyril steadfastly proclaimed Your Son, Jesus Christ, to be one person, fully God and fully man. By Your infinite mercy, keep us constant in faith and worship of Your Son, who lives and reigns with You and the Holy Spirit, one God, now and forever. Amen.

28
JUNE

This day, the Church rejoices to remember **St. Irenaeus of Lyons, Pastor.**

Irenaeus (ca. AD 130–200) was a hearer of Polycarp, who was in turn a hearer of St. John the apostle. Irenaeus's writings, as a result, form an important witness in how the apostolic teaching shaped the Church in the decades following the deaths of the apostles.

According to tradition, Irenaeus was a Greek born in Smyrna, where Polycarp was bishop. He was ordained a presbyter and served in the Church of what is today Lyons in France. His bishop, Pothinus, sent a letter by his hand to the pope of Rome in AD 177, regarding the false teaching of the Montanists. While in Rome, his bishop was martyred together with many others in the persecution enacted under Emperor Marcus Aurelius. Upon his return, Irenaeus was elected bishop.

Following that bitter and intense persecution, the Church experienced a period of relative relief. Most of Irenaeus's work as bishop and theologian was carried out in that peace. He wrote a famous work *Against Heresies*, which survives. In it he cataloged the corruptions of apostolic truth that he had encountered or heard of, most of which were gnostic in origin.

One statement of Irenaeus in *Against Heresies* is of particular importance to the Lutheran confession of the Lord's Supper. In Book IV, chapter 18, he wrote: "For as the bread, which is produced from the earth, when it receives the invocation of God, is no longer common bread, but the Eucharist, consisting of two realities, earthly and heavenly; so also our bodies, when they receive the Eucharist, are no longer corruptible, having the hope of the resurrection to eternity." This was used polemically to refute the false teaching of transubstantiation (that the earthly elements no longer remained in the Eucharist, having been replaced by the body and blood of

Lord, keep us steadfast in Your Word;
Curb those who by deceit or sword
Would wrest the kingdom from Your Son
And bring to naught all He has done.
Lord Jesus Christ, Your power make known,
For You are Lord of lords alone;
Defend Your holy Church that we
May sing Your praise eternally. (LSB 655:1–2)

---

the Lord) and affirm the Lutheran teaching that in the Eucharist the bread and the wine are present together with the body and blood of Christ.

When the question of the proper date to celebrate Easter rocked the Early Church, Irenaeus was the voice of reason. He wrote to Pope Victor at the time that "diversity concerning fasting does not destroy the harmony of faith," urging him not to break fellowship with the churches in Asia Minor over this question. The Lutheran Church cites this saying of the great Church Father with favor in the Augsburg Confession (Article XXVI, paragraph 44).

Nothing is known about Irenaeus's death with certainty. Some hold that he died a martyr, confessing the resurrection of the body even as had his predecessor in office. He was buried in the church that later was named after him in Lyons. Sadly, his grave was desecrated in disturbances of the radical Huguenots in the sixteenth century.

Almighty God, You upheld Your servant Irenaeus with strength to confess the truth against every blast of vain doctrine. By Your mercy, keep us stead-fast in the true faith, that in constancy we may walk in peace on the way that leads to eternal life through Jesus Christ, our Lord, who lives and reigns with You and the Holy Spirit, one God, now and forever. Amen.

29
JUNE

On this day, the Church celebrates with great joy the Festival of **St. Peter and St. Paul, Apostles.**

The Festival of Saints Peter and Paul is one of the very oldest saints' days in the Church's calendar. Christians have remembered these two on June 29 since at least AD 250. A very old tradition holds that both apostles were martyred the same day under orders from Emperor Nero in AD 68.

Peter, of course, during Christ's Passion had denied his Lord three times out of fear. When Christ restored Peter in John 21, He asked him if he loved Him three times. Three times Peter confessed that he loved Christ like a brother. He apparently hesitated to use the word for love (*agape*) that entails willingness to lay down one's life. Christ charged him to feed His lambs and tend His flock. The Lord Jesus, however, did go on to tell Peter that the day would come when he *will* stretch out his hands, have another dress him, and lead him where he does not want to go. "This He said to show by what kind of death he was to glorify God" (John 21:19) and added the invitation: "Follow Me." Peter was thus given the promise that he would die a martyr for his Master.

When that time came, Peter was in Rome (called by the code name "Babylon," 1 Peter 5:13). He had witnessed Christ's resurrection to Jews and Gentiles for many years, confessing to one and all, "We believe that we will be saved through the grace of the Lord Jesus Christ" (Acts 15:11). He was arrested and sentenced to death by crucifixion. He reportedly begged only the favor of being crucified upside down. He did not feel worthy to die in the exact same manner as the One he had once denied.

Paul, when last heard of in Acts, was under house arrest in Rome. Tradition suggests that he may have been released from that initial

We praise You for Saint Peter;
  We praise You for Saint Paul;
They taught both Jew and Gentile
  That Christ is all in all.
To cross and sword they yielded
  And saw Your kingdom come;
O God, these two apostles
  Reached life through martyrdom. (LSB 518:19)

---

imprisonment and fulfilled his desire to preach the Good News in Spain. But under fickle Nero, the apostle landed in prison yet again a short while later and this time received the death sentence. Because he was a Roman citizen, Paul was not crucified, but given a relatively merciful death through a swift beheading. He had long contemplated this final victory: "With full courage now as always Christ will be honored in my body, whether by life or by death. For to me to live is Christ, and to die is gain" (Philippians 1:20–21). Paul knew that the death that awaited him was already a vanquished enemy.

The remains of the two apostles are said to be interred beneath the original St. Peter's Basilica in Rome. Together they await the joyous resurrection that they fearlessly proclaimed.

Merciful and eternal God, Your holy apostles Peter and Paul received grace and strength to lay down their lives for the sake of Your Son. Strengthen us by Your Holy Spirit that we may confess Your truth and at all times be ready to lay down our lives for Him who laid down His life for us, even Jesus Christ, our Lord, who lives and reigns with You and the Holy Spirit, one God, now and forever. Amen.

READINGS
ACTS 15:1–12 (13–21) / GALATIANS 2:1–10 / MATTHEW 16:13–19

2
JULY

With overflowing joy, the Church of Jesus Christ celebrates today the Feast of **the Visitation of Our Lord** (one-year lectionary).

St. Luke's Gospel records in chapter 1 the visit of Mary to her kinswoman, Elizabeth, when Mary was newly with child and Elizabeth in her sixth month. It would be the first meeting of John the Baptist and the Lord whom he was to serve.

From within the house, Elizabeth hears the greeting of her kinswoman and a miracle happens. The child within her leaps for joy. Elizabeth is herself filled with the Spirit and speaks, as she greets Mary.

It was a fearful secret Mary had been carrying. But she knows from the look of astonishment on Elizabeth's face that she, too, was in the know. God had let Elizabeth in on the great secret of the ages. She cries out, "Blessed are you among women, and blessed is the fruit of your womb! And why is this granted to me that the mother of my Lord should come to me? For behold, when the sound of your greeting came to my ears, the baby in my womb leaped for joy."

Perhaps she gave a knowing glance over at Zechariah, sitting silently in his corner—silent since he had doubted the words of Gabriel. Her next words seemed aimed at him: "And blessed is she who believed that there would be a fulfillment of what was spoken to her from the Lord." You can almost see Zechariah laughing silently in agreement.

The young Mary melts into a song of praise that is reminiscent of Hannah's hymn in 1 Samuel 2. We call Mary's song her Magnificat, from the first words of the song in Latin. In it, she praises God for His kind regard of her, a lowly and despised person. She praises His upside-down way of working where He fills the hungry with good and sends the rich away empty, lifts up the lowly and tumbles the mighty from their thrones. Above all, she

Praise, all you people, the name so holy
  Of Him who does such wondrous things!
All that has being, to praise Him solely,
  With happy heart its amen sings.
Children of God, with angel host
Praise Father, Son, and Holy Ghost!
  Alleluia, alleluia! (LSB 797:5)

---

rejoices in how the fruit of her womb, the child whose heart now beats beneath her own, is the fulfillment of God's great promise to Abraham about the Seed who would come to bring blessing to all.

Mary's song of praise is the traditional canticle the Church delights to sing at Vespers or Evening Prayer, even as Zechariah's canticle is sung in the morning. By singing it with her, we confess that we, too, are among those for whom the Lord has done great things, and what is greater than the Son of God becoming flesh for us in Mary's womb to bring us all the blessing of eternal life?

Almighty God, You chose the Virgin Mary to be the mother of Your Son and made known through her Your gracious regard for the poor and lowly and despised. Grant that we may receive Your Word in humility and faith, and so be made one with Jesus Christ, Your Son, our Lord, who lives and reigns with You and the Holy Spirit, one God, now and forever. Amen.

READINGS
ISAIAH 11:1–5 / ROMANS 12:9–16 / LUKE 1:39–45 (46–56)

6
JULY

With thanks and praise to God, we today remember the holy prophet **Isaiah.**

Among the writing prophets, surely none is greater or more beloved than Isaiah. He prophesied in the Southern Kingdom, particularly in Jerusalem, from about 740–700 BC. He was thus a contemporary of the other eighth-century-BC prophets: Amos, Hosea, and Micah. The corpus of Isaiah's writing, however, is far larger than all of theirs combined. He wrote the longest prophecy in the entire canon.

Although Isaiah clearly addressed the contemporary issues of Judah's idolatry and her attempt to substitute military savvy for trust in the Lord, his writings look beyond the current challenges toward the time of the promised Messiah and the fulfillment of His kingdom. This is a reminder that God in the flesh is the answer to the pressing problems that continue to surround and plague the people of God. Isaiah is cited more than any other prophet in the pages of the New Testament. He foretells the birth of the Messiah from a Virgin and His identity as Emmanuel, God with us (Isaiah 7). He plumbs the mystery of the divine person who becomes a human child (Isaiah 9). Christian art usually depicts the ox and donkey at the manger in which the Christ Child lays because Isaiah proclaimed that the ox knew its owner and the donkey its master's crib (Isaiah 1). He predicts the visit of the Magi (Isaiah 60). He foretells the ministry and work of St. John the Baptist (Isaiah 40). He foretells the mighty miracles that our Lord would perform among mankind—the blind seeing, the deaf hearing, the lame walking (Isaiah 35)—and these miracles largely transpiring in Galilee (Isaiah 9). He predicts and explains the purpose of the Passion of our Lord and His resurrection in amazing detail (Isaiah 53). He clearly foretells

Isaiah 'twas foretold it,
The rose I have in mind;
With Mary we behold it,
The virgin mother kind.
To show God's love aright,
She bore to us a Savior,
When half-spent was the night. (LSB 359:2)

---

the ingathering of the Gentiles (Isaiah 2). He foresees a new heaven and new earth where Eden would be restored (Isaiah 65).

His book justly has been called the Old Testament Gospel because of the comfort in which it abounds. Indeed, the prophet's greatest task is to "comfort, comfort My people" (Isaiah 40). Martin Luther found great significance in particular in Isaiah 28 and God speaking of His strange or alien work (to terrify and to condemn) being always in the service of His proper work (to comfort and forgive). Isaiah also is a mighty teacher of divine monergism: "You have indeed done for us all our works!" (Isaiah 26).

According to tradition, the great prophet met a martyr's death by being sawn in half. It is believed that Hebrews 11:37 refers to Isaiah: "They were sawn in two." He surely has joined in the company of those who ceaselessly hear the song of the seraphim, "Holy, holy, holy!" (Isaiah 6).

Lord God, heavenly Father, through the prophet Isaiah You continued the prophetic pattern of teaching Your people the true faith and demonstrating through miracles Your presence in creation to heal it of its brokenness. Grant that Your Church may see in Your Son, our Lord Jesus Christ, the final end-times prophet whose teaching and miracles continue in Your Church through the healing medicine of the Gospel and the Sacraments; through Jesus Christ, our Lord. Amen.

16
JULY

On this day, we praise God for an ancestress of our Lord Jesus Christ, **Ruth**.

"But Ruth said, 'Do not urge me to leave you or to return from following you. For where you go I will go, and where you lodge I will lodge. Your people shall be my people, and your God my God. Where you die I will die, and there will I be buried. May the LORD do so to me and more also if anything but death parts me from you'" (Ruth 1:16–17). With those stirring words of devotion, Ruth bound herself to Naomi, her dead husband's mother. Evidently during their sojourn in Moab, Naomi and her family had shared Israel's faith in the true and living God. Ruth had heard, listened, and believed. She loved her mother-in-law and wanted to be part of the people of God, who waited together in faith and hope for the coming of the Promised One. Together, then, Naomi and Ruth returned to Naomi's hometown of Bethlehem.

Ruth set to work in the fields to support Naomi and herself. Her devotion to her mother-in-law, and by implication to her dead husband and father-in-law, became well-known in the village. The pious Boaz, a near relative, provided for the two widows by allowing Ruth to glean, that is, to pick up the leftovers in his fields (and even ordered his servants to leave extra wheat for Ruth to find). Emboldened by this sign of Boaz's tender care, Naomi instructed Ruth to appeal to Boaz for "redemption": Ruth asked to be taken under his protection as his wife, since in Hebrew law the nearest kinsman had an obligation to raise up children for their near relatives who left childless widows.

Boaz was touched by Ruth's appeal, for he was an older man and humble. When a nearer relative refused the right of redemption, Boaz then took

118

Lord, 'tis not that I did choose Thee;
That, I know, could never be;
For this heart would still refuse Thee
Had Thy grace not chosen me.
Thou hast from the sin that stained me
Washed and cleansed and set me free
And unto this end ordained me,
That I ever live to Thee. (LSB 573:1)

Ruth as his wife, Moabite though she was. Their first child was named Obed. He became the father of Jesse, who was the father of King David, ancestor of the Lord Jesus Christ.

Could Ruth have ever guessed the truth? She was joined by faith to the people who awaited the gift of a Savior, the advent of the Promised Seed of the woman who would crush the serpent's head. Her hope was in the Seed of Abraham who would bring blessing to all the families of earth. And this child, so desired and longed for, would come from her very own body! For faithful Ruth, ancestress of Christ, all glory to God!

Faithful God, You promised to preserve Your people and save Your inheritance, using unlikely and unexpected vessels in extending the genealogy that would bring about the birth of Your blessed Son. Give us the loyalty of Ruth and her trust in the one true God, that we, too, might honor You through our submission and respect and be counted among Your chosen people, by the grace of Jesus Christ, our Lord, and the Holy Spirit, who reign together with You, now and forever. Amen.

20
JULY

Today, we rejoice to remember the holy prophet **Elijah.**

Elijah was the Lord's great prophet to the Northern Kingdom (Israel), mostly during the reign of the evil king Ahab (874–853 BC). It is a great comfort that at a time when the nation had outwardly embraced idolatry and sought to worship Yahweh as one god among many, the true God did not abandon His people, but sent to them a mighty prophet to call them to repentance.

Elijah and his successor, Elisha, were great miracle-working prophets, prefiguring our Lord's own miracles. It is, however, instructive to note the differences. Both Elijah and Elisha pray that a dead child be restored to life and both children are raised from death; Jesus, however, doesn't pray—He simply speaks and causes the dead to live.

Elijah was a mighty man of prayer. He asked God that it not rain and for three years, and no rain fell upon Israel. He gathered Ahab and all the false prophets to a mighty confrontation on Mount Carmel. He urged them to call upon their false god, Baal, to accept the sacrifice they had prepared by sending fire from heaven. Silence was the only answer, for Baal is no true god. Then he prepared a sacrifice for Yahweh and called upon His name, and fire fell from heaven and consumed the offering. The people were moved to confess: Yahweh, He is God!

Elijah then prayed for rain to come again upon the land and it did. Yet, even as he was exulting in this stupendous revelation of the true God's power, Ahab's wicked wife, Jezebel, sent the prophet a message that he was now under the death warrant. In fear and trembling, Elijah fled to the wilderness. An angel sustained him with miraculous food, and he finally made his way to Horeb, the mountain of God.

Now our heavenly Aaron enters
With His blood within the veil;
Joshua now is come to Canaan,
And the kings before Him quail.
Now He plants the tribes of Israel
In their promised resting place;
Now our great Elijah offers
Double portion of His grace. (LSB 494:4)

A mighty wind and fire shook the mountain. God finally spoke in "a quiet whisper." In the face of the prophet's despair over the outcome of his ministry, God sent him back with more promises. He wasn't done with Elijah yet! He was to anoint two kings and the man who would be his successor, Elisha.

At the end of his life, the miracles continued. Elijah with his servant Elisha crossed the Jordan after striking it with his rolled up cloak. Elijah was then swept up into heaven by horses and chariots of fire ("Swing low, sweet chariot!"). Elijah's cloak fell back to the earth and a double portion of Elijah's spirit then rested upon Elisha.

Malachi foretold that Elijah was to come again before the time of Messiah. Jesus explained that John the Baptist fulfilled this prophecy by coming in the power and spirit of Elijah. Yet, Elijah did also appear with our Lord on the Mount of Transfiguration. For this prophet in whom the Spirit worked so mightily and who yet knew the discouragement of rejection and hatred, the Church renders her thanks this day!

Lord God, heavenly Father, through the prophet Elijah You continued the prophetic pattern of teaching Your people the true faith and demonstrating through miracles Your presence in creation to heal it of its brokenness. Grant that Your Church may see in Your Son, our Lord Jesus Christ, the final end-times prophet whose teaching and miracles continue in Your Church through the healing medicine of the Gospel and the Sacraments; through Jesus Christ, our Lord. Amen.

21
JULY

Today, we rejoice to remember the holy prophet **Ezekiel.**

Ezekiel served the Lord as a prophet primarily to the Judean exiles at the time of the Babylonian Captivity, having been carried captive by Nebuchadnezzar in 597 BC. He was the son of Buzi and thus part of the priestly family. Familiarity with the liturgy and ritual of the temple stamp his prophecy.

His initial prophecies were warnings to the Judeans that Jerusalem and the temple would be destroyed. He repeatedly had to counter false prophets who prophesied an eminent return from exile. In contrast, Ezekiel prophesied a long exile and complete destruction of the city. After his prophecies came true about the final destruction of the Holy City and its temple, Ezekiel's words turned mainly to comfort. He foretold the destruction of the enemies of God's people and a restoration to the land with a new temple.

Most intriguing were his words about how God would rescue His scattered people and bring them home by giving them a new heart and putting His own Spirit within them (Ezekiel 36). He foretold that God would sprinkle them with clean water to accomplish this, a prophecy of the grace of Baptism.

In his famous vision of the valley of dry bones (chapter 37), Ezekiel is given a glimpse of the resurrection where, as C. S. Lewis would put it centuries later, "death works backwards." A valley of dead bones stretches before him. Many bones. All bleached white. The Lord challenges the prophet, "Can these bones live?" It is *the* question. The best the prophet can do is to refer the question back to God, "O Lord GOD, You know." At the command of the Lord he prophesies over the dry bones and the bodies

This is He whom seers in old time
Chanted of with one accord,
Whom the voices of the prophets
Promised in their faithful word.
Now He shines, the long-expected;
Let creation praise its Lord
Evermore and evermore. (LSB 384:3)

---

reassemble. At another command, he summons the breath, the Spirit of the Lord, and the dead bodies come to life and stand on their feet, a vast army. In such a way, the Lord promises Ezekiel that He will raise His people from their graves.

Another vision of the prophet is particularly important. He foresees the restored temple and, from the altar, a stream of water. It starts small, but it grows. It becomes a mighty river. Wherever it flows, everything lives. When we remember the promise of our Lord that His body is the true temple, this vision becomes clear. From Him, our living temple, flows the water (mingled with the blood!) that brings divine life to everything it touches. This is the image of Holy Baptism itself, flowing from the Lord's body on His cross. That water brings to life those whom it touches. In fact, it makes them part of the very temple of God Himself.

Some of the odd symbolism that Ezekiel employs finds an echo in the Revelation to St. John. The living creatures he saw surrounding the throne of God recur there. His prophecies about the battle between the enemies of God, Gog and Magog, find an answering echo as well. Both Ezekiel and St. John declare that the final victory in history belongs to the God who visits His people to wash them in living water and make them His very temple.

Lord God, heavenly Father, through the prophet Ezekiel You continued the prophetic pattern of teaching Your people the true faith and demonstrating through miracles Your presence in creation to heal it of its brokenness. Grant that Your Church may see in Your Son, our Lord Jesus Christ, the final end-times prophet whose teaching and miracles continue in Your Church through the healing medicine of the Gospel and the Sacraments; through Jesus Christ, our Lord. Amen.

22
JULY

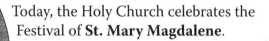

Today, the Holy Church celebrates the
Festival of **St. Mary Magdalene**.

Honored as "the apostle to the apostles," Mary
Magdalene was among the first to see the risen Lord.
John (chapter 20) relates the account of the women
coming to the tomb to anoint the Lord's body, finding
the tomb empty, and running to tell the apostles. Peter
and John confirm the women's witness: the body of Jesus
was no longer in the tomb. They went away, but Mary
lingered, weeping outside the grave in the garden.

As she stooped to look in, a veritable vision of the Holy of Holies greeted
her. Two angels, one at the head and one at the feet of the place where
Jesus' body had been, were clothed in white array. They asked her, "Woman,
why do you weep?" Her grief is so overwhelming, she doesn't even seem to
register that she's speaking with angels. "They've taken away my Lord and I
don't know where they've laid Him."

She turned about and saw someone standing there. She thought he was
the gardener. The question again: "Woman, why are you weeping? Whom
are you seeking?" She thought that the gardener, if anyone, would know
what had happened. "Sir, if you have carried Him away, tell me where you
have laid Him, and I will take Him away." Striking that she doesn't refer to a
body, but to *Him*.

And then in a single word the revelation happened. "He calls His own
sheep by name," He had foretold (John 10). "Mary!" He calls. And suddenly
she knows. The body is not in the tomb because her Lord is standing before
her, alive and never to die again. She lunges at Him: "Rabboni!" That is, "my
teacher." She wants to hold Him so that He can never get away from her ever

All praise for Mary Magdalene,
*   Whose wholeness was restored*
By You, her faithful master,
*   Her Savior and her Lord.*
On Easter morning early
*   A word from You sufficed;*
For she was first to see You,
*   Her Lord, the risen Christ.* (**LSB** *518:20*)

---

again. You can almost hear her thinking, "It will be like before! I'll never let You go ever again!"

But He wanted to be much more Jesus for her than that. He tells her, "Do not cling to Me, for I have not yet ascended to the Father; but go to My brothers and say to them, 'I am ascending to My Father and your Father, to My God and your God.'" Off she runs and tells the apostles all that she has seen and heard. Thus Christ chose this lowly woman, from whom He had once cast out seven demons to be the first witness to the resurrection, and dispatched her with a joyous message to the apostles.

Modern fiction often suggests that Mary is the wife of Jesus, but our Lord has only one Bride, and that is the Church. Mary is honored in the Church as one of our Savior's close companions, a sinner whom He in love set free.

Almighty God, Your Son, Jesus Christ, restored Mary Magdalene to health and called her to be the first witness of His resurrection. Heal us from all our infirmities, and call us to know You in the power of Your Son's unending life; through the same Jesus Christ, our Lord, who lives and reigns with You and the Holy Spirit, one God, now and forever. Amen.

READINGS
PROVERBS 31:10–31 / ACTS 13:26–31 / JOHN 20:1–2, 10–18

25
JULY

Today, the Holy Church celebrates the Festival of **St. James the Elder, Apostle**.

The Gospels tell that among the first disciples Christ called to Himself were the two sons of Zebedee and Salome: the fishermen James and John. This James is often called the "elder" to distinguish him from James the "less," or "the younger, the littler," whose feast day is on May 1.

Though present at some of the most significant events in our Lord's ministry, James is strangely silent in the Scriptures. He was one of the favored three blessed to witness the raising of Jairus's daughter, the glory of the Transfiguration, and the agony in the Garden.

The Gospels recount how James and John, either directly or through their mother, asked of the Lord the favor of sitting in the chief places, on His right and left, when He entered into His glory. Our Lord bluntly tells them, "You don't know what you are asking." They were thinking in a worldly way, but the Lord's glory was mysterious and utterly unexpected. "Are you able to drink the cup that I am to drink and to be baptized with the Baptism I am to undergo?"

In boundless self-confidence they both affirm that they are able. It is as though our Lord looked down through the years and saw. He nodded. He told them, "You will indeed drink from My cup and share My Baptism, but to sit at My right and left is not Mine to grant. It is for those for whom it has been prepared by My Father." Most probably Jesus was speaking of the thieves crucified with Him, one on the right and one on the left. For the glory of Jesus was, above all, the cross, where He reigned as king. "Jesus of Nazareth, King of the Jews."

But with His long sight, Jesus did see them sharing His cup of suffering. He saw John outliving all the other disciples and suffering anxieties for

O Lord, for James we praise You,
Who fell to Herod's sword;
He drank the cup of suffering
And thus fulfilled Your word.
Lord, curb our vain impatience
For glory and for fame,
Equip us for such sufferings
As glorify Your name. (LSB 518:21)

---

the churches beset by heresies as he lived in exile on Patmos and received strange visions. And James? How could He not have seen that among the chosen Twelve, James would be the very first to be martyred? Herod Agrippa I had him slain around a decade after the crucifixion of our Lord. James was beheaded for the crime of witnessing to others of the risen Lord, whose blood blots out the world's sin and whose resurrection sets free His baptized from death itself. These even occurred around the same time as our Lord's Passion: it was Passover. Except for John, tradition states that all the company of the Twelve met a similar fate, just as the Lord had foretold: "If they hate Me, they will hate you."

For silent James, the holy martyr whose blood speaks boldly of the defeat of death, all glory to You, Lord Jesus!

O gracious God, Your servant and apostle James was the first among the Twelve to suffer martyrdom for the name of Jesus Christ. Pour out upon the leaders of Your Church that spirit of self-denying service that they may forsake all false and passing allurements and follow Christ alone, who lives and reigns with You and the Holy Spirit, one God, now and forever. Amen.

READINGS
ACTS 11:27–12:5 / ROMANS 8:28–39 / MARK 10:35–45

28
JULY

Today, we remember and thank God for the ministry and music of **Johann Sebastian Bach, Kantor**.

Upon this day in 1750, the great kantor Johann Sebastian Bach died. The heritage of music he left is so great that when the *Voyager* space probes were sent out, they carried on them the joyous strains of the famed Brandenburg Concertos as representative of the noblest and greatest music of planet earth. But what is the key to the greatness of this composer?

If we take his own writings seriously, we realize that first and foremost he was a convinced and devout Lutheran. His edition of the Luther Bible has his notes scribbled throughout. Luther and the Lutheran Church highly valued music, reckoning it after the Word of God as God's greatest gift to man. And it was to be offered to God's glory. The music from Bach's pen invariably invokes Jesus at the beginning, "Help, Jesus!" and concludes, "All glory be to God alone!"

Johann was born into a musical family in the city of Eisenach. His father was director of the musicians in the town and all his uncles were professional musicians. Bach, too, grew up to be a professional musician for the Church, and his ministry culminated in Leipzig, where he organized the musical offerings in the city's churches. There he sought to forge what he regarded as "a well-regulated church music." By this he meant a series of poetic songs that interacted with the chief hymn of each Sunday and festival. The music was designed to preach and thus complement the Word read in the Divine Service and proclaimed from the pulpit. For Lutheran musicians, this "praise of God" as "proclaiming the great things He has done" was key to all music in the Church.

Now let all the heav'ns adore Thee,
Let saints and angels sing before Thee
*   With harp and cymbals' clearest tone.*
Of one pearl each shining portal,
Where, joining with the choir immortal,
*   We gather round Thy radiant throne.*
No eye has seen the light,
No ear has heard the might
*   Of Thy glory;*
Therefore will we
Eternally
Sing hymns of praise and joy to Thee! (LSB 516:3)

At times irascible in his insistence that music be fully funded and staffed, Bach became known as an ardent and uncompromising defender of the noble work of kantor. He fathered many children, several of whom continued to serve in the family tradition of making music for the Church. During his own lifetime, Bach achieved renown as a gifted organist. His compositions have enriched the Church ever since they were written. The depth of His musical painting in the "B Minor Mass" is still unrivaled, and his cantatas bring joy to the heart of those who hear in them the sweet Gospel message matchlessly paired with notes.

Almighty God, beautiful in majesty and majestic in holiness, You have taught us in Holy Scripture to sing Your praises and have given to Your servant Johann Sebastian Bach grace to show forth Your glory in his music. Continue to grant this gift of inspiration to all Your servants who write and make music for Your people, that with joy we on earth may glimpse Your beauty and at length know the inexhaustible richness of Your new creation in Jesus Christ, our Lord, who lives and reigns with You and the Holy Spirit, one God, now and forever. Amen.

29
JULY

On this day, we remember three friends of Jesus: **Mary, Martha, and Lazarus of Bethany**.

How perplexing it must have been for them: that mysterious delay. Mary and Martha sent word to Jesus because they knew that His very word could drive sickness away and force encroaching death to step back. And yet silence. No response from their beloved friend and Teacher. Their frustration turned to terror as they watched their brother literally failing before their eyes, and themselves helpless. At last, Lazarus closed his eyes and his breathing ceased. Their hearts were broken. Jesus had not come.

They tenderly washed him, bound him in grave clothes, and carried him to the tomb. The townsfolk joined them in the procession. The stone was rolled in place. The darkness took their brother and their own hearts. Lazarus was buried. Jesus had not come.

The grief only grew as the sisters wept. Over and over again their hearts questioned, "Why? Why no answer? Why had He not come? Did He not love them anymore? Had they offended Him? Angered Him in some way? Why had Jesus not come?" Mary, who had sat so attentively at His feet and learned of the unshakable love of the heavenly Father for the fallen lot of humanity turned His words over in her mind repeatedly, searching for some clue to make sense of it all. Martha, no doubt, kept busy to keep her mind off the same conundrum. And then Martha heard the shouts, and as the name "Jesus" caught her between fear and hope, she marched off to meet the Master.

"If you had been here, my brother would not have died. And even now, I know God will give You whatever You ask." Jesus looks at her in compassion. "Your brother will rise." She dismisses this, "Yes, at the resurrection." The implication being, "That's a long way off. What about now?" Jesus offers the startling answer, "I am the resurrection and the life." Mary runs to meet Him

Jesus has come! Now see bonds rent asunder!
Fetters of death now dissolve, disappear.
See Him burst through with a voice as of thunder!
He sets us free from our guilt and our fear,
Lifts us from shame to the place of His honor.
Jesus has come! Hear the roll of God's thunder! (LSB 533:2)

---

and again He is moved to comfort His friend. At last they take Him to the tomb, where Jesus weeps. With the command to open the tomb, His voice rings out, "Lazarus, come out!" And out he comes. Not a dead man walking, but a live man wrapped in the clothes of death.

Why the delay? Why put them through it? Jesus never answers except this: all that happens is so that His Father may be glorified. He truly loved these three, just as He truly loves you. Awful things may befall, but knowing that His love is sure, His tears for you genuine, and His power over death invincible, faith holds tight to the words and promises of Jesus. And Lazarus is just a foretaste of what's about to happen when that unshakable love of His brings Him to cross, tomb, and resurrection. The resurrection on the last day is a comfort, but the presence of Him who is the resurrection and the life brings true peace. Fear not, then; you have a friend in high places, and He will raise you on the last day with His friends from Bethany.

Heavenly Father, Your beloved Son befriended frail humans like us to make us Your own. Teach us to be like Jesus' dear friends from Bethany, that we might serve Him faithfully like Martha, learn from Him earnestly like Mary, and ultimately be raised by Him like Lazarus. Through their Lord and ours, Jesus Christ, who lives and reigns with You and the Holy Spirit, one God, now and forever. Amen.

30
JULY

Today, we remember and thank God for His servant
Robert Barnes, Confessor and Martyr.

Robert Barnes was an Englishman and by conviction a Lutheran. He was born in 1495 in Norfolk and educated at Cambridge. He joined the Augustinian friars where he came to hear and know of another famous Augustinian Eremite: Martin Luther. Barnes was soon made a doctor of theology and became the prior for the Cambridge convent. In 1525, he preached a homily that historians regard as the first Reformation message publicly proclaimed from a pulpit in England. He was detained for this and charged with teaching heresy. He providentially escaped his imprisonment and crossed the channel to Antwerp.

Once on the continent, he made his way to Wittenberg and became a personal acquaintance of Martin Luther and a dinner guest in his home. Barnes would not stay in the relative safety of Germany. He determined to return to England in 1531 and hoped to convince his beloved king of the truth of the Reformation Gospel. At first, matters looked hopeful. He rose to government office and was sent back to Europe to possibly secure the blessing of Luther and other Lutheran theologians for his king's desire to divorce and remarry. This, of course, was a failure, and Henry VIII quickly soured on Lutheran theology when it would not serve his personal ends.

Traditionalist forces in England that opposed Barnes's avowed Lutheran teaching and preaching resulted in Barnes being imprisoned and finally burned at the stake on July 30, 1540. The martyr's love for his king showed to the very end. His final prayer was, "Lord, open the King of England's eyes!"

Luther wrote upon hearing of Barnes's martyrdom, "This Dr. Robert Barnes we certainly knew, and it is a particular joy for me to hear that our good, pious dinner guest and houseguest has been so graciously called by God to pour out his blood and to become a holy martyr for the sake of

Amen, Lord Jesus, grant our prayer;
Great Captain, now Thine arm make bare,
*   Fight for us once again!*
So shall Thy saints and martyrs raise
A mighty chorus to Thy praise,
*   Forevermore. Amen. (LSB 666:4)*

His dear Son. . . . Hope betrayed him. For he always hoped his king would become good in the end. Let us praise and thank God! This is a blessed time for the elect saints of Christ, and an unfortunate time for the devil, for blasphemers and enemies, and it is going to get worse. Amen."

Barnes was but one of six men who were executed upon this day. Luther gladly published Barnes's *Confession of Faith* and wrote the dedicatory preface. For those Lutherans who live in English-speaking lands, Robert Barnes is a particularly beloved herald of God's Word whom neither torture nor fear could dissuade from proclaiming the joyous truth of the saving Gospel.

Almighty God, heavenly Father, you gave courage to Your servant Robert Barnes to give up his life for confessing the true faith during the Reformation. May we continue steadfast in our confession of the apostolic faith and suffer all, even death, rather than fall away from it; through Jesus Christ, our Lord. Amen.

31
JULY

Today, the Holy Church rejoices to remember **Joseph of Arimathea**.

Joseph of Arimathea is mentioned by all of the evangelists: Matthew, Mark, Luke, and John. He hailed from a small village called Arimathea in the Judean hills. An honored member of the Jewish Sanhedrin, he was wealthy and had for himself a tomb already prepared. He bravely came forward to Pilate and asked for permission to take the Savior's body to bury it in his own new tomb.

John reports in his Gospel (chapter 19) that Joseph assisted Nicodemus in the bloody task of taking our Lord's body off His cross. Together they brought His body to the tomb that belonged to Joseph, along with many spices. They laid Him hastily to rest, wrapped in clean white linen, as the Sabbath was upon them with the setting of the sun. The women who followed our Lord saw the place and would return after Sabbath to finish caring for the Savior's body and encounter the great surprise of the Lord's resurrection.

Many note the public bravery shown by Nicodemus and Joseph in contrast to the fearful reaction of the Lord's disciples. These brave members of the Jewish Sanhedrin did not hesitate to ask the Roman Governor, Pilate, for permission to bury the "King of the Jews" and received his blessing to do so.

Their honoring of the Lord's body was in itself a confession of the resurrection of the dead. In a similar way, the dead bodies of the saints are not litter to be disposed of, but truly holy relics awaiting the joyous resurrection. As we remember Joseph and his service to the body of our Lord

Were you there when they laid Him in the tomb?
Were you there when they laid Him in the tomb?
  Oh . . .
Sometimes it causes me to tremble,
          tremble,
     tremble.
Were you there when they laid Him in the tomb? (**LSB** *456:3*)

---

at His tomb, we also remember the task we as Christians have of honoring the dead remains of Christ's saints. We confess before an unbelieving world that these remains are to be honored, for joined to Christ, they *will* be raised in glory on the Last Day when our Lord will appear again, raise all the dead, and give to all believers in Christ a life that never ends.

Merciful God, Your servant Joseph of Arimathea prepared the body of our Lord and Savior for burial with reverence and godly fear and laid Him in his own tomb. As we follow the example of Joseph, grant us, Your faithful people, the same grace and courage to love and serve Jesus with sincere devotion all the days of our lives; through Jesus Christ, our Lord, who lives and reigns with You and the Holy Spirit, one God, now and forever. Amen.

3
AUGUST

Today, we remember and thank God for His servants **Joanna, Mary, and Salome, Myrrhbearers**.

The sun fell lower in the sky as Joseph and Nicodemus trudged along with the body of Jesus. They thought Joseph's new tomb would serve as a resting place for His body until the flesh was consumed and His bones could be given final burial in an ossuary. Behind them came the women in sad procession: Mary Magdalene and the three women commemorated today. Joanna was a wife of the steward of Herod's household. Mary was the mother of James. Salome was the mother of Zebedee's children, James and John. And while they walked, the shadows lengthened and the mandatory Sabbath rest loomed.

The men only had time to spread out the linen and lay Jesus' body upon it. No time even to wash the corpse and prepare it properly. It would have to wait. Perhaps they tied a band around His head to keep the slack jaw closed; perhaps they spread the linen atop His body and bound it with bands. It might at least soak up some of the blood and fluid and make their work easier when Sabbath was done. As the sun sank, the men rolled the stone before the tomb and left. In tearful silence, the myrrhbearers watched it all. That unfinished final act of love—preparing the body—consumed their hearts and minds all the Sabbath. As soon as sun had set that Saturday they hurried to purchase more myrrh and spices so that they'd be ready to tend to their Master come the first hint of dawn.

With the gift of love, they make their way in dawn's first light, only to be met with utter confusion. The tomb was open and no body was in it. Yet, angels announced they were looking in the wrong spot for Jesus of Nazareth, for He was no longer dead, but had risen as He promised. In fear

I am content! My Jesus is my light,
My radiant sun of grace.
His cheering rays beam blessings forth for all,
Sweet comfort, hope, and peace.
This Easter sun has brought salvation
And everlasting exultation.
I am content!
I am content! (LSB 468:3)

---

and trembling they ran from the tomb, unable to process what they had heard. Matthew records this as the moment when Jesus met them and bid them to rejoice and hurry to tell His disciples the good news of resurrection.

They had come to bring the spices that would somewhat cover up the stench of death. He had risen to deliver to them and to us all the source of unending joy: the spice that dissipates the rank odor of sin and death itself. He had risen to pour over them the sweet anointing of His everlasting righteousness and life. Yet, the Church rejoices to remember the love and devotion of Joanna, Mary, and Salome (along with Mary Magdalene commemorated on her own day). Still among us in the Church are those who tend the suffering, dying, and dead. Their love and care remind those who suffer and mourn of the nail-scarred hands of the One whom death could not defeat and His promise of everlasting life to all who believe in His name.

Mighty God, Your crucified and buried Son did not remain in the tomb for long. Give us joy in the tasks before us, that we might carry out faithful acts as did Joanna, Mary, and Salome, offering to You the sweet perfume of grateful hearts, so that we, too, may see the glory of Your resurrection and proclaim the Good News with unrestrained eagerness and fervor worked in us through our Lord Jesus Christ, who rose and reigns with You and the Holy Spirit, one God, now and forever. Amen.

10
AUGUST

Today, we remember and thank God for **Lawrence, Deacon and Martyr.**

The apostles established the office of deacon. Deacons helped their bishops and presbyters (pastors) by tending to the collection, management, and distribution of alms (gifts for the poor, those in crisis, and for the clergy). Since the bread and wine that were used in the Eucharist were gifts of the people, the deacons also had the responsibility to prepare them, set the table, and even help distribute them. Many large congregations copied the example of the apostles in Acts 6 and appointed seven deacons, the head of which organized their work and connected them to the bishop.

Lawrence was such a deacon. Most likely born in Spain toward the early part of the third century, he met and became fast friends with the man who would end up being Pope Sixtus II, bishop of Rome. Together they journeyed to Rome. When Sixtus was elected the bishop of the city, he appointed his friend Lawrence to be his chief deacon.

In those days, the Roman Emperor Valerian made it policy that whoever was denounced as a Christian was to be summarily executed. All his possessions would be given over to the empire's treasury. It was further ordered that all the Christian clergy should be killed. Sixtus had not been bishop even for a whole year. He and many of his clergy with him were denounced and taken custody while celebrating a liturgy in a cemetery. It was August 6, 256.

After the death of his friend and spiritual father, Lawrence was brought before the prefect of Rome. He was ordered to turn over to the Roman treasury all the treasures of the church. The prefect understood that deacons handled the church's wealth. Lawrence asked for three days to assemble the treasure. He spent those days giving away to the poor as much of the

Teach us the lesson Thou hast taught:
To feel for those Thy blood hath bought,
That every word and deed and thought
*   May work a work for Thee.*
All are redeemed, both far and wide,
Since Thou, O Lord, for all hast died.
Grant us the will and grace provide
*   To love them all in Thee. (LSB 852:3–4)*

---

church's material wealth as he could. On the third day, he appeared before the prefect, who again demanded the church's treasure. The gutsy deacon then called forth an assembly of the poor folk whose lives the church's charity had touched. He brought in the disabled and the sick. He said to the prefect, "*These* are the treasures of the Church."

The enraged prefect ordered a gridiron prepared and well heated. Lawrence was placed over the fire. After he had endured the agony a time, he quite cheerfully called out, "You can turn me over; I'm done on this side." He was a mighty witness to Nehemiah's words: "The joy of the Lord is your strength."

The story of Lawrence's martyrdom was seared into the memory of the young and growing Church. The commemoration of his death this day was observed in Rome right away and soon spread to other places. In Frankenmuth, Michigan, stands a large and lovely Lutheran Church named in honor of the cheerful deacon, devoted to mercy: St. Lorenz.

Almighty God, You called Lawrence to be a deacon in Your Church to serve Your saints with deeds of love, and You gave him the crown of martyrdom. Give us the same charity of heart that we may fulfill Your love by defending and supporting the poor, that by loving them we may love You with all our hearts; through Jesus Christ, our Lord, who lives and reigns with You and the Holy Spirit, one God, now and forever. Amen.

15
AUGUST

Today, the Holy Church rejoices to celebrate the Festival of **St. Mary, Mother of Our Lord**, remembering her falling asleep in faith (dormition).

I remember it all as I lay down my head in death.

I remember when the angel came and told me, and my heart burst with joy and terror.

I remember when I came to the door of Zechariah's house and Elizabeth knew my secret and my heart melted and my eyes burned with tears and my mouth prophesied.

I remember when I felt Your movement first inside my body, and I realized that I was the living ark of the living God.

I remember when first I saw Your face, and touched Your hands, and looked into my Joseph's eyes.

I remember when they came creeping in to see You, to worship You, the shepherds of the night, and told me of angel songs and glory in the highest and peace on earth.

I remember when we brought You to the temple and the old man took You in his arms and blessed God, ready to die, and told me of pain yet to come.

I remember when they came from the East, and as I held You, they bowed before You and gave their gifts—the gold, the incense, and the myrrh, while the star's light shone upon us.

I remember when he woke me and we fled into the night ahead of the terror of Herod's sword.

I remember when we came home at last, and people looked and talked, but You were all our joy.

I remember when You stayed behind, when You left us, and we found You in the temple and my heart rose up in fear, realizing that You chose to abide in the place of sacrifice and death.

O higher than the cherubim,
More glorious than the seraphim,
Lead their praises: "Alleluia!"
Thou bearer of the eternal Word,
Most gracious, magnify the Lord:
"Alleluia, alleluia!
Alleluia, alleluia, alleluia!" (LSB 670:2)

I remember when You spoke to me in roughness and yet made the water into wine.

I remember when we came to make You take Your rest, and You taught me that all these in need were dear to You as Your own family.

I remember when they took You, tortured You, and crucified You; before my eyes rose up the memory of the old man in the temple—his words haunted me still—and as I watched You dying it was as if a sword ran me through.

I remember when You looked on the beloved one and me and gave us to each other for all our days.

I remember when the light died in Your eyes and my heart sank beyond tears and words.

I remember after the empty days when they came and told me that You lived again, and joy flooded my heart, and I knew then what I had always known—Your every promise was true.

I remember when we prayed together after You had gone into heaven and the Spirit came in wind and flame.

I remember how they went and told the news to all the world. And I welcomed each new believer as my beloved child, a brother of my Son, the King of all.

I remember it all.

My Son, now as I die, I am not afraid. I go to You, to You who has conquered death, to You who is the forgiveness of all sins. Receive me, child. Receive me. I remember. I remember. I remember.

Almighty God, You chose the Virgin Mary to be the mother of Your only Son. Grant that we, who are redeemed by His blood, may share with her in the glory of Your eternal kingdom; through Jesus Christ, our Son, our Lord, who lives and reigns with You and the Holy Spirit, one God, now and forever. Amen.

READINGS
ISAIAH 61:7–11 / GALATIANS 4:4–7 / LUKE 1:(39–45) 46–55

16
AUGUST

Today, we remember the holy patriarch **Isaac**, the ancestor of Christ.

To old Abram God gave the promise: you will have a son. To older Abraham God clarified: you will have a son through Sarah. Sarah, listening at the tent door, laughed as only a ninety-year-old can laugh. God heard her. He thought that was as good a name as any for the child: Isaac, which in Hebrew is "laughter" (Genesis 18).

Here was a living reminder in flesh and blood that nothing is too hard for the Lord. No human incapacity stands in His way. In fact, He swept aside every effort Abraham had ever made to "help" God fulfill the promise. No to Lot, no to Eliezer, no to Ishmael. God waited until they had to despair of their own schemes. The name Isaac reminds his parents of the joyfully unexpected way He loves to give.

With Isaac we cannot but remember how the Lord who gives is also the Lord who takes away. Abraham, in his obedience to the divine command, prepared to offer his only-begotten son. And here, even more than in his joy-filled name, Isaac serves as a type of his descendant, Jesus. The donkey, the wood laid on his back, the question about the lamb—these all point to the final Promised Seed of Abraham who would die on Golgotha's hill, the Lamb that God did finally provide as the substitute (Genesis 22). Every time we approach the altar to receive the blessed Sacrament, what do we receive but the Lamb of God who takes away the sin of the world. Indeed, God still provides.

As Isaac grew to manhood, Abraham took care to provide him a wife from his own clan. The beautiful story of how the Lord guided Abraham's servant Eliezer and answered his prayer is told in Genesis 24. Here is

A multitude comes from the east and the west
  To sit at the feast of salvation
With Abraham, Isaac, and Jacob, the blest,
  Obeying the Lord's invitation.
    Have mercy upon us, O Jesus! (**LSB 510:1**)

---

yet another beautiful type of Christ, as Isaac welcomes and treasures his beloved and laughs with her. In it we see a picture of the Savior's delight in His Bride, the Holy Church.

Like his father, Isaac prayed for his wife, for she was barren. She conceived and bore the twins Jacob and Esau. She consulted God as she was with child and heard from God that the older would serve the younger. Her conviction that this was so explains her complicity in the deception of her blind husband. The birthright went not to Isaac's favorite but to the wily Jacob. Isaac lived a long life and finally was gathered to His people. But his name of laughter is forever remembered. The God who can make a ninety-year-old woman conceive and bear a child is the God who will later make a virgin who knows not a man to conceive and bear the final Promised Seed. And He will bring joyful laughter to all the earth in the defeat of death and the forgiveness of sin. For Your holy servant Isaac, kind Father, all glory and thanks!

Almighty God, heavenly Father, through the patriarch Isaac You preserved the seed of the Messiah and brought forth the new creation. Continue to preserve the Church as the Israel of God as she manifests the glory of Your holy name by continuing to worship Your Son, the child of Mary; through Jesus Christ, our Lord. Amen.

17
AUGUST

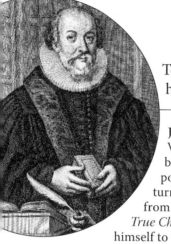

Today, we remember and thank God for His holy servant **Johann Gerhard, Theologian**.

Johann Gerhard was born in Quedlinburg in 1582. When he was fourteen or fifteen, he was stricken by a serious disease and had to face the very real possibility of his own mortality. In this time of spiritual turmoil and fear, he received comfort and counsel from his pastor (the famous Johann Arndt, author of *True Christianity*). He resolved after his recovery to devote himself to the study of theology and the Bible.

Gerhard studied both at Wittenberg and at Jena, from which he graduated in 1605. He accepted an appointment by Johann Casimir to serve as superintendent of Heldburg. In short time, the gifts of the man were so evident that he was appointed the superintendent of the entire duchy. He remained in this position until 1616, after which he became a professor at Jena and remained there till his death, despite numerous calls to serve elsewhere.

His early brush with death and the great comfort he received from his pastor left their mark on him. Out of the furnace of that affliction, the Lord raised up a mighty servant of the Word. Gerhard never let piety come unglued from dogma. He was first and foremost a man of prayer. It breathes from start to finish in all his writings. Still in his youth, he wrote his *Sacred Meditations*, which have remained a beloved and treasured classic of Christian devotional literature. His sermon collections (*postilla*) are noteworthy for his consistent discovery in the Old Testament of foreshadowings of Christ. His longest work was his massive *Loci Communes Theologici*. In the tradition of Melanchthon and Chemnitz, every doctrine of theology was traced to its roots in Scripture and its apprehension and

I know my faith is founded
On Jesus Christ, my God and Lord;
And this my faith confessing,
Unmoved I stand on His sure Word.
Our reason cannot fathom
The truth of God profound;
Who trusts in human wisdom
Relies on shifting ground.
God's Word is all-sufficient,
It makes divinely sure;
And trusting in its wisdom,
My faith shall rest secure. **(LSB 587:1)**

---

misapprehension across the centuries of the Church's history investigated. Unlike earlier Lutheran theological books, Gerhard freely employed all the categories of Aristotelian philosophy. The result was a crisp, lucid expression of the doctrine of Scripture as articulated by the Lutheran Church. It ran to some twenty-two volumes.

Gerhard was truly a great teacher, a preacher of Christ, a man of prayer who teaches us how to meditate upon the commands and promises of God so as to be comforted in conscience and strengthened in faith. As a theologian of the Lutheran Church he is usually ranked right behind Martin Chemnitz. He died this day in 1637. O God, for the witness of Your faithful servant Johann, all glory and praise!

Almighty God, heavenly Father, through the ministry and teaching of Johann Gerhard You have blessed Your Church and built up Your people in the holy faith. Continue to provide to Your Church teachers who will proclaim Your truth with zeal and with great kindness and love; through Jesus Christ, our Lord. Amen.

19
AUGUST

Today, the Holy Church rejoices to remember **Bernard of Clairvaux, Hymnwriter and Theologian.**

Bernard is one of the beloved saints of the Church from the Middle Ages. He was born in 1090 to a noble family in Burgundy, France. Yet, at the age of 22 he chose to turn his back on the path of wealth and power. As many would before and after him, he became a monk. Bernard asked admittance to the monastery of Citeaux in the Cistercian Order. This monastery was devoted to a strict observance of the Rule of St. Benedict.

After only two or so years there, Bernard was dispatched to form a new monastery at Clairvaux. The monastery's founding was quite trying. Benedict's strictness resulted in damaged health and it finally took intervention from his friends to have Benedict reconsider the extreme asceticism he was enjoining. The monastery then grew by leaps and bounds.

Instead of the intellectually heavy approach to theology characterized by Scholasticism, Bernard was a champion of a warm faith that stressed trust in the Crucified. The hymns "O Jesus, King Most Wonderful!" and "O Sacred Head, Now Wounded" derive from the heritage left us by Bernard.

His typically comforting, Gospel-drenched preaching stood at times in tension with the blindness of the age. He could preach the sweet comfort of the blood of Christ and then urge the recruits to the second crusade to atone their sin and appease God's wrath by bloodying their swords.

There is in all of this a parallel with Martin Luther. Though not a noble, when he chose the monastery against his parent's will, he chose the toughest one. He ruined his health as a monk with his austere practices. He had a fire of love when he preached that focused upon Christ and Him crucified. He

O Jesus, King most wonderful!
O Conqueror renowned!
O Source of peace ineffable,
In whom all joys are found;
When once You visit darkened hearts,
Then truth begins to shine,
Then earthly vanity departs,
Then kindles love divine. (LSB 554:1–2)

---

brought comfort to the troubled conscience through Christ's loving sacrifice. Luther wrote hymns that celebrated his Lord. And while he could write the most beautiful and comforting words, he also was capable of spewing out horrific things against the Jews and against the peasants at their revolt. Both men were called upon by civil authorities to help with various political troubles. Both were finally men who were indeed "earthen vessels" through whom God delighted to give His Church great treasures.

We do not commemorate any of the saints because they were perfect. We commemorate them because they were forgiven and through them God has given us a mirror of His grace.

O God, enkindled with the fire of Your love, Your servant Bernard of Clairvaux became a burning and shining light in Your Church. By Your great mercy, grant that we also may be aflame with the spirit of love and discipline and ever walk in Your presence as children of light; through Jesus Christ, our Lord, who lives and reigns with You and the Holy Spirit, one God, now and forever. Amen.

20
AUGUST

Today, we remember and thank God for His servant, the holy prophet and judge of Israel, **Samuel**.

Samuel was Israel's last judge. His father, Elkanah, had two wives, Hannah and Peninnah. Peninnah bore Elkanah many children, but Hannah was barren. The family was pious and went up to the yearly sacrifice in Shiloh. One day, after eating there, Hannah went to the place where God was worshiped. She was deeply distressed and prayed silently to the Lord as she wept. Eli, the priest, after first mistaking her condition, realized she was in great anguish. He assured her that the Lord would hear and answer her prayer. Hannah vowed that if she bore a son, she would lend him to the Lord as a Nazirite all his days.

Her prayer was answered, and she gave birth to her little child whom she named Samuel, because the Lord had heard her prayer (Samuel means "the Lord hears"). When he was still a lad, newly weaned, she went with Elkanah to the sacrifice and presented the lad to Eli. She explained that the Lord had given this child to her in response to her prayer; now she was giving back to the Lord. So the little boy stayed and ministered to Eli.

The day came when God revealed Himself to Samuel, calling to him three times. At first, Eli thought the boy was dreaming, but when he persistently returned, saying, "Here I am, for you called me," Eli realized that God was speaking to the lad. He told him how to answer. God called Samuel yet again and pronounced judgment against Eli's house. Samuel was hesitant to tell the old man the words of God but finally did so.

As Samuel grew up, all Israel realized that he was a prophet of the Lord, for the Lord "let none of his words fall to the ground" (1 Samuel 3:19). Samuel judged Israel for many years, but sadly, his sons (like Eli's before him) did not follow the Lord as their father had. The people demanded that

Speak, O Lord, Your servant listens,
Let Your Word to me come near;
Newborn life and spirit give me,
Let each promise still my fear.
Death's dread power, its inward strife,
Wars against Your Word of life;
Fill me, Lord, with love's strong fervor
That I cling to You forever! (LSB 589:1)

Samuel give them a king. Samuel was displeased and warned the people what a king would do. Still they insisted on having one so that they could be like the other nations around them. First, at God's instruction, he anointed Saul of Benjamin as Israel's king. When Saul proved unfaithful and turned from the Lord, Samuel anointed Jesse's youngest son, David. Samuel died prior to Saul, and Saul, in great dismay at having no guidance from God, sought to call up Samuel's spirit. The apparition told Saul that he would be with him by the next day, together with his sons.

Samuel is remembered as a man of prayer whose intercession for the people of God was constant. He is remembered above all for his statement "to obey is better than sacrifice." This would be a theme that the later prophets would constantly repeat.

Almighty God, in Your mercy You gave Samuel courage to call Israel to repentance and to renew their dedication to the Lord. Keep us and all Your people in the grace of repentance, that by the blood of Jesus, the Son of David, we may continually receive and rejoice in the forgiveness of all our sins; through the same Jesus Christ, our Lord. Amen.

24
AUGUST

Today, the Holy Church rejoices to celebrate the Festival of
St. Bartholomew, Apostle.

St. Bartholomew (also called Nathanael) was one of the first of our Lord's disciples. His home was in Cana of Galilee, where the Lord performed His first miracle. According to St. John's Gospel, Philip sought to introduce his friend to Jesus in Judea. Nathanael was more than a little skeptical about a Messiah who hailed from the town of Nazareth (a town not even mentioned in the Old Testament). But Philip urged him, "Come and see." He did, and as so many have done since, he left a changed person.

When he approached Jesus, the Lord said, "Behold, an Israelite indeed, in whom there is no deceit!" Nathanael didn't understand how the Lord could possibly know him. Jesus answered, "Before Philip called you, when you were under the fig tree, I saw you." This elicits the powerful confession from Nathanael, "Rabbi, You are the Son of God! You are the King of Israel!" Jesus then promised that he would see greater things than this. "You will see heaven opened, and the angels of God ascending and descending on the Son of Man." Jesus promised him something better than Jacob's vision at Bethel.

Bartholomew was with the other disciples, except for Thomas, behind the locked doors on Easter evening when our Lord appeared, and then again with them a week later when Thomas was called from unbelief to faith. In John 21, he went fishing with Peter, Andrew, James, and John. The risen One called to them from the shore, blessed them with a miraculous catch of 153 fish, and then shared a breakfast with them. Thus, at least three times after the resurrection, the Lord revealed Himself to Bartholomew. He was, of course, with the Twelve and Mary in the Upper Room on Pentecost and so a recipient of the Spirit's flame and a participant in the miraculous speaking in various tongues.

All praise for him whose candor
Through all his doubt You saw
When Philip at the fig tree
Disclosed You in the law.
Discern, beneath our surface,
O Lord, what we can be,
That by Your truth made guileless,
Your glory we may see. (LSB *518:23*)

According to very old tradition in the Church, St. Bartholomew carried the Gospel of Jesus to Armenia. There he had success in converting the king, but the king's brother was reportedly so angered at this that he had Bartholomew flayed alive. He died a witness to the resurrection. The terrible torture lasted only for a time, but the eternal life His Savior had won was forever. His symbol in the art of the Church is a flaying knife.

For Your servant St. Bartholomew and for his steadfastness in the face of suffering and of death, glory to You, Lord Jesus Christ!

Almighty God, Your Son, Jesus Christ, chose Bartholomew to be an apostle to preach the blessed Gospel. Grant that Your Church may love what he believed and preach what he taught; through Jesus Christ, Your Son, our Lord, who lives and reigns with You and the Holy Spirit, one God, now and forever. Amen.

READINGS
PROVERBS 3:1–8 / 2 CORINTHIANS 4:7–10 / LUKE 22:24–30
OR JOHN 1:43–51

27
AUGUST

Today, we remember and thank God for the life of His maidservant **Monica, Mother of Augustine.**

St. **Monica, mother** of St. Augustine, was a native of North Africa and lived from about AD 333 to 387. She has ever been regarded as an inspiring example of a godly mother who persists in prayer. She spent her life seeking the spiritual welfare of others, above all her husband, her children, and her friends.

Augustine relates in his *Confessions* much of what we know of her extraordinary character and piety. She won her husband to Christ by her kindness and humility. Before he died, he was baptized and named Christ's own. This comforted her in her widowhood. But she still had her errant child, Augustine, to worry about.

When Augustine left North Africa for Rome and later for Milan, she followed. In Milan, her prayers were at long last answered when the Holy Spirit through Archbishop Ambrose brought her son to faith and he was baptized along with several of his company. While there, she also inquired of the Archbishop about the divergent fasting practices she'd encountered between Rome and Milan. The Archbishop's famous answer to her was, "When in Rome, I do as the Romans do." In other words, don't raise scruples about divergent spiritual disciplines, but cheerfully join in whatever you find the Christians doing at a given locale.

Her long travels had wearied her, and she died May 4 (her traditional commemoration) in Ostia, Italy, on a journey she had hoped would take her back to her beloved Africa. Because of her close association with her son's story, many modern church calendars have transferred her commemoration to the day next to her son's death.

Oh, blest the parents who give heed
Unto their children's foremost need
And weary not of care or cost.
May none to them and heav'n be lost! (LSB 862:3)

When Augustine reflected back upon his mother, he remembered several things about her. She was a patient wife with her sometimes wayward husband before his conversion. She always was a consummate peacemaker. When she heard bitter things from either side about the other in a dispute, she never disclosed to the other party anything hurtful, but only what would tend toward mending the strained relationship. She delighted to be a servant to all the servants of God. Augustine said those who met her delighted to honor her, "for they felt Your presence in her heart, witnessed by the fruits of her holy way of life" (*Confessions*, IX:21–22). She welcomed all believers as though they were her children and served them all as if she were their daughter.

Above all, Monica is remembered as the very flesh and blood image of the widow our Lord described in His parable (Luke 18:1–8). We remember her dogged persistence in prayer for the salvation of her family and most of all for the salvation of that brilliant, but undisciplined son, Augustine. She banged upon heaven's door until her request was granted, and for it she was thankful the rest of her days.

O Lord, You strengthened Your patient servant Monica through spiritual discipline to persevere in offering her love, her prayers, and her tears for the conversion of her husband and of Augustine, their son. Deepen our devotion to bring others, even our own family, to acknowledge Jesus Christ as Savior and Lord, who with You and the Holy Spirit, lives and reigns, one God, now and forever. Amen.

28
AUGUST

Today, we remember and thank God for the life of His servant
Augustine of Hippo, Pastor and Theologian.

St. Augustine is one of four so-called Doctors of the Western Church, the others being Saints Ambrose, Jerome, and Gregory the Great. Yet, among the four, Augustine is generally regarded as the greatest theologian and the one individual who had the most significant impact upon the theology of the Church of anyone save St. Paul. St. Jerome said of him that he "established anew the ancient faith" (see *Letter* 195).

Born in North Africa in 354, Augustine's brilliance was early recognized. He studied rhetoric and advanced readily as an instructor. He was intrigued by various worldly philosophies: first, Manichaeism with its dualism; then Plotinus's version of Neo-Platonism. Christianity seemed to him quite impoverished when it came to its philosophical depth. He lived a morally dissolute life, as he freely admits in his *Confessions*, taking a concubine and fathering a son out of wedlock.

God answered his mother's fervent prayers through encountering St. Ambrose, Archbishop of Milan. Here was a man who knew rhetoric and was conversant in the various philosophies and yet who wholeheartedly embraced the Christian faith. Augustine, under his catechesis, soon became a Christian and was baptized. "Late have I loved Thee!" he cried out in his *Confessions*.

Ordained a priest and later consecrated a bishop of Hippo (in modern-day Algeria), Augustine turned that remarkable intellect toward the task of expounding the Sacred Scriptures and governing the Church. He vigorously confronted the Donatist schism and showed its errors from the Scripture, and he later did the same for the Pelagian controversy. His defense of salvation being by grace alone earned him the moniker "The Doctor of

By grace I'm saved, grace free and boundless;
My soul, believe and doubt it not.
Why stagger at this word of promise?
Has Scripture ever falsehood taught?
No! Then this word must true remain:
By grace you too will life obtain.
By grace! None dare lay claim to merit;
Our works and conduct have no worth.
God in His love sent our Redeemer,
Christ Jesus, to this sinful earth;
His death did for our sins atone,
And we are saved by grace alone. (LSB 566:1–2)

Grace." His major writings include not only the aforementioned *Confessions*, but also *City of God* (in which he offers a biblical understanding of history as a battle between two cities), *Enchiridion* (a handbook for expounding the Christian faith), *On the Spirit and the Letter* (where he treats the proper distinction between Law and Gospel), and a *Harmony* of the four Gospels.

The great man died upon this day in AD 430 as the Germanic Vandals besieged his beloved Hippo. When they finally took the city, all of it was burned save St. Augustine's cathedral and library. He was early commemorated as a great gift of God to His Church.

O Lord God, the light of minds that know You, the life of souls that love You, and the strength of hearts that serve You, give us strength to follow the example of Your servant Augustine of Hippo, so that knowing You we may truly love You and loving You we may fully serve You—for to serve You is perfect freedom; through Jesus Christ, our Lord, who lives and reigns with You and the Holy Spirit, one God, now and forever. Amen.

29
AUGUST

Today, the Holy Church rejoices to celebrate the Festival of the
Martyrdom of St. John the Baptist.

He worked no mighty miracles. He had neither wife nor child nor place he
could call home. He lived in the desert wilderness of Judea and ate insects
and wild honey growing up. He dressed in a rough fashion reminiscent
of Elijah (in whose spirit he served, turning the hearts of fathers to their
children, and children to the obedience of the just). His life prepared him
for a ministry that lasted at most a year and half. He was jailed for daring to
criticize King Herod Agrippa I and telling him that it was not lawful for him
to take his brother's wife as his own.

It was at this stage of his life, as he was in prison, that Jesus said of him,
"Among those born of women there has arisen no one greater than John the
Baptist." Under unjust arrest for speaking truth, John no doubt knew exactly
what awaited him. After all, from the time he baptized Jesus and heard the
Father's voice and saw the Spirit descend, he had proclaimed that Jesus was
"the Lamb of God" (John 1:29). John knew that "He must increase, but I
must decrease" (John 3:30), since he was the one who prepared the way, the
forerunner. Lambs were for slaughter, and to be a forerunner is to go ahead
on the way the Lord Himself was to travel. John knew it wouldn't end well
for him in this world. Yet, Jesus had sent him the comfort, "Go and tell John
. . . the dead are raised up, and the poor have good news preached to them"
(Matthew 11:4–5).

Did he whisper that promise to himself as the executioner came with
sword in hand? Herodias's daughter's swirling and salacious hints had
captured the old man's lust. Herod made his foolish promise and Herodias
finally had her revenge. The regretful king handed the grisly platter with the
prophet's head upon it to the girl, who gave it to her mother. When word
reached John's disciples, they came and took away the body and buried it.

Our thanks for John the Baptist
Who, till his dying day,
Made straight paths for the Savior
And heralded His way!
In witnessing to Jesus
Through times of threat or shame
May we with faith and courage
The Lamb of God proclaim. (LSB 518:24)

Then they went to Jesus.

That is what John had taught them to do. Go to Jesus. And hear from Him the words that will sustain when all else fails. They were words John clung to as he entered into the darkness, forerunner in death as he had been in life. Did he announce to the dead, "Fear not! The Death of death, the Lamb of God, lives! I've seen Him. Soon He will bring light to those who sit in darkness, in the shadow of death. He will free us, raise us, bring us to His kingdom!"? So today we commemorate the death of the greatest born of women in the natural way and last prophet of the Old Testament: John the Baptist.

Almighty God, You gave Your servant John the Baptist to be the forerunner of Your Son, Jesus Christ, in both his preaching of repentance and his innocent death. Grant that we, who have died and risen with Christ in Holy Baptism, may daily repent of our sins, patiently suffer for the sake of the truth, and fearlessly bear witness to His victory over death; through the same Jesus Christ, our Lord, who lives and reigns with You and the Holy Spirit, one God, now and forever. Amen.

READINGS
REVELATION 6:9–11 / ROMANS 6:1–5 / MARK 6:14–29

1
SEPTEMBER

Today, we remember and thank God for the successor to Moses, **Joshua**.

Joshua (also named Hoshea in Numbers 13:8) was the son of Nun of the tribe of Ephraim. He was one of the twelve representatives sent to spy out the land of Canaan. Only Joshua and Caleb brought a good report back to the people; the rest sought to discourage the Israelites from going up to take the land. The people sided with the ten and rebelled against God's command. God then decreed that the Israelites would have to wander for forty years in the wilderness until almost the entire generation that had refused the good land died. Joshua and Caleb alone would be permitted to enter Canaan and help secure Israel's possession of the land.

Joshua served Moses throughout those years of wandering as his personal assistant. When Moses himself was forbidden to enter the land of promise, Joshua was appointed to lead the people into the land of Canaan. The Lord told him, "Be strong and courageous. Do not be frightened, and do not be dismayed, for the LORD your God is with you wherever you go" (Joshua 1:9).

With a miracle parallel to that of crossing the Red Sea, Joshua commanded the ark of the covenant to enter the flooded Jordan and the waters to stand in a heap to the north, while to the south they drained away. Israel crossed over on dry ground. Joshua commanded that stones be taken from the dry bed of the Jordan and set up as a memorial on the east side of the river. With instruction from the Lord he waged war on Jericho with trumpets rather than swords, and the walls of the city fell as the Lord promised. City after city, territory after territory, Joshua gave to the children of Israel. At the end of the major conquests, he summoned Israel to himself at Shechem to renew Israel's covenant with the Lord. Here he urged the people to decide what God or gods they were intending to serve. "But as for

Now our heavenly Aaron enters
  With His blood within the veil;
Joshua now is come to Canaan,
  And the kings before Him quail.
Now He plants the tribes of Israel
  In their promised resting place;
Now our great Elijah offers
  Double portion of His grace. (LSB 494:4)

---

me and my house," said Joshua, "we will serve the LORD" (Joshua 24:15). He died at the age of 110 and was buried in the hill country of Ephraim, north of the mountain of Gaash (Joshua 24:29–30).

Joshua is the Hebrew form of Jesus' name. The Church has long seen significance in the fact that Moses got the people of God *to* the Promised Land, but couldn't get them possession *of* it. That was the work of Joshua. So the Law can only get a person so far. It cannot bring them into possession of the land of promise. That is the work of a latter-day Joshua, the Lord Jesus Christ. St. Mark's Gospel especially depicts our Lord following along in Joshua's path: He crosses the Jordan after a time of testing in the wilderness and then proceeds to drive out the demons and restore God's people to their heritage.

Lord Jesus Christ, Your servant Joshua led the children of Israel through the waters of the Jordan River into a land flowing with milk and honey. As our Joshua, lead us, we pray, through the waters of our Baptism into the promised land of our eternal home, where You live and reign with the Father and the Holy Spirit, one God, now and forever.

2

SEPTEMBER

Today, we remember and thank God for the mother of the prophet Samuel, **Hannah**.

Hannah was one of two wives of Elkanah. His other wife, Peninnah, taunted Hannah when they went up to the yearly sacrifice at Shiloh. She mocked her barrenness, perhaps intimating that while Hannah might be more beloved of Elkanah than she, God obviously didn't love or care for her since He had withheld the fruit of the womb. Hannah's grief was inconsolable. Elkanah asked her, "Hannah, why do you weep? And why do you not eat? And why is your heart sad? Am I not more to you than ten sons?" (1 Samuel 1:8).

Hannah took her sorrow in hand and went to pray before the ark. She stood outside the door of the temple praying in her heart and weeping bitterly. She promised that if the Lord remembered her in her affliction and gave her a son, she would give him to the Lord all his days. He would be a perpetual Nazirite.

As she prayed and wept, her mouth moved, but she didn't speak aloud. Eli, the priest, beholding her standing there and muttering, mistook her for a drunkard: "How long will you go on being drunk? Put away your wine from you." She told the priest that she was not drunk, but speaking to God out of "great anxiety and vexation." Eli then looked kindly upon her: "Go in peace, and the God of Israel grant your petition that you have made to Him." She replied, "Let your servant find favor in your eyes" (1 Samuel 1:14–18). Then she went her way at peace and hopeful.

In time, the Lord remembered Hannah. She gave birth to a little boy and gave him a fitting name: Samuel, that is, God has heard. When he had been weaned, she went up with a three-year-old heifer and a skin of wine and presented him to the priest in Shiloh. "As you live, my Lord, I am the woman who was standing here in Your presence, praying to the LORD. For

Are we weak and heavy laden,
  Cumbered with a load of care?
Precious Savior, still our refuge—
  Take it to the Lord in prayer.
Do thy friends despise, forsake thee?
  Take it to the Lord in prayer.
In His arms He'll take and shield thee;
  Thou wilt find a solace there. (LSB 770:3)

---

this child I prayed, and the LORD granted me my petition that I made to Him. Therefore I have lent him to the LORD. As long as he lives, he is lent to the LORD" (1 Samuel 1:26–28).

Hannah then prayed and sang a song of fierce beauty, foreshadowing the Magnificat of the blessed Virgin. Among its memorable lines: "My heart exults in the LORD; my horn is exalted in the LORD. . . . There is none holy like the LORD; for there is none besides You; there is no rock like our God" (1 Samuel 2:1–2).

God the Father Almighty, maker of all things, You looked on the affliction of Your barren servant Hannah and did not forget her but answered her prayers with the gift of a son. So hear our supplications and petitions and fill our emptiness. Grant us trust in Your provision, so that we, like Hannah, might render unto You all thankfulness and praise, and delight in the miraculous birth of Your Son, Jesus Christ, who lives and reigns with You and the Holy Spirit, one God, now and forever. Amen.

3
SEPTEMBER

Today, the Holy Church rejoices to remember the sixth-century bishop of Rome, **Gregory the Great, Pastor**.

Gregory the Great (c. AD 540–604) was the last of the four great Doctors of the Western Church (together with the earlier Saints Ambrose, Augustine, and Jerome). Gregory was a capable administrator, having served earlier in his life as mayor of Rome, a post he assumed at the young age of 33. He restored a measure of prosperity and order to the decimated city, weakened by waves of barbarian invasions and plague. His successful civil service could not still an inner yearning. He felt a calling to serve in the Church. He sold off his sizable holdings, donated the money to the assistance of the poor, and founded a monastery in what had been his father's villa.

Pope Pelagius II ordained him a deacon and then appointed him to be the ambassador of the Roman bishop to the imperial court in Constantinople. While there he engaged in a disputation with Eutychius, bishop of Constantinople, and vanquished his opponent simply by quoting the Scripture: "Touch me, and see. For a spirit does not have flesh and bones as you see I have" (Luke 24:39). He later returned to Rome, where upon the death of Pelagius II due to plague, Gregory was acclaimed bishop of the city. That took place this day in the year AD 590.

Gregory, even as a deacon and presbyter, had a great heart for mission work. Due to his determination, the Gospel's proclamation was strengthened in England. He had noted a young lad in the marketplace for sale and remarked upon his beautiful countenance. He asked from whence he came and whether his people were Christians or still heathen. Upon finding that they were heathen, he asked the name of their race. "Angles" he was told, upon which he remarked that it was fitting, for they have angelic faces. He wished the country to be delivered from God's wrath and brought into the unity of the catholic faith. Toward that end, he begged the pope (this was

All-holy Father, Son, and equal Spirit,
Trinity blessed, send us Thy salvation;
Thine is the glory, gleaming and resounding
    Through all creation. (LSB 875:3)

---

before his own elevation) for leave to preach the Gospel in that land. The pope, however, was not about to lose his right-hand man. It would fall to St. Augustine of Canterbury to preach the Gospel and begin organizing the Church among the Germanic tribes that had invaded and largely displaced the original Britons.

Gregory is remembered also for bringing order and discipline to the music of the Latin Church, for adding the Lord's Prayer to the order of service in the Roman Church (bringing it into conformity with wider Christian practice), and for writing *The Pastoral Office*, a handbook on the ministry that continued in use for a millennium.

Almighty and merciful God, You raised up Gregory of Rome to be a pastor to those who shepherd God's flock and You inspired him to send missionaries to preach the Gospel to the English people. Preserve in Your Church the catholic and apostolic faith that Your people may continue to be fruitful in every good work and receive the crown of glory that never fades away; through Jesus Christ, our Lord, who lives and reigns with You and the Holy Spirit, one God, now and forever. Amen.

4
SEPTEMBER

Today, the Holy Church remembers and thanks God for the great prophet and deliverer of His people, **Moses**.

The first of the great prophets, Moses was born in Egypt long after Joseph and his service to the Egyptian people had faded in memory. Under the harsh conditions at the time, all Jewish male children were ordered drowned in the Nile. This was an order with which Moses' mother, Jochebed, could not comply. She hid her little boy for three months and then finally put him in a basket, made watertight, and placed him upon the Nile. In time, the daughter of Pharaoh heard the baby crying and sent her servant to fetch him. She recognized that he was one of the Hebrew children, but chose to adopt him and raise him as her own.

When he was forty, Moses visited his own people. He saw an Egyptian abusing one of them. He killed the Egyptian and hid his body in the sand. When he visited them the next day, he saw two Hebrews fighting and urged them to stop. They asked him who had appointed him ruler and judge over them and if he intended to kill them as he had the Egyptian. Realizing his deed was known, Moses fled to the wilderness.

There a Midianite priest took him in and gave him his daughter Zipporah in marriage. Moses stayed there for forty years. Then God appeared to him in a burning bush, revealing Himself as "I AM." He sent a reluctant Moses back to Egypt to bring out the children of Israel from their slavery and gave him his brother Aaron as a helper and spokesperson.

Pharaoh was not at all inclined to let Israel go. Yet, through a series of escalating, miraculous disasters, God finally forced Pharaoh's hand. The final disaster was the death of the firstborn of all the Egyptians, but the saving of all Israelites who sheltered beneath the blood of the Passover lamb. Pharaoh

His wondrous works and ways
He made by Moses known,
But sent the world His truth and grace
By His beloved Son. (LSB 814:6)

---

then changed his mind and pursued the Hebrews. He cornered them by the Red Sea, but with a mighty miracle the sea divided and Israel crossed, the waters a wall on either side. When Pharaoh and his army attempted to follow, the waters crashed over them. Thus Moses led the Israelites through the sea as on dry ground. He brought them to Sinai where he received the Ten Commandments and the regulations regarding worship. Due to their faithlessness, Israel was condemned to wander forty years in the wilderness. During this whole time, Moses constantly interceded for them and pleaded with God to forgive them and to fulfill His promises to them. Moses was not allowed to enter the land of promise. He viewed it from the top of Mount Pisgah and there died. The first five books of the Bible are attributed to his authorship. In the Gospels, Moses was a witness of the glory of Christ in the Transfiguration.

Lord God, heavenly Father, through the prophet Moses You began the prophetic pattern of teaching Your people the true faith and demonstrating through miracles Your presence in creation to heal it of its brokenness. Grant that Your Church may see in Your Son, our Lord Jesus Christ, the final end-times prophet whose teaching and miracles continue in Your Church through the healing medicine of the Gospel and the Sacraments; through Jesus Christ, our Lord. Amen.

5
SEPTEMBER

Today, we remember and thank God for the righteous parents of St. John the Baptist, **Zacharias and Elizabeth.**

When we meet Zacharias and Elizabeth in the first chapter of Luke's Gospel, they are already advanced in years. Zacharias is a priest of the division of Abijah, and his wife also was a descendant of Aaron. Like Abraham and Sarah many centuries before them, they had no children; Elizabeth was barren.

It was Zacharias's turn to burn incense in the temple as the people prayed outside. As the sweet smoke began to rise from the hot coals, the old priest had an odd feeling and looked up, startled. Indeed, he was not alone. Gabriel, the angel of the Lord, stood before him.

"Do not be afraid . . . your prayer has been heard."

Prayer? he wonders. What prayer could the angel be referring to?

"Your wife Elizabeth will bear you a son . . ."

Did he immediately think, "But that prayer was years ago!"?

The angel was still speaking: ". . . and you shall call his name John. And you will have joy and gladness, and many will rejoice at his birth, for he will be great before the Lord. . . . He will be filled with the Holy Spirit, even from his mother's womb. And he will turn many of the children of Israel to the Lord their God, and he will go before Him in the spirit and power of Elijah" (Luke 1:13–17).

It was all too much for Zacharias. He wanted to know how he would know it. Gabriel was riled that his good news was met with doubt and disbelief. The sign, then, will be silence. Zacharias would no longer be able to speak until Gabriel's words were fulfilled.

The old priest had been too long in the temple. The people were getting

Come, Thou long-expected Jesus,
Born to set Thy people free;
From our fears and sins release us;
Let us find our rest in Thee.
Israel's strength and consolation,
Hope of all the earth Thou art,
Dear desire of every nation,
Joy of every longing heart. (LSB 338:1)

---

restive. Yet, when he came out, he could not talk. He made a sign, and they gradually realized he'd had a vision. He went home and his wife, Elizabeth, conceived. Five months she kept herself hidden, marveling that the Lord had done such a thing in her. In the sixth month, Mary came calling and the Miracle of all miracles entered their home in Mary's womb. Mary stayed with them for three months, perhaps long enough to see the birth of little John. At John's circumcision, the townsfolk wished to name the child after his father, but first Elizabeth and then Zacharias insisted that "his name is John." Immediately, Zacharias could speak again. He blessed God in the words that we know as the Benedictus: "Blessed be the Lord . . ."

Zacharias and Elizabeth are thus both remembered as examples of patient faith and godliness. Some think that this Zechariah is who our Lord referred to in Matthew 23:35. If so, he died a martyr's death.

O God, who alone knits all infants in the womb, You chose improbable servants—old and childless—to conceive and parent the forerunner of Christ and, in so doing, demonstrated again Your strength in weakness. Grant us, who are as unlikely and unworthy as Zacharias and Elizabeth, the opportunity to love and serve You according to Your good and gracious will; through Jesus Christ, our Lord, who lives and reigns with You and the Holy Spirit, one God, now and forever. Amen.

14
SEPTEMBER

Today, the Holy Church celebrates in awe and reverence the festival of the exaltation of the **Holy Cross**.

This day originally commemorated what was considered the discovery of the original cross of our Lord Jesus Christ. In the early fourth century AD, St. Helena, mother of Emperor Constantine, discovered the cross. She thought it was authenticated when it effected a miraculous healing. The Church of the Holy Sepulchre in Jerusalem was then constructed on the site where it was found. This building was dedicated on September 13, 335, but the Holy Cross was exposed for public veneration for the first time on the next day, September 14, hence the present festival.

Martin Luther was no great lover of the feasts dedicated to the holy cross. He saw in them the danger of superstition akin to the relic trafficking he so long had opposed. He once quipped that if all the alleged pieces of the "true cross" were gathered together, it would constitute a pretty massive object! Rather than fixating on the relics, he directed attention to the crucified and risen Christ.

Still, many Lutheran Church orders intentionally chose to retain the festival, and "Holy Cross" continues to be a popular name for Lutheran congregations to this day. What Lutherans celebrate on Holy Cross Day, however, is not primarily the history of a rediscovered relic attested by miracles. Rather, we celebrate the triumph of our Lord upon the indisputably real cross that once stood on Golgotha. There in love the Father's eternal Son and the Son of the blessed Virgin Mary poured out His life. His blood blotted out the sin of the world. His death proved death's destruction, as His divine life and love were finally and gloriously indigestible. We celebrate on this festival the way God used and uses suffering to bring blessing; the way

Faithful cross, true sign of triumph,
Be for all the noblest tree;
None in foliage, none in blossom,
None in fruit thine equal be;
Symbol of the world's redemption,
For the weight that hung on thee! (LSB 454:4)

He worked and works so contrary to anything human reason could or would ever conceive or anticipate.

Lutherans, of course, do not deny the possibility that the original cross was the one discovered by St. Helena. Yet, to us, whether that relic is authentic is not of prime importance. What does matter is that many years ago, under Pontius Pilate, our Lord Jesus was nailed to a tree through His hands and His feet. He was lifted up just as He foretold He would be. And through this unfathomable act of divine love, He still draws all people to Himself through the redemption that is in His blood, the forgiveness of our sins according to the riches of His grace. Better than any relic is the living body and blood which He imparts to us in the Eucharist as the lasting memorial of the holy cross.

Merciful God, Your Son, Jesus Christ, was lifted high upon the cross that He might bear the sins of the world and draw all people to Himself. Grant that we who glory in His death for our redemption may faithfully heed His call to bear the cross and follow Him, who lives and reigns with You and the Holy Spirit, one God, now and forever. Amen.

READINGS
NUMBERS 21:4–9 / 1 CORINTHIANS 1:18–25 / JOHN 12:20–33

16
SEPTEMBER

Today, we remember and thank God for His servant **Cyprian of Carthage, Pastor and Martyr** in the third century.

Cyprian was born toward the beginning of the third century in North Africa, possibly in the city he would later serve as bishop: Carthage. His birth name was Thascius, but after being converted to the catholic faith by a presbyter named Cyprian, he honored his father in the faith by taking his name. Before his conversion, he had been an orator and teacher of rhetoric (quite like another famous North African, St. Augustine, would be years later).

Cyprian was converted when he was approximately thirty-five years old, receiving the grace of Holy Baptism. Only a short time later, he was made a deacon and then ordained a presbyter. About AD 248, he was acclaimed the bishop of Carthage. This rapid rise in churchly office was not without some significant opposition, however, and for years people murmured against him for it.

During the persecution under Emperor Decius, he fled Carthage. He returned when the storm had ended and then had to deal with the aftermath. What should be done for those Christians who had lapsed in fear during the persecution, yet now in repentance begged readmission to the Church? Cyprian walked a middle way between severe strictness and simply ignoring what they'd done. He helped forge a penitential discipline that would welcome them back as members of the Church and yet only fully restore them after they had given suitable demonstration of their faithfulness to Christ.

St. Cyprian wrote many important theological works. His treatise *On the Unity of the Catholic Church* remains a great classic. There he insists that no one can have God for his father who does not have the Church as his mother and that there simply is no salvation outside the Church of Christ.

Yet she on earth has union
With God, the Three in One,
And mystic sweet communion
With those whose rest is won.
O blessèd heav'nly chorus!
Lord, save us by Your grace
That we, like saints before us,
May see You face to face. (LSB 644:5)

He also wrote a fine treatise on the Lord's Prayer. After Tertullian, he was one of the chief forgers of the Church's Latin theological vocabulary.

In AD 256, a new persecution broke out under Emperor Valerian. Popes Stephen I and Sixtus II both fell to martyrdom. When the persecution spread to North Africa, Cyprian was among those who simply refused to sacrifice to the emperor. In AD 258, he was arrested and finally beheaded. His only response to the sentence of death was, *"Deo gratias!"* that is, "Thanks be to God!" He stripped his own clothes off, put on the blindfold, and stretched out his neck for the sword.

Almighty God, You gave Your servant Cyprian boldness to confess the name of our Savior, Jesus Christ, before the rulers of this world and courage to die for the faith he proclaimed. Give us strength always to be ready with a reason for the hope that is in us and to suffer gladly for the sake of our Lord Jesus Christ, who lives and reigns with You and the Holy Spirit, one God, now and forever. Amen.

21
SEPTEMBER

Today, the Holy Church rejoices to celebrate the Festival of
St. Matthew, Apostle and Evangelist.

St. Matthew was also known by the name Levi in the Gospels. He was originally a tax collector by trade and thus would have been viewed by the Jewish populace as a traitor and sell-out to the Romans. The account of the Lord Jesus calling Matthew is found in his own Gospel in chapter 9. Matthew was sitting at his tax booth one day when Jesus passed by. The Lord simply said, "Follow Me." The man who had devoted himself to acquiring money at the expense of his own people got up and walked away from his table, his money, his old life.

Jesus joined him at his house for a meal that celebrated Matthew's newfound calling. Many of his friends, who were also tax collectors, joined in the feast. At this the Pharisees grumbled that Jesus was not more discriminating in His choice of dinner guests: "Why does your teacher eat with tax collectors and sinners?" When He heard it, Jesus responded, "Those who are well have no need of a physician, but those who are sick. Go and learn what this means: 'I desire mercy, and not sacrifice.' For I came not to call the righteous, but sinners" (Matthew 9:9–13).

Not only was Matthew then one of the Lord's disciples, but he was also sent as an apostle and finally used by the Holy Spirit as the evangelist who wrote the Gospel that appears first in the New Testament. Matthew's Gospel portrays Christ as the prophet greater than Moses. It divides into five sections, reminiscent of the five Books of Moses. Its first long discourse, given on a mountain, relates how Christ explicates the spiritual meaning of the Law. He alone recounts the perspective of Joseph in the account of our Lord's infancy (the dreams of Joseph by which the angel directs his actions, the visit of the Magi, the slaughter of the innocents, the flight to Egypt). Matthew's Gospel contains the fullest version of the Beatitudes and of the

Praise, Lord, for him whose Gospel
Your human life declared,
Who, worldly gain forsaking,
Your path of suffering shared.
From all unrighteous mammon,
O raise our eyes anew
That we in our vocation
May rise and follow You. (LSB 518:25)

Lord's Prayer. He portrays Christ always as the fulfillment of various Old Testament prophecies, whose blood of the New Testament inaugurates the age of grace. His account of the postresurrection command of Christ to make disciples of all nations by baptizing in the triune name and teaching the baptized to hold on to all that Jesus commanded guides the Church's mission to this day.

The Church's traditions speak variously about his field of labors, but nearly all agree that he died a martyr's death.

O Son of God, our blessed Savior Jesus Christ, You called Matthew the tax collector to be an apostle and evangelist. Through his faithful and inspired witness, grant that we also may follow You, leaving behind all covetous desires and love of riches; for You live and reign with the Father and the Holy Spirit, one God, now and forever. Amen.

READINGS
EZEKIEL 2:8–3:11 / EPHESIANS 4:7–16 / MATTHEW 9:9–13

22
SEPTEMBER

Today, we remember and thank God for His servant, the prophet **Jonah**.

Jonah, the son of Amittai, was a prophet from Gath-hepher (see 2 Kings 14:25), about an hour's walk from Nazareth, in the Northern Kingdom. He ministered apparently in the days of Jeroboam II at the time King Uzziah reigned in Judah. Thus, he was a contemporary of Isaiah, who prophesied in the Southern Kingdom.

Jonah is chiefly remembered for the commission he received to call Nineveh, the capital of the Assyrian Empire, to repentance. He ran from this call, taking a ship in the opposite direction into the Mediterranean. God, however, caused a great storm to arise. The sailors, by casting lots, determined that the storm was due to Jonah's presence. He finally confessed himself to be a disobedient prophet of the Lord of all creation and told them the sea would grow calm if they threw him into the sea. They strove to find another way, but finally they threw him overboard, praying God for forgiveness. Immediately the sea grew calm and a great fish swallowed Jonah. There in the belly of the fish Jonah repented and prayed; the Lord heard and answered. The fish disgorged the prophet near the land, and he went his reluctant way.

When Jonah arrived in Nineveh, he proclaimed its imminent destruction. The people, hearing and heeding the prophetic warning, repented. Even the king joined in the fast, begging that this temporal punishment might be averted. God heard and relented. This angered the prophet a great deal. He wanted God to punish Nineveh and her people.

As the prophet sulked outside the great city, God caused a plant to grow up overnight that shaded the prophet from the heat. But then He also

Are we weak and heavy laden,
Cumbered with a load of care?
Precious Savior, still our refuge—
Take it to the Lord in prayer.
Do thy friends despise, forsake thee?
Take it to the Lord in prayer.
In His arms He'll take and shield thee;
Thou wilt find a solace there. (LSB 770:3)

---

caused it to be attacked by a worm and die. Jonah was very angry. God asked the prophet if he had a right to be angry. It was only a plant, after all, but Nineveh was a great city filled with people who were ignorant of the Lord's ways. God asked if it wasn't right that He have mercy upon them (and their cattle!).

In the New Testament, Jesus refers to the sign of Jonah as portending His resurrection. As Jonah was three days in the belly of the fish, so the Son of Man would be three days in the belly of the earth. This picture prophecy is all the more striking if Jonah in fact died in the fish and then was raised from the dead and sent on his mission of proclaiming repentance. Jesus also specifically mentions the people of Nineveh repenting at the preaching of Jonah, promising them an easier time in the judgment than the cities where He long labored and yet who did not repent.

Lord God, heavenly Father, through the prophet Jonah You continued the prophetic pattern of teaching Your people the true faith and demonstrating through miracles Your presence in creation to heal it of its brokenness. Grant that Your Church may see in Your Son, our Lord Jesus Christ, the final end-times prophet whose teaching and miracles continue in Your Church through the healing medicine of the Gospel and the Sacraments; through Jesus Christ, our Lord. Amen.

29

SEPTEMBER

With great joy, the Holy Church celebrates on this day the Feast of **St. Michael and All Angels**.

Originally, this was just the Feast of St. Michael, the archangel. The idea of including all the angels on this day arose among the Anglican Christians and was carried over by English-speaking Lutherans. This was an easy adaptation since Lutherans from the time of the Reformation had used the feast to set forth the biblical teaching on the service of the holy angels to the children of God.

The name Michael in Hebrew means "Who is like God?" We first meet this angel by name in the Book of Daniel. He appears again in the New Testament in Jude and in the twelfth chapter of Revelation. He is depicted as warring with Satan and the fallen angels and serving and protecting the people of God.

In Church tradition, Michael is most often joined to Gabriel (mentioned in Luke's Gospel) and Raphael (from the Apocrypha). These are the latter creatures referenced in the Church's great Proper Preface during the Divine Service: "with angels and archangels."

On this day, we remember how Scripture relates angels constantly weaving in and out of the Gospel itself. An angel announces the impending birth of Christ to Mary in person and to Joseph in a dream. An angel announces the birth of Christ as good news of great joy to the shepherds. Angels sing glory to God and peace on earth on Christmas night. Angels direct Joseph's trip to Egypt and back. Our Lord teaches that the angels who serve the little ones constantly behold the Father's face in heaven. Angels are present at our Lord's Passion in Gethsemane. They announce His

Ye watchers and ye holy ones,
Bright seraphs, cherubim, and thrones,
Raise the glad strain: "Alleluia!"
Cry out, dominions, princedoms, powers,
Virtues, archangels, angels' choirs:
"Alleluia, alleluia!
Alleluia, alleluia, alleluia!" (LSB 670:1)

---

resurrection on Easter morning. They speak to the disciples at the Ascension. They free Peter from prison. They speak to Paul. They long to look into the mysteries that are revealed now through the Church's proclamation. We gather with them when we worship. They appear throughout the Revelation to St. John.

The Old Testament is as replete as the New Testament with references to them. Their special task regarding believers is given in Psalm 34:7: "The angel of the LORD encamps around those who fear Him, and delivers them." We remember them in our morning and evening prayers when we pray to the heavenly Father, "Let Your holy angel be with me, that the evil foe may have no power over me." We ask God to send His holy angels to accompany us along our life's journey and know that in the end of our days, we will join them in singing His praises forever.

Everlasting God, You have ordained and constituted the service of angels and men in a wonderful order. Mercifully grant that, as Your holy angels always serve and worship You in heaven, so by Your appointment they may also help and defend us here on earth; through Your Son, Jesus Christ, our Lord, who lives and reigns with You and the Holy Spirit, one God, now and forever. Amen.

READINGS
DANIEL 10:10–14; 12:1–3 / REVELATION 12:7–12 / MATTHEW 18:1–11
OR LUKE 10:17–20

30
SEPTEMBER

Today, we remember and thank God for one of the four great Doctors of the Western Church, His servant **Jerome, Translator of Holy Scripture**.

Jerome is the only Doctor of the Western Church who was not a bishop. He was born in a village on the Adriatic Sea around the middle of the fourth century. As a young man, he traveled to Rome, where he was baptized into Christ. He continued studying pagan literature for a time but eventually studied the sacred writings of the Old and New Testaments exclusively.

He was ordained a priest (against his own will) by Bishop Paulinus in Antioch. Jerome traveled to Constantinople to study Scripture under the tutelage of its bishop, Gregory of Nazianzus. He ended up serving for some time as secretary to the bishop of Rome, Pope Damasus I. At the time of his service to Damasus, he undertook an extensive revision of the old Latin translation of the New Testament and the Psalter. This was the beginning of what eventually would become the Vulgate, Jerome's masterful translation of Scripture, which became standard throughout the Western Church for more than a thousand years.

His love for the ascetic life, coupled with calumnious rumors about his relationship with a godly widow, Paula, led to dissatisfaction remaining in the capital. In August 385, Jerome left Rome with a small company of friends and returned to Antioch. He traveled throughout Palestine and down to Egypt, even hearing the famous catechist Didymus the Blind. In the summer of 388, he returned to Palestine and lived as a hermit near Bethlehem the remainder of his life.

He devoted his remaining days in Bethlehem to writing voluminous correspondence; rendering into Latin the Old Testament, for the first time based upon the Hebrew rather than the Greek; and writing various polemical theological treatises. His letters back and forth to St. Augustine are particularly rich in theological reflection.

Preserve Your Word and preaching,
The truth that makes us whole,
The mirror of Your glory,
The pow'r that saves the soul.
Oh, may this living water,
This dew of heav'nly grace,
Sustain us while here living
Until we see Your face. (LSB 658:4)

He died on this day in AD 420 and was originally buried near his cell. His relics were later transferred to various places, including Rome. His Scripture translation (the Vulgate) and his treatise *On the Perpetual Virginity of Mary* were among his most significant contributions to the Church. Martin Chemnitz, in his treatise *On the Reading of the Church Fathers,* notes that Jerome's particular genius is in his attention to the grammar of the Sacred Scriptures, while he is most unreliable when he veers too near topics dealing with various bodily disciplines (fasting, continence, buffeting of the body, etc.).

O Lord, God of truth, Your Word is a lamp to our feet and a light on our path. You gave Your servant Jerome delight in his study of Holy Scripture. May those who continue to read, mark, and inwardly digest Your Word find in it the food of salvation and the fountain of life; through Jesus Christ, our Lord, who lives and reigns with You and the Holy Spirit, one God, now and forever. Amen.

7

OCTOBER

Today, we remember the tireless efforts of **Henry Melchior Muhlenberg, Pastor**, to establish, strengthen, and provide for congregations of the Lutheran confession in North America in the eighteenth century.

Though he was not the first Lutheran in North America, Henry Muhlenberg was the first to endeavor to establish the Lutheran Church and gather the scattered Lutherans into their own church body. Born September 6, 1711, in the duchy of Brunswick, Muhlenberg studied theology at Göttingen. He was ordained in Leipzig in 1739 and worked for a few years in an orphanage. But in 1741, he accepted a call from German-speaking Lutherans in the commonwealth of Pennsylvania. He and his wife and family moved to America.

In this land, Muhlenberg truly came into his own. He worked tirelessly to plant and strengthen Lutheran congregations, traveling far and wide through the colonies. He led the effort to create the first organization for Lutheran pastors in America: the Ministerium of Pennsylvania and Adjacent States, founded in 1748. He imparted to that organization his own zeal for missions. He valued greatly the gift of music in worship, at times serving as his own organist. He led the preparation of the first American Lutheran liturgy, translated from German into English (to which very clearly our later Common Service was indebted). His dream was that one day there would be one Lutheran hymnbook, one Lutheran liturgy used by one Lutheran Church in all of North America. That dream still awaits its fulfillment.

Poor health at last curtailed his efforts and forced his retirement from the ministry. He died in 1787 in Trappe, Pennsylvania. He was buried within Augustus Lutheran Church next to his beloved wife. Yet, before his death he had seen his work here bear significant fruit. He left behind a distinctly American Lutheran Church.

It is also worthy of note that his sons were prominent in the government of the early days of the United States. A statue of his son John Peter stands

Rise! To arms! With prayer employ you,
O Christians, lest the foe destroy you;
For Satan has designed your fall.
Wield God's Word, the weapon glorious;
Against all foes be thus victorious,
For God protects you from them all.
Fear not the hordes of hell,
Here is Emmanuel.
Hail the Savior!
The strong foes yield
To Christ, our shield,
And we, the victors, hold the field. **(LSB 668:1)**

---

in the crypt of the Capitol in Washington DC, and a portrait of his son Frederick, the first speaker of the House, hangs in a lobby of the House of Representatives. His daughter Maria married a US congressman, and his daughter Eve was eventually the mother of the governor of Pennsylvania, John Schulze.

Lord Jesus Christ, the Good Shepherd of Your people, we give You thanks for Your servant Henry Melchior Muhlenberg, who was faithful in the care and nurture of the flock entrusted to him. So they may follow his example and the teaching of his holy life, give strength to pastors today who shepherd Your flock so that, by Your grace, Your people may grow into the fullness of life intended for them in paradise; for You live and reign with the Father and Holy Spirit, one God, now and forever. Amen.

9
OCTOBER

Today, we remember and thank God for His friend, the holy patriarch and ancestor of Christ, **Abraham**.

Born in Ur of the Chaldeans around 2000 BC, Abram (as his name was originally) received a call from the Lord to leave his country and go to a land God would show him. There God promised he would become a great nation and through his seed blessing would come to all the families of the earth. At the age of 75, Abram obeyed and began his journey. He stopped for a time in Haran but eventually arrived in Canaan. With him came his wife, Sarai, and his nephew, Lot.

In that land, God appeared to him over a number of years, reiterating the promise and clarifying it. Abram at first seemed to think that Lot would be his heir, but the Lord made it clear that neither Lot nor his servant Eliezer would be heirs. Instead, a child coming from his own body would inherit. Abram believed the Lord's promise, and the Lord credited that faith to him as righteousness. Still, when nothing had happened for a number of years and Abram and Sarai had grown tired of waiting, they took matters into their own hands. Sarai gave her handmaid, Hagar, into Abram's embrace and Ishmael was born. Yet, God again made it clear that the child He promised would be born from Sarai. In token of His promise, God changed their names to Abraham (father of a people) and Sarah.

At last, when all human ingenuity had failed, God visited the old man and his wife yet again and said that the birth of the promised child would take place within the next year. Sarah, overhearing this in her tent, laughed at the thought. The name stuck. The Lord decreed the child would be named Laughter, or Isaac. And it did indeed come to pass, just as God had promised.

The God of Abraham praise,
Whose all-sufficient grace
Shall guide me all my pilgrim days
In all my ways.
He deigns to call me friend;
He calls Himself my God.
And He shall save me to the end
Through Jesus' blood. (LSB 798:3)

One day God asked a fearful thing of Abraham. He told Abraham to give the child back to Him through sacrifice. Obediently, Abraham and Isaac with some servants ventured to the place God had indicated. Isaac noticed that the lamb for the offering was missing. Abraham spoke the prophecy, "God will provide for Himself a lamb for the offering, my only son." Though Abraham was prepared to sacrifice the child, he believed in his heart that God would raise the lad from the dead to keep His promises. At the last minute, an angel stayed the old man's hand. Isaac was spared and a ram offered in his place as an offering.

Abraham's prompt obedience and faith in the unseen promises of God marked his life from the time of his call. Our Lord even says that Abraham rejoiced to see His day and that, seeing it, he was glad.

Lord God, heavenly Father, You promised Abraham that he would be the father of many nations. You led him to the land of Canaan and You sealed Your covenant with him by the shedding of blood. May we see in Jesus, the Seed of Abraham, the promise of the new covenant of Your Holy Church, sealed with Jesus' blood on the cross and given to us now in the cup of the New Testament; through the same Jesus Christ, our Lord, who lives and reigns with You and the Holy Spirit, one God, now and forever. Amen.

11

OCTOBER

Today, we remember and thank God for His faithful servant
Philip the Deacon.

In Acts 6, St. Luke relates how a disturbance arose in the early congregation at Jerusalem. The Greek-speaking Christians murmured that their widows were neglected in the daily distribution of food, in favor of the Aramaic-speaking widows. The apostles, rather than sort the matter out themselves, wisely instituted what became the first auxiliary office in the Church. "Pick out from among you seven men of good repute, full of the Spirit and of wisdom, whom we will appoint over this duty," the apostles advised. "But we will devote ourselves to prayer and to the ministry of the word" (Acts 6:3–4).

The suggestion was pleasing to the congregation and they selected seven men, including Stephen (the first martyr) and the man whom we commemorate today, Philip. The seven were presented to the apostles, who laid their hands upon them and put them into office. Many regard this as the start of the diaconate in the Church.

After Stephen's martyrdom and the beginning of persecution in the city, many members of the Jerusalem congregation were scattered. Wherever they went, though, they carried the Good News about Jesus on their lips. Philip went to a city of Samaria and proclaimed the Good News there. Through his preaching and the miracles the Lord Jesus performed through him, the townsfolk were brought to faith, including the infamous Simon the Magician. According to Luke, "there was much joy in that city" (Acts 8:8) upon the advent of the Gospel.

After Peter and John came to Samaria and confirmed the work of Philip, the Spirit sent Philip on another task. He was the man chosen to bring the Good News to the Ethiopian eunuch, servant and treasurer of the queen of the Ethiopians. He had been to Jerusalem to worship and was returning home in his chariot, puzzling over the meaning of Isaiah 53. Philip drew

Come, holy Fire, comfort true,
Grant us the will Your work to do
And in Your service to abide;
Let trials turn us not aside.
Lord, by Your pow'r prepare each heart,
And to our weakness strength impart
That bravely here we may contend,
Through life and death to You, our Lord, ascend.
Alleluia, alleluia! (LSB 497:3)

---

alongside the chariot and preached the Good News of Christ to him and baptized him. And again we are told he "went on his way rejoicing" (Acts 8:39).

On St. Paul's final journey to Jerusalem, which led to his arrest, he was a guest for some days at Philip's house (Acts 21:8–15). Philip had four unmarried daughters who were prophetesses. It was while Paul was staying there with them that the prophet Agabus foretold Paul's imminent arrest and imprisonment if he journeyed to Jerusalem. Philip and the others begged him not to go, but Paul was determined. He was ready even to die for the Lord Jesus. Philip and the others finally ceased begging and said, "Let the will of the Lord be done."

Almighty and everlasting God, we give thanks to You for Your servant Philip the Deacon. You called him to preach the Gospel to the peoples of Samaria and Ethiopia. Raise up in this and every land messengers of Your kingdom, that Your Church may proclaim the immeasurable riches of our Savior, Jesus Christ, who lives and reigns with You and the Holy Spirit, one God, now and forever. Amen.

17
OCTOBER

Today, the Holy Church rejoices to remember **Ignatius of Antioch, Pastor and Martyr.**

Ignatius was one of the Apostolic Fathers, that generation immediately following the apostles who personally knew and interacted with them. He was born sometime around AD 35 in the province of Syria. Ignatius was a student of St. John, the apostle and evangelist. Some have even suggested he was one of the little children that Christ took in His arms and blessed. According to the Eusebius's history of the Church, Ignatius became the third bishop of the great church at Antioch (after St. Peter and Evodius). Ignatius knew and corresponded with Polycarp, the bishop of Smyrna.

When persecution arose under the Roman Emperor Trajan, Ignatius was arrested and brought in chains to Rome to be fed to the wild beasts in the Colosseum. This likely took place in AD 107 or 108. During the long journey, Ignatius had time to write to six different churches and to his beloved Polycarp, and it is from these letters that we learn much of what we know of this saint and martyr.

In these letters several themes emerge. Ignatius urges for the sake of unity that the churches submit in humility to their bishops. As befits a disciple of St. John, he constantly urges the churches toward love for one another, a genuine love that befits the name of "Christian." He speaks of the Eucharist often and always in terms of it being the self-same body and blood that were offered on Calvary for the redemption of the world. He warns against false teachers. He urges the Christians to shut their ears if anyone should come preaching to them something other than Jesus Christ, descended from David, born of the Virgin, crucified for the world, and raised from the dead. His letter to the Romans is perhaps his most influential, extolling the glory of martyrdom. He begs the church there not to interfere, but rather to pray that he may indeed die a death that bears witness to the Lord Jesus and His

Apostles, prophets, martyrs,
And all the noble throng
Who wear the spotless raiment
And raise the ceaseless song—
For these, passed on before us,
We offer praises due
And, walking in their footsteps,
Would live our lives for You. (LSB 517:4)

---

resurrection victory. They heeded his wishes, and this great saint, one of the living links to the apostles, was fed to the wild beasts in Rome.

After his martyrdom, his friends gathered what remained of his bones and carried them back as a precious treasure to Antioch, where they were interred. His remains were later moved twice, finally ending up in Rome's Basilica San Clemente. To his life's end he lived his own words: "Be a follower of Christ even as He is of His Father" (*Epistle to the Philadelphians* 7).

Almighty God, we praise Your name for Ignatius of Antioch, pastor and martyr. He offered himself as grain to be ground by the teeth of the wild beasts so that he might present to You the pure bread of sacrifice. Accept the willing tribute of all that we are and all that we have, and give us a portion in the pure and unspotted offering of Your Son, Jesus Christ, who lives and reigns with You and the Holy Spirit, one God, now and forever. Amen.

18
OCTOBER

Today, the Holy Church celebrates with great joy the Festival of **St. Luke, Evangelist.**

St. Paul once called Luke "the beloved physician" (Colossians 4:14). He was, thus, a doctor of the body, but even more has so the Church honored him as a doctor of the soul. Aside from accompanying St. Paul on some of his missionary travels, St. Luke wrote more than one-third of our New Testament. He carefully researched and set in order an extensive account of the life of our Lord Jesus, the third canonical Gospel. He also researched the spread of the Gospel from Jerusalem through Judea and Samaria and to the ends of the earth, adding his own memoirs of his time with St. Paul.

Luke's Gospel is unique in several features. First, he begins with information that could only have come from the blessed Virgin Mary herself. He intimates as much when he notes that the Virgin "treasured up all these things in her heart" (Luke 2:51), holding the words and sayings that at first she could not understand. She then must have opened up her heart to Luke and told him the events surrounding our Lord's birth. So only from his Gospel do we come to know the details of the annunciation, the visitation, the conception and birth of John the Baptist, the trip to Bethlehem, the manger and the shepherds, the angels and their song, Simeon and Anna, and the trip to Jerusalem when our Lord was twelve. Second, Luke's Gospel contains some unique teachings of Christ: only there do we read the parable of the Good Samaritan, the account of the rich man and Lazarus, the prodigal son, the Pharisee and the tax collector. In Luke, we find Christ persistently warning against the dangers of trust in riches and elevating the role of women. Mary sitting at Jesus' feet to hear His teaching is only in

For that belov'd physician
All praise, whose Gospel shows
The Healer of the nations,
The one who shares our woes.
Your wine and oil, O Savior,
Upon our spirits pour,
And with true balm of Gilead
Anoint us evermore. (LSB 518:26)

Luke. Luke literally frames his Gospel with the temple in Jerusalem, both starting and ending there, and from Luke's Gospel the Church has taken numerous canticles into her worship: the Ave Maria, the Magnificat, the Benedictus, the Nunc Dimittis.

Luke's second work, the Book of Acts, is the account of the spread of the Gospel after the Ascension to Paul's imprisonment in Rome. It provides us invaluable information about all that the exalted Lord Jesus *continued* to do and to teach through His apostles. As in his Gospel, Luke highlights especially the work of the Holy Spirit and the constant joy that the Good News brings as it releases people from their bondage to sin and the fear of death.

Luke's joy-filled witness to our Lord's life and to the Spirit's work in the Church is truly one of the greatest treasures of the Church, and for the man who researched and collected this history for us, we give praise to God this day!

Almighty God, our Father, Your blessed Son called Luke the physician to be an evangelist and physician of the soul. Grant that the healing medicine of the Gospel and the Sacraments may put to flight the diseases of our souls that with willing hearts we may ever love and serve You; through Jesus Christ, Your Son, our Lord, who lives and reigns with You and the Holy Spirit, one God, now and forever. Amen.

READINGS
ISAIAH 35:5–8 / 2 TIMOTHY 4:5–18 / LUKE 10:1–9

23
OCTOBER

Today, the Holy Church celebrates with great joy the Festival of **St. James of Jerusalem, Brother of Jesus and Martyr**.

Raised in the same household as our Lord, James is identified by Paul in Galatians as "the Lord's brother" (Galatians 1:19), yet in his epistle James refers to himself as "a servant of God and of the Lord Jesus Christ" (James 1:1).

Although modern scholarship has tended toward the assumption that James is a son of the Virgin Mary and Joseph, this is denied throughout most of Church history and among the vast majority of Christians today. James is identified as the son of that Mary who was either sister or sister-in-law to Joseph. This is the Mary that was mentioned in Matthew 27:56, who watched the hasty burial of Christ on that first Good Friday: "among whom were Mary Magdalene and *Mary the mother of James and Joseph* and the mother of the sons of Zebedee" (emphasis added). It would be extremely odd for Mary, the mother of our Lord, not to be referred to in such a context as "His mother" (as in John 19).

James, as a child of the same household, apparently did not believe in Jesus until after the resurrection (see John 7:3–5). After a special appearance of the risen Christ to him (1 Corinthians 15:7), James was brought to faith. In the early congregation at Jerusalem, he appears to have been (with Peter and John) one of the three "pillars" (Galatians 2:9). This is evident at the Jerusalem Council (Acts 15), where James's word is decisive and final. He quotes the prophets that it was foretold that the Gentiles would also be called by the name of the Lord and be saved.

Throughout Paul's ministry, he faced those who claimed to be representing James in opposition to him. Yet, James and Paul were always at one in Christ and the Gospel. Some people—including Dr. Luther—

We sing of James, Christ's brother,
*   Who at Jerusalem*
Told how God loved the Gentiles
*   And, in Christ, welcomed them.*
Rejoicing in salvation
*   May we too, by God's grace,*
Extend Christ's invitation
*   To all the human race. (LSB 518:27)*

---

have thought that James's teaching in James 2:24 ("you see that a person is justified by works and not by faith alone") is contradictory to St. Paul's teaching in Romans and Galatians. Yet, the contradiction is only apparent. James operates with a different definition of faith than Paul, since for James even the demons "believe" (James 2:19). Both are concerned that a genuine faith issues forth in repentant fruits of faith, and without this the faith is "dead" or a sham.

According to Josephus, the first-century historian of the Jewish people, James the Just was martyred by being stoned to death in Jerusalem in AD 62. Josephus believed that the destruction of Jerusalem was, in part, a punishment from God for the wrongful death of that just man.

Heavenly Father, shepherd of Your people, You raised up James the Just, brother of our Lord, to lead and guide Your Church. Grant that we may follow his example of prayer and reconciliation and be strengthened by the witness of his death; through Jesus Christ, Your Son, our Lord, who lives and reigns with You and the Holy Spirit, one God, now and forever. Amen.

READINGS
ACTS 15:12–22A / JAMES 1:1–12 / MATTHEW 13:54–58

25
OCTOBER

Today, we remember and give thanks to God for His holy maidservants **Dorcas (Tabitha), Lydia, and Phoebe, Faithful Women.**

Though the New Testament nowhere shows women serving in the office of the ministry as presbyters (and in fact explicitly *forbids* such), it does show how very active in the life of the Early Church were any number of holy women. Three of these faithful and loving servants of the Lord we commemorate this day.

Dorcas, from the city of Joppa, was also known as Tabitha. St. Luke described Dorcas as "full of good works and acts of charity." When Dorcas grew sick and then suddenly died, the disciples who knew her were grief-stricken. Hearing that Peter was nearby, they begged him to come. He visited her home, as the widows showed him the clothing that she had made when she was still with them. Peter asked them all to leave. He knelt beside her bed and prayed God to restore the life of his servant. He called to her, "Tabitha, arise." She opened her eyes, saw Peter, and sat up. Peter raised her from the bed and presented her to those who had called him. The news of the miracle spread and many more believed in the Lord Jesus (Acts 9:36–42).

Lydia was from the city of Thyatira and was a seller of purple goods. Yet, when we meet her, she is living in the Roman colony of Philippi in Macedonia (see Acts 16:11–15). She had gathered with some Jews on the outskirts of the city for a time of prayer on the Sabbath Day, when Saints Paul and Silas joined the crowd and proclaimed Jesus as the Christ. Through their message, the Holy Spirit opened Lydia's heart to believe. She was baptized into Christ and begged Paul and Silas to come and stay at her house while they sojourned in Philippi. The Church there was thus sheltered beneath her roof.

Phoebe was another faithful servant and co-worker of St. Paul. She was a deaconess from Cenchreae, the port that served Corinth. He entrusted

Be of good cheer, for God's own Son
Forgives all sins which you have done;
And, justified by Jesus' blood,
Your Baptism grants the highest good.
If you are sick, if death is near,
This truth your troubled heart can cheer:
Christ Jesus saves your soul from death;
That is the firmest ground of faith. (LSB 571:4–5)

---

her with his epistle to the Romans and writes of her in Romans 16:1–2: "I commend to you our sister Phoebe, a servant of the church at Cenchreae, that you may welcome her in the Lord in a way worthy of the saints, and help her in whatever she may need from you, for she has been a patron of many and of myself as well."

In all three holy women, we see an image of the Church of Christ, devoting herself to the service of her Lord. For them and their unsung sisters in Christ, we give glory to the blessed Trinity!

Almighty God, You stirred to compassion the hearts of Your dear servants Dorcas, Lydia, and Phoebe to uphold and sustain Your Church by their devoted and charitable deeds. Give us the same will to love You, open our eyes to see You in the least ones, and strengthen our hands to serve You in others, for the sake of Your Son, Jesus Christ, our Lord, who lives and reigns with You and the Holy Spirit, one God, now and forever. Amen.

26
OCTOBER

Today, the Holy Church rejoices to remember and give thanks to God for His musical servants **Philipp Nicolai, Johann Heermann**, and **Paul Gerhardt, Hymnwriters**.

The Church has always been marked by its joy in gathering to sing praises to the blessed Trinity. The first heathen description of Christian worship (by Pliny the Younger) is that "they sing a hymn of praise to Christ as to God." To assist the people of God in this high calling, God has continually raised up servants who are skilled and gifted in music, "who prophesied with the lyre in thanksgiving and praise to the LORD" (1 Chronicles 25:3) and "were trained in singing to the Lord" (1 Chronicles 25:7). Such were the men we commemorate this day.

Philipp Nicolai (1556–1608) was a pastor in Germany, serving at the time a great plague devastated his parish and community. In the midst of a tidal wave of death, he wrote a book on the glories and joys of eternal life and appended to it several hymns of his own composition. Two of these became known as "the King and Queen of the Chorales." They are regarded as the greatest hymns ever written in the Western Church: "Wake, Awake, for Night is Flying" and "O Morning Star."

Johann Heermann (1585–1647) also served as pastor. Beset with poor health and serving during the ravages of the Thirty Years' War, he wrote numerous hymn texts that express a depth of piety and devotion to the Lord that delights any devout Christian to this day. Among his great works are "O Dearest Jesus, What Law Hast Thou Broken" and "O God, My Faithful God."

The final musician we commemorate today was probably the greatest poet of all three and is sometimes reckoned the greatest hymnwriter of all time. Paul Gerhardt, yet another pastor of the Lutheran Church, suffered

My heart with joy is springing;
I am no longer sad.
My soul is filled with singing;
Your sunshine makes me glad.
The sun that cheers my spirit
Is Jesus Christ, my King;
The heav'n I shall inherit
Makes me rejoice and sing. (LSB 724:10)

---

enormously. Though quite irenic in character, he was drawn into theological controversy and his steadfast adherence to the Lutheran Confessions resulted in him being dismissed from his church. He lost four of his five children and his beloved wife. He wrote 133 hymns of outstanding beauty and firm faith. His classics include "Why Should Cross and Trial Grieve Me?", "O Sacred Head, Now Wounded," and the joyful Easter hymn "Awake, My Soul, with Gladness." Upon his grave are marked the words: "A theologian sifted in Satan's sieve."

All three servants of the Church's song show us that in the Lutheran Church music is for proclamation. It praises God by recounting the wonderful things He has done and continues to do in His Son. The congregation exercises its royal priesthood by lifting voices to praise the blessed Trinity in this way.

Almighty God, the apostle Paul taught us to praise You in psalms and hymns and spiritual songs. We thank You this day for those who have given to Your Church great hymns, especially Your servants Philipp Nicolai, Johann Heermann, and Paul Gerhardt. May Your Church never lack hymnwriters who through their words and music give You praise. Fill us with the desire to praise and thank You for Your great goodness; through Jesus Christ, our Lord, who lives and reigns with You and the Holy Spirit, one God, now and forever. Amen.

28
OCTOBER

Today, the Holy Church offers God praise
and thanks for His servants **St. Simon
and St. Jude, Apostles**.

Whenever the twelve apostles are listed, Judas
Iscariot is listed last. Immediately before him are
Simon the Zealot and Jude (or Judas, son of James),
apparently also called Thaddeus.

The New Testament itself records little about these
men other than their names as being among the Twelve
and therefore witnesses to much of our Lord's ministry and,
above all, the events of Holy Week and Easter. They would have
eaten the Supper with their Master and heard the farewell discourse on
Holy Thursday, during which John records Jude asking a question of the Lord
(John 14:22). They would have accompanied Christ to the garden and then
run away following His arrest. They would have been in the Upper Room
on Easter evening when the Lord first appeared to the gathered apostles,
and likewise the following week when He revealed Himself again to beckon
Thomas from his unbelief. They would have witnessed the Ascension of
their Lord. They participated in the election of Matthias to complete their
number. They were present at the miracle of Pentecost when the risen Lord
poured out His Spirit upon them and they proclaimed the praises of God in
languages they had never learned. They were arrested when the high priest
sought to silence all the apostles, but they were released from prison by an
angel who instructed them, "Go and stand in the temple and speak to the
people all the words of this Life" (Acts 5:17–21).

According to the tradition of the Church, after the dispersion of the
apostles, Saints Simon and Jude traveled together as far as Persia, bringing
the message of salvation to any who would hear. While there, both suffered
martyrdom for the holy name of Jesus.

Praise, Lord, for Your apostles,
Saint Simon and Saint Jude.
One love, one hope impelled them
To tread the way, renewed.
May we with zeal as earnest
The faith of Christ maintain,
Be bound in love together,
And life eternal gain. (LSB 518:28)

The symbol the Church employs for St. Simon is a fish on top of a book. This reminds us that he went forth as a fisher of men, proclaiming the Good News of Christ from the divine Word.

The symbol of St. Jude, or Thaddeus, in the Church is a ship with the wind filling its sail and upon the sail the sign of the holy cross. This is a reminder of the great distances that Jude traveled with his friend St. Simon, filled with the Holy Spirit, to bring the Good News of salvation and gather heathen into the saving ark of the Christian Church.

Surely it was a comfort to these two, as they faced death, to recall the gracious promise they had heard from the Lord's lips on the night of His betrayal: "I go to prepare a place for you."

Almighty God, You chose Your servants Simon and Jude to be numbered among the glorious company of the apostles. As they were faithful and zealous in their mission, so may we with ardent devotion make known the love and mercy of our Lord and Savior Jesus Christ, who lives and reigns with You and the Holy Spirit, one God, now and forever. Amen.

READINGS
JEREMIAH 26:1–26 / 1 PETER 1:3–9 / JOHN 15:(12–16) 17–21

31
OCTOBER

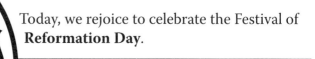

Today, we rejoice to celebrate the Festival of **Reformation Day**.

On October 31, 1517, an Augustinian monk crossed a leaf-strewn courtyard to stand before the door of the Castle Church in Wittenberg, Saxony. There he posted a series of ninety-five statements, or theses, for debate among the theologians of the Church. Little did the poor monk know that he had just set in motion a series of events that would rock the Church in Europe to its core. The monk, of course, was Martin Luther, an Augustinian Eremite. Printers soon grabbed up his theses and had them translated into German and many other languages of Europe. Soon everyone knew who Martin Luther was and joined in the debate.

The Roman curia, at the time quite hopelessly corrupt, had no interest in debate. They wanted the monk and his concerns to be silent and go away. He was interfering with the money that indulgences were intended to raise in Germany, money that funded finally the construction of the greatest Church Christendom had ever seen to honor the graves of Saints Peter and Paul in the city of Rome. But the monk wouldn't go away or be silent.

He was judged a heretic by Church officials and excommunicated by the pope. Luther was then summoned for trial before the secular authority, Emperor Charles V, at the Diet of Worms in 1521. Luther's study of the Scriptures had utterly convinced him that he was not wrong to teach that salvation was by grace alone through faith in Christ alone, and he knew that this was, in fact, what the Church had anciently taught. He refused to recant his writings in the famous words: "I am bound by the Scriptures I have quoted and my conscience is captive to the Word of God. I cannot and will not retract anything. I cannot do otherwise, here I stand, may God help me, Amen."

Lord, keep us steadfast in Your Word;
Curb those who by deceit or sword
Would wrest the kingdom from Your Son
And bring to naught all He has done.
Lord Jesus Christ, Your power make known,
For You are Lord of lords alone;
Defend Your holy Church that we
May sing Your praise eternally.
O Comforter of priceless worth,
Send peace and unity on earth;
Support us in our final strife
And lead us out of death to life. (LSB 655)

The Lutheran movement grew and spread like wildfire. Nine years after the monk stood all alone at Worms, numerous princes and representatives of the free cities stood before the same emperor at Augsburg on June 25, 1530. They proclaimed their faith in the words of the Augsburg Confession. They indicated they would rather suffer martyrdom than lose the precious Gospel of the sinner's free justification, a doctrine which had brought such consolation to them and the people of their lands. A distinctly Lutheran Church was taking shape. The heritage received from the medieval catholic Church was purified in one territory after another according to the divine Word and in conformity with the saving Gospel.

Almighty and gracious Lord, pour out Your Holy Spirit on Your faithful people. Keep us steadfast in Your grace and truth, protect and deliver us in times of temptation, defend us against all enemies, and grant to Your Church Your saving peace; through Jesus Christ, Your Son, our Lord, who lives and reigns with You and the Holy Spirit, one God, now and forever. Amen.

READINGS
REVELATION 14:6–7 / ROMANS 3:19–28 / JOHN 8:31–36
OR MATTHEW 11:12–19

1 NOVEMBER

With overflowing joy, the Church of Jesus Christ celebrates the Feast of **All Saints' Day**.

The Feast of All Saints' is one of the principal feasts of Christ. Many congregations observe the custom of transferring it to the first Sunday in November each year so that a maximal number of people may join in its joyful celebration.

All Saints' was originally observed in the West as All Martyrs' in the spring. Since the number of those who have laid down their lives in the confession of Christ far outnumbers the days available in the Church's yearly round, All Martyrs' served as a sort of catchall. Pope Gregory III, bishop of Rome from AD 731 to 741, expanded the feast further to embrace all saints and ordered it observed on November 1. A similar Feast of All Saints' is observed in the Eastern Church calendar on the Sunday following Pentecost.

The joy of this particular feast is in its celebration of the unity of the Church Triumphant (the saints gathered already into rest) and the Church Militant (the present and future Church that struggles still under daily crosses). Together, both constitute but one communion, one fellowship.

They are the crowd glimpsed in the reading from Revelation for this day, a vast multitude beyond human numbering and calculation. What makes them one is what they have received from the Lord: They have washed their robes and made them white in the blood of the Lamb. Their sins are forgiven and they hold the palm of victory He has placed in their hand.

If you look at the crowd, you can readily discern that some were among earth's famous and powerful. Most were quite unknown to history. There are some black, some white, and every color of the flesh of humanity.

For all the saints who from their labors rest,
Who Thee by faith before the world confessed,
Thy name, O Jesus, be forever blest.
Alleluia! Alleluia!
O blest communion, fellowship divine,
We feebly struggle, they in glory shine;
Yet all are one in Thee, for all are Thine.
Alleluia! Alleluia! (LSB 677:1, 4)

Some were very wealthy upon earth; most quite poor. Some spoke this language, others that. They come from every nation and tribe. What is most captivating about them, however, isn't their diversity; it's the unity of their attention. They aren't paying the least bit of attention to themselves. They are united in their gaze upon the Lamb on His throne, the Lord Jesus Christ victorious in His sacrifice of love. And therein lies the secret to becoming part of that crowd. You do so not by squeezing in and trying to imitate the look of astonishment and awe upon their faces. Rather you share their blessedness by joining in what they are so fixated upon: Jesus Christ, who humbled Himself to become what they were (a child of man) in order to lift them up to become what He is (children of God).

Almighty and everlasting God, You knit together Your faithful people
of all times and places into one holy communion, the mystical Body of Your
Son, Jesus Christ. Grant us so to follow Your blessed saints in all virtuous
and godly living that, together with them, we may come to the unspeakable
joys You have prepared for those who love You; through Jesus Christ, our Lord,
who lives and reigns with You and the Holy Spirit, one God, now and forever.
Amen.

READINGS
REVELATION 7:(2–8) 9–17 / 1 JOHN 3:1–3 / MATTHEW 5:1–12

8

NOVEMBER

This day, the Holy Church rejoices to remember the life of **Johannes von Staupitz, Luther's Father Confessor**.

Johannes von Staupitz was born in the 1460s in Saxony. His family was originally Czech. In 1485, he was accepted into the Augustinian Order. He was made a doctor of theology in 1500 and made dean of theological faculty of the newly founded University of Wittenberg. He was then elected in 1503 as Vicar General of the Augustinian Order throughout German-speaking lands. He resigned his professorship in 1512. In 1520, he officially resigned as Vicar General. Two years later, he accepted an invitation from the Benedictines to become Abbot of St. Peter's Archabbey in Salzburg. There he died in 1524.

It was in his service as the Vicar General of the Augustinian Order in Germany that Staupitz took in hand the spiritual care of one very troubled young Eremite. His name was Martin Luther. Luther had become a monk to save his soul after making a hasty vow to St. Anne. He tried every remedy the Church suggested to him, and yet his brutal self-honesty led him to doubt his own repentance and God's love. He lived in constant fear of damnation. He would confess his sins for hours, but he could always think of more he had forgotten when he left.

Staupitz believed that the cure for what ailed young Luther lay in the Sacred Scriptures and the picture of Christ that is there found—a Lord who welcomes sinners to Himself and shows them divine mercy. Staupitz determined that the young man would earn his doctorate in theology and replace him as professor of the Bible at the University of Wittenberg. It was a move both wise and fateful.

"What you will bind, that bound shall be;
What you will loose, that shall be free;
To My dear Church the keys are giv'n
To open, close the gates of heav'n."
The words which absolution give
Are His who died that we might live;
The minister whom Christ has sent
Is but His humble instrument. (LSB 614:4–5)

In the Sacred Scriptures, Luther did indeed find at long last the peace that had eluded him as he realized that the righteousness of the Gospel is not a human achievement but a divine gift. He realized at last that his salvation, indeed, all people's salvation, depended entirely upon the obedience and righteousness of Jesus Christ alone, which can only be believed and rejoiced in. This set Luther on a collision course with the authorities of the Church.

Staupitz released his star pupil and troubled friend from obedience to the Augustinian Order. Though Staupitz never embraced the Reformation and remained loyal to the Roman pope till his death, he served a crucial role by turning the great Reformer to Scripture, where Luther found consolation and joy in the Lamb of God who truly has taken away the sins of the world.

Almighty, everlasting God, for our many sins we justly deserve eternal condemnation. In Your mercy, You sent Your dear Son, our Lord Jesus Christ, who won for us forgiveness of sins and everlasting salvation. Grant us a true confession so that dead to sin we may hear the sweet words of Absolution from our confessor, as Luther heard them from Johannes von Staupitz, and be released from all our sin; through Jesus Christ, our Lord, who lives and reigns with You and the Holy Spirit, one God, now and forever. Amen.

9
NOVEMBER

Today, we remember and thank God for the life and work of **Martin Chemnitz, Pastor and Confessor.**

Born this day in 1522 was perhaps the greatest theologian the Lutheran Church could ever boast—Martin Chemnitz. So significant was his life's work on the lasting success of the Reformation that it became a Lutheran proverb: if the second Martin (Chemnitz) had not come, the first Martin (Luther) would hardly have lasted.

This humble and irenic man was born in Brandenburg and, after some initial education at Magdeburg, apprenticed to become a weaver. Chemnitz followed this calling for a few years but at last returned to studies at age 20. He studied until his funds ran dry, and then he taught. In 1545, he went to Wittenberg and studied under both Luther (shortly) and Melanchthon. He graduated from Konigsberg in 1548 and ended up in a post as librarian. He taught some, but mostly he could read. And read he did. It was regarded as one of the finest libraries of the day. His interest in reading shifted from astrology (which he had studied at Magdeburg) to divinity. Chemnitz worked through the Scriptures in their original languages, studying matters that had long puzzled him. He worked through the extant writings of the great Fathers of the Church. He then studied the great controversies of the day, concluding that the Lutheran position was, in fact, biblically and historically grounded.

He was ordained November 25, 1554, and was made coadjutor of the superintendent of the duchy of Brunswick. In 1567, he became superintendent and remained in the post till his death. His years of careful study enabled him to write voluminous theological tomes. He gave a critical read of the Canons and Decrees of the Council of Trent in his *Examination of*

O little flock, fear not the foe
Who madly seeks your overthrow;
　Dread not his rage and pow'r.
And though your courage sometimes faints,
His seeming triumph o'er God's saints
　Lasts but a little hour.
Be of good cheer; your cause belongs
To Him who can avenge your wrongs;
　Leave it to Him, our Lord.
Though hidden yet from mortal eyes,
His Gideon shall for you arise,
　Uphold you and His Word. (LSB 666:1–2)

---

the Council of Trent. He prepared his own annotated version of Melanchthon's *Loci Communes*, called *Loci Theologici.* He prepared a handbook for the examination of the pastors in Brunswick. He wrote definitive treatises on the Lord's Supper and Christology.

His irenic spirit, encyclopedic mind, and humble submission to the Sacred Scriptures soon made him a leading theological force in the troubled years after Luther's death. He was the major contributor to the work that resulted in the Formula of Concord. At the end of his life, he experienced increasing forgetfulness, surely a great trial to a man who had always had what he needed neatly stored away in his mind. He died April 8, 1586.

Lord God, heavenly Father, through the teaching of Martin Chemnitz,
You prepare us for the coming of Your Son to lead home His Bride, the Church,
that with all the company of the redeemed we may finally enter into His
eternal wedding feast; through the same Jesus Christ, our Lord, who lives and
reigns with You and the Holy Spirit, one God, now and forever. Amen.

11
NOVEMBER

Today, we remember **St. Martin of Tours, Pastor**.

Martin was born into a heathen family in present-day Hungary around AD 316. His father, a senior officer in the Roman army, was transferred to Lombardy. There Martin grew to manhood. He was reportedly but ten when (against his parent's wishes) he began attending church and even enrolled as a catechumen. When the young lad was but fifteen, he was conscripted to join the cavalry according to the custom of the time for children of officers. At eighteen, he was stationed in Gaul, present-day France. As a soldier, he once came upon a poor beggar, wrapped in meager rags, on a cold winter's day. Martin is said to have used his sword to slice his own cloak in two parts, giving half of it to the freezing beggar to wrap up in.

Once in the course of his military service, Martin felt that he could not join in a particular battle. "I am a soldier of Christ," he protested. He was immediately arrested and jailed until it befell that the battle did not actually take place, the enemy suing for peace instead. Martin was eventually released both from prison and from all obligation of military service.

Freed at last to pursue his faith in freedom, he made his way to Poitiers. There he studied with the great Hilary, a famous teacher of the faith and confessor of the orthodox teaching of the Holy Trinity. Martin joined in the orthodox resistance to the Imperial embrace of Arianism. In 371, he was lured to Tours on the pretense of visiting and praying with a sick man. Once there, he was acclaimed the city's bishop, a position he accepted only reluctantly.

As bishop, Martin gave his energies toward the spread of Christianity among the natives of Gaul and the alleviation of the suffering of captives. He reportedly once ordered a pine tree chopped down that the locals worshiped. They agreed only if he would stand in the path. He did so and the tree missed him as it fell. He thus won over the heathen to Christ.

Oh, may Thy soldiers, faithful, true, and bold,
Fight as the saints who nobly fought of old
And win with them the victor's crown of gold.
Alleluia! Alleluia! (LSB 677:3)

He was also remembered (with Ambrose of Milan) for unyielding opposition to the notion that the state should ever execute people for heresy. He experienced great sorrow when the Emperor did not finally heed his warning and executed some of the Priscillian heretics.

St. Martin died this day in 397, a man much loved and revered. The account of his charity in the gift of his cloak made the saint quite popular. The Frankish kings treasured his piece of the cloak, which they kept as a relic.

It was on the day of this popular saint in 1483 that Hans and Margaret Luther brought their one-day-old son to the saving waters of Baptism. Since it was St. Martin's day, the child was named in honor of Martin of Tours: Martin Luther.

Lord God of hosts, Your servant Martin the soldier embodied the spirit of sacrifice. He became a bishop in Your Church to defend the catholic faith. Give us grace to follow in his steps so that when our Lord returns we may be clothed with the baptismal garment of righteousness and peace; through Jesus Christ, our Lord, who lives and reigns with You and the Holy Spirit, one God, now and forever. Amen.

14
NOVEMBER

Today, we remember and thank God for the life of his holy servant **Emperor Justinian, Christian Ruler and Confessor of Christ**.

Justinian was emperor of the Eastern Roman Empire from AD 527 to 565. He was born about 482 to a peasant family. His uncle Justin, who had served in the Imperial Guards and later became the Emperor, adopted him. His uncle brought the young lad to Constantinople and had him well schooled in history, theology, and law. A contemporary described the young man as short of stature, fair-skinned, round of face, and curly haired. Significantly, Justinian is regarded as the last emperor of the Roman Empire to be a native Latin speaker.

Although the empire had been in steady decline, Justin and his wife, Theodora, strove to regain control of the West and to restore something of the splendor and dignity that had once characterized the Byzantine court. He was truly a workaholic and earned the nickname "the emperor who never sleeps" for his great energy in governing. His great and lasting achievement in government was the promulgation of a revised and comprehensive code of law, the *Codex Iustinianus*.

After the untimely death of Theodora in 548, Justinian devoted ever more time and energy to theology and the problems of the Church. Under him, the fifth ecumenical council had been convened in Constantinople (Constantinople II) in 533, and he remained committed to extending the Church's rights and influence his whole reign.

To this day, the Eastern rite churches sing in their Divine Liturgy a song of praise to Christ that is known as the hymn of St. Justinian. It encapsulates in the liturgy the point at issue at Constantinople II:

Christians, this Lord Jesus
Shall return again
In His Father's glory,
With His angel train;
For all wreaths of empire
Meet upon His brow,
And our hearts confess Him
King of glory now. (LSB 512:6)

Only-begotten Son and Word of God, immortal as You are, You condescended for our salvation to take flesh from the holy mother of God and ever-virgin Mary, and without undergoing change You were made man. You were crucified for us, O Christ our God, and crushed death by Your death. You are One of the Holy Trinity, equal in glory to the Father and the Holy Spirit: save us!

This is the liturgical confession of a teaching that Lutherans gladly embrace: in the incarnation, the Second Person of the Godhead, the eternal Word, takes to Himself a human nature, with all the attributes of that nature. But the person acting through that human nature is that of God the Son.

Justinian died upon this day in the year 565. He sadly did not live to see his dream fulfilled of a reunion between the parties who embraced the Council of Chalcedon and those who rejected it, yet he left behind a Church strengthened in the true confession of Christ and a comprehensive law code for the empire.

Lord God, heavenly Father, through the governance of Christian leaders such as Emperor Justinian, Your name is freely confessed in our nation and throughout the world. Grant that we may continue to choose trustworthy leaders who will serve You faithfully in our generation and make wise decisions that contribute to the general welfare of Your people; through Jesus Christ, our Lord. Amen.

19
NOVEMBER

Today, we thank God for His humble maidservant **Elizabeth of Hungary**.

Elizabeth was born into Hungary's royal family in 1207, the daughter of King Andrew II and his wife, Gertrude. She was only fourteen when she was given in marriage to Louis of Thuringia, the same year he was made Landgrave.

Although their marriage was not destined to be a long one, it was quite blessed. In their happy home at Wartburg Castle (where Luther would later be kept in friendly imprisonment and would begin his translation of the Scriptures), the young couple had two children and devoted themselves to lives of Christian charity. Elizabeth is even said to have once given up her own bed to a passing leper. When a time of plague and famine hit Thuringia while her husband was away at court, Elizabeth took charge. She distributed alms to the needy, selling off some of the castles' treasures. She also had a hospital constructed at the foot of the Wartburg. There she daily attended the sick and dying.

Elizabeth was pregnant with a third child when sad word reached her that her beloved husband had died of a fever on a journey to Italy. Her heart was crushed. She said it was to her as if the entire world had died.

Before Louis's death, Elizabeth had already come under the spiritual care of a rather harsh priest, Konrad von Marburg. He was made her confessor. With Louis gone, Elizabeth vowed absolute obedience to Konrad, whom she trusted to look after her soul. The priest insisted upon such a severely ascetic way of life that her health began to fail. She had promised the priest that she would live in celibacy all her days. This set her in opposition to her family, who wanted to see her married again. She steadfastly refused. She entrusted the care of her little ones to various relatives at Konrad's insistence.

In sickness, sorrow, want, or care,
May we each other's burdens share;
May we, where help is needed, there
  Give help as unto Thee!
And may Thy Holy Spirit move
All those who live to live in love
Till Thou shalt greet in heav'n above
  All those who live in Thee. (LSB 852:5–6)

She took the money from her dowry and built a hospital in Marburg where she and her companions lived, caring for the sick. At last, this austere life of penance took its toll. Her health was broken beyond repair. She died this day in 1231, only twenty-four years old.

Hospitals throughout the world are often named in memory of this brave young woman, St. Elizabeth. She was a living icon of the truth of Matthew 25: "As you did it to the least of these My brothers, you did it to Me." Though her years of earthly pilgrimage were few, her example has inspired countless others in the following centuries to serve Christ in the poor and sick.

Mighty King, whose inheritance is not of this world, inspire in us the humility and benevolent charity of Elizabeth of Hungary. She scorned her bejeweled crown with thoughts of the thorned one her Savior donned for her sake and ours, that we, too, might live a life of sacrifice, pleasing in Your sight and worthy of the name of Your Son, Christ Jesus, who with the Holy Spirit reigns with You in the everlasting kingdom. Amen.

23
NOVEMBER

Today, the Holy Church rejoices to remember
St. Clement of Rome, Pastor.

Clement served as an early bishop of the Roman Church from approximately AD 92 to 99. Early succession lists place him as either the second or third bishop after Peter (or Peter and Linus), but these are probably anachronistic. At the end of the first century, a council of presbyters or bishops apparently jointly governed the Roman Church. The early Christian writing *Shepherd of Hermas* mentions a Clement as the bishop who was charged with correspondence with other churches. This fits with the fact that we have from his hand only one piece of writing, and it is a letter to the Church of Corinth.

Clement is regarded as first among the Apostolic Fathers, that generation following the apostles who had personal connections with the Twelve and St. Paul. Some believe that Clement of Rome is the very man St. Paul referred to in Philippians 4:3 as one of his fellow workers with whom he labored side by side with Euodia and Syntyche.

In the letter we have from his hand, Clement urges the Corinthians not to be in rebellion against the men appointed to watch out for their souls and extols instead the virtues of humility and unity. He finds these exemplified in Christ and the saints. He urged the Corinthian congregation: "Let us fix our eyes on the blood of Christ, realizing how precious it is to His Father, since it was poured out for our salvation and has brought the grace of repentance to the whole world." As an official of that Church to which St. Paul addressed the lengthy discourse on justification in Romans, it should not surprise anyone that Clement would also write about that topic. "And we, in the same way, being called by His will in Christ Jesus, are not justified

Elect from ev'ry nation,
* Yet one o'er all the earth;*
Her charter of salvation:
* One Lord, one faith, one birth.*
One holy name she blesses,
* Partakes one holy food,*
And to one hope she presses
* With ev'ry grace endued. (LSB 644:2)*

---

by ourselves, nor by our own wisdom, or understanding, or godliness, or works which we have done in holiness of heart. No, we are instead justified by that faith through which, from the very beginning, Almighty God has justified all men, to whom be glory forever and ever. Amen!"

According to tradition, Clement sealed his confession of Christ with a martyr's death under the reign of Emperor Trajan. He was reportedly tied to an anchor and tossed into the sea. His symbol is, therefore, an anchor on a white background.

Almighty God, Your servant Clement of Rome called the Church in Corinth to repentance and faith to unite them in Christian love. Grant that Your Church may be anchored in Your truth by the presence of the Holy Spirit and kept blameless in Your service until the coming of our Lord Jesus Christ, who lives and reigns with You and the Holy Spirit, one God, now and forever. Amen.

29
NOVEMBER

Today, we remember and thank God for faithful **Noah**.

Noah descended from the godly line of Seth. His father was Lamech, his grandfather Methuselah, and his great-grandfather was Enoch, who "walked with God." Lamech named his son Noah, saying, "Out of the ground that the LORD has cursed, this one shall bring us relief from our work and from the painful toil of our hands" (Genesis 5:29). When Noah had already lived a very long time, five hundred years, he became a father to three sons: Shem, Ham, and Japheth.

The Scriptures tell how God with sadness and regret beheld the great wickedness of humanity upon the earth. The fallen state of man's heart is described this way: "Every intention of the thoughts of his heart was only evil continually" (Genesis 6:5). Yet, the bright spot was Noah and his family: "Noah found favor in the eyes of the LORD." Thus, when God decided to wipe out the world with a flood because of the great sinfulness of mankind, in mercy He spared believing Noah and his family, eight souls in all.

Noah was instructed to prepare a large ark, and God commanded the animals to come to him two by two, a male and his mate, with seven pairs of the "clean" animals (suitable for sacrifice). After the animals had been gathered into the ark, God shut the door behind Noah and his family. The great flood began. Rain poured from the sky, and "the fountains of the great deep burst forth." The dry land disappeared as the waters prevailed over the earth. It was a return to the primordial chaos when the Spirit of God hovered over the face of the waters.

After a long time, the rain stopped and the waters began to subside. Noah's ark came to rest on the mountains of Ararat. He sent forth first a

There's nothing that can sever
From this great love of God;
No want, no pain whatever,
No famine, peril, flood.
Though thousand foes surround me,
For slaughter mark His sheep,
They never shall confound me,
The vict'ry I shall reap. (LSB 746:2)

---

raven and then a dove. When the dove returned with a freshly plucked olive leaf, he knew that it would soon be safe to leave. When his family left the boat, he took some of the clean animals and offered them in a sacrifice of thanksgiving to God, who had brought them safely through the great flood. This sacrifice of thanksgiving pleased the Lord, and He promised never again to wipe the earth out with a flood. As a sign of His covenant, He hung up His bow in the clouds.

Before the flood, God had restricted mankind's diet solely to vegetation. Afterward, He permitted man to eat every moving thing that lives, with the provision that man could not eat a live animal, but must kill it first (hence, not eating flesh with its "life," that is, its blood).

From Noah's children the earth was repopulated. All mankind descends from this family that was graciously saved through the waters.

Almighty and eternal God, according to Your strict judgment You condemned the unbelieving world through the flood, yet according to Your great mercy You preserved believing Noah and his family, eight souls in all. Grant that we may be kept safe and secure in the holy ark of the Christian Church, so that with all believers in Your promise, we would be declared worthy of eternal life; through Jesus Christ, our Lord. Amen.

30
NOVEMBER

Today, the Holy Church rejoices in the Festival of **St. Andrew, Apostle**.

Andrew was among the first of our Lord's disciples. He was the son of Jonah and brother of Simon, whom Jesus renamed Peter. The family was from Bethsaida in Galilee. With his brother, Andrew was a fisherman by trade.

In the Gospel of John, we find Andrew introducing others to the Lord Jesus. Andrew had apparently been a follower of St. John the Baptist. Upon hearing John point to Jesus as "the Lamb of God who takes away the sin of the world," Andrew and another disciple followed Jesus and spent the day with Him. Later, Andrew "first found his brother Simon and said to him, 'We have found the Messiah' (which means Christ). He brought him to Jesus'" (John 1:41–42). Thus, Andrew is regarded as the first "home missionary," recognizing the importance of telling those closest to him about the Lord and introducing them to Him.

Some time later in Galilee, Jesus would specifically summon Peter and Andrew, James and John from their vocation as fishermen to follow Him (see Mark 1:16). He would promise them that from now on they would become fishers of men.

In John 12, some Greeks who had come to Jerusalem for the Passover desired to see Jesus. They first approached Philip (also a native of Bethsaida), and Philip turned to Andrew for assistance. Andrew and Philip brought word to Jesus, who exulted that as He is lifted up from the earth, He will draw all people to Himself. Thus, Andrew may also be regarded as the first "foreign missionary," recognizing the need for introducing those who come from distant lands to Jesus.

All praise, O Lord, for Andrew,
The first to welcome You,
Whose witness to his brother
Named You Messiah true.
May we, with hearts kept open
To You throughout the year,
Confess to friend and neighbor
Your advent ever near. (LSB 517:5)

Andrew witnessed his Lord's resurrection, being with the others in the Upper Room on Easter evening and the week following. After Pentecost and the dispersion of the apostles, Andrew is said to have preached his Master's resurrection as far as Scythia or Thrace. According to tradition, he was martyred by crucifixion in Patras in Achaea.

Because Andrew felt unworthy to die upon the same kind of cross as his Lord had, he begged to be crucified on an X-shaped cross. This was granted him. Hence his symbol in church art is a cross in that particular shape. After his death, his bones were at one time interred in Constantinople and later transferred to the cathedral of Amalfi in Italy.

St. Andrew's Day always determines the beginning of Advent, for the first Sunday in Advent falls on the Sunday nearest to his festival.

Almighty God, by Your grace the apostle Andrew obeyed the call of Your Son to be a disciple. Grant us also to follow the same Lord Jesus Christ in heart and life, who lives and reigns with You and the Holy Spirit, one God, now and forever. Amen.

READINGS
EZEKIEL 3:16–21 / ROMANS 10:8B–28 / JOHN 1:35–42A

4
DECEMBER

Today, we remember and give thanks to God for **St. John of Damascus, Theologian and Hymnwriter.**

John was born (ca. AD 675) and raised in Damascus. His considerable gifts landed him a position as an administrator in the Muslim caliphate in that city. Yet, his love for his Lord and his devotion to the Church led him to forsake this position of worldly wealth and influence, enter a monastery (ca. AD 716), and finally be ordained a presbyter.

As a custodian of the apostolic doctrine, he forcefully resisted when the Byzantine Emperor Leo the Isaurian tried to outlaw the use of images in the Church. John constantly taught that once the eternal Word had become flesh, that flesh could be depicted and the depiction could be honored. And similarly, the flesh of Christ's saints could be depicted and grace the walls of the churches and the homes of Christians. The Church's use of iconography was simply a consequence of the incarnation itself. Luther would later express quite similar teachings against the radical reformers who sought to remove art from the churches.

As a theologian, John is often regarded as the last of the great Church Fathers of the antiquity. His work *On the Orthodox Faith* summarized the dogmatic tradition that he had received, and it is cited more than once by Martin Chemnitz in his great work on Christology. In his book on the faith, John freely confesses, "It is impossible either to say or fully to understand anything about God beyond what has been divinely proclaimed to us, whether told or revealed, by the sacred declarations of the Old and New Testaments" (Book 1, chapter 2).

Similarly, his *Fount of Wisdom* was a massive compendium of the work of previous theologians. Melanchthon and other Lutheran theologians used its structure and form as a guideline in the construction of their *Loci Communes*.

Alleluia! Now we cry
* To our King immortal,*
Who, triumphant, burst the bars
* Of the tomb's dark portal.*
Come, you faithful, raise the strain
* Of triumphant gladness!*
God has brought His Israel
* Into joy from sadness! (LSB 487:5)*

As a hymnwriter, John perfected the form of song in the East known as the canon. John's compositions remain beloved in both East and West. Lutherans in English-speaking lands are particularly familiar with some of his Easter hymnody: "Come, You Faithful, Raise the Strain" and "The Day of Resurrection." Perhaps his most hauntingly beautiful piece is this reflection on the contrast between the passing joys of earth and the lasting blessedness of the beatific vision:

> What earthly joy remains untouched by grief?
> What glory stands forever on the earth?
> Frail shadows—all, delusive dreams;
> Which death will one day sweep away.
> But in the light of Your countenance, O Christ,
> And in the enjoyment of Your beauty,
> Give rest to those whom You have chosen and taken
> For You are the Lover of mankind.
> (St. John of Damascus, Friday Evening Aposticha Verse)

He could well have had such words on his lips when he died in 749, a teacher of the Church revered and loved.

O Lord, through Your servant John of Damascus You proclaimed with power the mysteries of the true faith. Confirm our faith so that we may confess Jesus to be true God and true man, singing the praises of the risen Lord, and so that by the power of the resurrection we may also attain the joys of eternal life; through Jesus Christ, our Lord, who lives and reigns with You and the Holy Spirit, one God, now and forever.

6
DECEMBER

This day, the Holy Church rejoices to remember **St. Nicholas of Myra, Pastor**.

Nicholas was born in Patara (present-day Turkey). Orphaned at an early age, he was adopted by his uncle, the bishop of that city. His piety marked him as one who would serve well in the Church. About 317, he was elected bishop of the city of Myra in Lycia (also part of present-day Turkey).

Tradition states that he was among the fathers who gathered for the first council of Nicaea and was a staunch anti-Arian. Nicholas confessed boldly the full deity of the eternal Word. Much later tradition tells that at the council he actually struck the heretic Arius, but this is apparently a medieval fabrication.

The stories of Nicholas's kindness to the poor became well-known throughout Christendom. Perhaps the most famous was the account of a poor man who had three daughters but no dowry to give any of them. The girls would most likely have ended up in slavery or prostitution. But the kind bishop, hearing of their plight, used funds from the church to secure their freedom from such a cruel fate. Under cover of night, he dropped into the house small bags of gold coins. According to some accounts, all three bags were delivered at once; according to others, the bags were delivered to each the day before a given daughter came of age. Either way, the young ladies were able to marry and thus rescued from lives of disgrace and hardship.

Nicholas became beloved by sailors due to an account of a sea voyage he once took. He was on a pilgrimage to the Holy Land when the ship he was traveling in fell into a fierce squall. The kindly bishop prayed to the Lord of wind and sea, the sea grew markedly calm, and the sailors rejoiced.

Love divine, all loves excelling,
Joy of heav'n, to earth come down!
Fix in us Thy humble dwelling,
All Thy faithful mercies crown.
Jesus, Thou art all compassion,
Pure, unbounded love Thou art;
Visit us with Thy salvation,
Enter ev'ry trembling heart. (LSB 700:1)

Because of the help given to the three daughters for their dowry, the saint came to be associated in many places with charitable giving and also with a special love for the Lord's little ones. His feast day is thus observed in many lands as a time for gift giving, especially to children. In Germany, it is common for the saint to arrive in full bishop's regalia and distribute small gifts to children on December 6. In North America, due to Clement Clark Moore's famous poem *A Visit from St. Nicholas,* the saint merged with certain other traditions to become the modern Santa Claus.

What lives on in the Church is a day to celebrate a man of orthodox faith and devout prayer, shaped by the love of Christ, who delighted to bestow gifts to bless children.

Almighty God, You bestowed upon Your servant Nicholas of Myra the perpetual gift of charity. Grant Your Church the grace to deal in generosity and love with children and with all who are poor and distressed and to plead the cause of those who have no helper, especially those tossed by tempests of doubt or grief. We ask this for the sake of Him who gave His life for us, Your Son, our Savior, Jesus Christ, our Lord, who lives and reigns with You and the Holy Spirit, one God, now and forever. Amen.

7
DECEMBER

Today, we remember and give thanks to God for **St. Ambrose of Milan, Pastor and Hymnwriter**.

Ambrose was born into a Christian family in Trier in AD 340. He followed his father's footsteps as a civil servant of the empire, and about 372 he was named the governor of the Roman province whose capital was Milan. He proved quite popular. He had been governor for but two years when the bishop of the city died, and he was acclaimed (to his shock) the new bishop. He was still a catechumen, had not yet been baptized, and had never really studied theology. Yet, the crowd would be not be denied. Within the week, Ambrose was hurriedly baptized, consecrated a deacon, ordained a presbyter, and then consecrated bishop on December 7, 374. He would later protest that the congregation had to be patient with him, as he was learning even as he was required to teach!

Nevertheless, despite this irregularity, Ambrose proved to be the first of the great Latin Doctors of the Church (the others being Saints Augustine, Jerome, and Gregory the Great), a theologian of highest rank. He strongly opposed Arianism from the first. He used his Greek-speaking background to study extensively the Eastern fathers in their biblical commentaries and theological treatises. He soon showed himself a faithful bishop and servant of Christ, and his sermons utilized to the full his classical learning.

He was not afraid to stand up to Emperor Theodosius when needed. The instance of the famous massacre at Thessalonica shows this. The emperor, in a fit of rage, had ordered thousands slaughtered. Ambrose met him at the door of the church in Milan and barred his entrance until he had publicly repented in the manner of King David.

Savior of the nations, come,
Virgin's Son, make here Your home!
Marvel now, O heav'n and earth,
That the Lord chose such a birth.
Not by human flesh and blood,
By the Spirit of our God,
Was the Word of God made flesh—
Woman's offspring, pure and fresh. (LSB 332:1–2)

Ambrose is also famous for his catechesis of Augustine. The learning of the Bishop of Milan brought Augustine and company to repentance and to the washing of Baptism. A medieval legend even attributes the text of the *Te Deum Laudamus* to the two great men at the time of Augustine's Baptism at Ambrose's hand.

While that is only a legend, it is true that Ambrose introduced into the West a form of antiphonal singing that remains quite popular. The great Advent hymn "Savior of the Nations, Come" is attributed to him and witnesses a decidedly anti-Arian confession of Christ. The form of "office hymn" is due directly to Ambrose's influence.

He died April 4, 397, in Milan.

O God, You gave Your servant Ambrose grace to proclaim the Gospel with eloquence and power. As bishop of the great congregation of Milan, he fearlessly bore reproach for the honor of Your name. Mercifully grant to all bishops and pastors such excellence in preaching and fidelity in ministering Your Word, that Your people shall be partakers of the divine nature; through Jesus Christ, our Lord, who lives and reigns with You and the Holy Spirit, one God, now and forever. Amen.

13
DECEMBER

Today, we give thanks to God for
St. Lucia, Martyr.

The young virgin commemorated this day was one of many martyred under Emperor Diocletian, the last great widespread persecution of Christians under Roman authority. Her martyrdom took place in her native Sicily in AD 304.

According to tradition, Lucia (or Lucy, which means "light") was born to wealthy and noble parents sometime around AD 280. Her father died when she was but a child. Lucia privately decided that she would never marry. She vowed to remain a virgin and to bestow the dowry her father had left her upon the poor. Her mother, unaware of her daughter's resolve and in poor health, betrothed her to a wealthy young pagan man.

Lucia and her mother visited the shrine of St. Agatha, who had died confessing Christ years before in the Decian persecution. They prayed for the gift of healing. Her mother was restored to health. With her mother's health no longer a concern, Lucia persuaded her mother to allow the distribution of the entirety of her dowry to the poor. When word reached the young man to whom she was betrothed that Lucy had given away what he regarded as his treasure, he was quite angry. He denounced her to the governor of Syracuse as a Christian. She was then executed according to imperial policy.

A later tradition says that before Lucia was slain with the sword, her eyes were gouged out. This was supposedly in retaliation for prophesying that the persecution would soon end and that the emperor who had commanded it would soon be dead himself.

Tell how, when at length the fullness
Of the appointed time was come,
He, the Word, was born of woman,
Left for us His Father's home,
Blazed the path of true obedience,
Shone as light amidst the gloom. (LSB 454:2)

Because her name means "light" and her commemoration falls at the time of year in the northern hemisphere when nights are longest, festivals of light commemorating the brave young virgin of Syracuse became popular and spread throughout Europe. In the far north, in Scandinavia, where the hours of darkness are greatest, a tradition arose of clothing young women in white with a red sash, symbolizing the blood of martyrdom. A crown of lighted candles would be placed upon their heads in honor of the martyr's name, and they would carry in to their family some tasty baked goods to give away, made especially in memory of St. Lucia.

O God, by whose grace and power Your holy martyr Lucia triumphed over suffering and remained faithful unto death, grant us, who now remember her with thanksgiving, to be so true in our witness to You in this world that we may receive with her new eyes without tears and the crown of light and life; through Jesus Christ, our Lord, who lives and reigns with You and the Holy Spirit, one God, now and forever. Amen.

17
DECEMBER

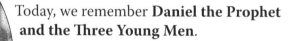

Today, we remember **Daniel the Prophet and the Three Young Men**.

At the time that he defeated Judah and captured Jerusalem, the Babylonian King Nebuchadnezzar took captive a number of young noblemen. He carried them back to Babylon to be brought up and trained in the literature and language of the Chaldeans. Among these were four of note: Daniel, Hananniah, Mishael, and Azariah. The king commanded them to be educated for three years and then to serve at his pleasure. They were to eat the king's food, all of which had been offered to his idols.

Though carried far away from their native land, Daniel and the others remained faithful to the God of Israel. They declined to eat the king's fare, surviving instead on vegetables and water, yet they were preserved in their health. Daniel was given the gift of interpreting dreams. When Nebuchadnezzar had a troubling dream, he refused to reveal it and demanded that his counselors tell him the dream and its interpretation or be killed. The four young Judeans prayed, and the dream and its meaning was revealed to Daniel. Daniel and the three received high office as a result.

The king famously demanded Hananniah, Mishael, and Azariah (all of whom he renamed in honor of his own gods) to bow down to an image he made. With great resolve, the Judeans stood fast and refused. They were tossed into a massively overheated furnace, but one "like the son of the gods" appeared in the furnace and sheltered them. They came out of the flames unhurt and even without the smell of smoke upon their clothes. The king was thus brought to confess that their God was indeed true and mighty.

Later, Daniel was maliciously accused under the reign of another king in the Persian Empire that succeeded the Babylonians. Despite a royal decree,

Praise, all you people, the name so holy
Of Him who does such wondrous things!
All that has being, to praise Him solely,
With happy heart its amen sings.
Children of God, with angel host
Praise Father, Son, and Holy Ghost!
Alleluia, alleluia! **(LSB 797:5)**

---

he continued to pray three times a day toward Jerusalem. He was thrown into a lions' den and left overnight. But the Lord shut the lions' mouths, and Daniel's life was spared. In both the fiery furnace and the lions' den, the Church has always seen types of Christ's victory over death and the grave and hints of the resurrection.

Daniel also had many visions about the end times. He foresaw the enthronement of the Son of Man, coming on clouds and with great glory. He foretold how the Lord would establish a kingdom that would last forever. He foresaw the resurrection of the dead, when the righteous would shine like stars.

The Greek translation of Daniel contains a canticle that the young men sang in the furnace, the *Benedicite Omnia Opera*, of which the hymn stanza above is a paraphrase.

Lord God, heavenly Father, You rescued Daniel from the lions' den and the three young men from the fiery furnace through the miraculous intervention of angels. Save us now through the presence of Jesus, the Lion of Judah, who has conquered all our enemies through His blood and taken away all our sins as the Lamb of God, who now reigns from His heavenly throne with You and the Holy Spirit, one God, now and forever. Amen.

19
DECEMBER

Today, we remember and give thanks to
God for the parents of the human race,
Adam and Eve.

The Lord God created humanity as the crown of His
creation, His final work on the sixth day. He made
us male and female, and told us to be fruitful and
multiply and to exercise dominion over all the earth.
The first man, called Adam (from the Hebrew *ademah*,
or earth), God formed from the dust of the earth. He
breathed into the man's nostrils the breath of life, and the
man became a living soul or being.

Causing a deep sleep to fall upon Adam, God took a rib from
the man and formed it into the woman and brought her to the man. Adam
received this gift with joy and named her "Woman [*ishah*], because she
was taken out of Man [*ish*]." Thus marriage was founded, the human family
established, and Adam's primordial headship shown by his naming the
woman as gift from the Lord.

Our first parents were placed into a paradise of plenty. It was a place
without fear, for there was no death yet. No sin to stain their conscience.
That soon changed. The serpent deceived the woman and led her (and the
man who was with her) to take the one fruit God had not given them, the
fruit from the tree of the knowledge of good and evil. Thus sin was ushered
into the world and brought with it death, separation from the God of life.
From that point, all born in the natural way would inherit a rebellious
human nature. Immediately, Adam and Eve knew shame and sought to hide
from each other behind fig-leaf aprons. When they heard the sound of God
in the evening, they ran into the trees and tried to hide.

God called the man to account. Adam blamed first God and then the
woman. The woman in turn blamed the serpent. God then spoke words of

'Tis He forgives thy sins;
'Tis He relieves thy pain;
'Tis He that heals thy sicknesses
And makes thee young again.
He crowns thy life with love
When ransomed from the grave;
He that redeemed my soul from hell
Hath sov'reign pow'r to save. (LSB 814:3–4)

---

judgment, but also of hope. He cursed the serpent and foretold the coming of the Seed of the Woman (who is our Lord Jesus) who would finally crush the serpent's head and undo the damage he inflicted. For the woman, He foretold pain in childbearing and child-rearing, and for the man, struggle and hard work. He took off their pitiful fig leaves and clothed them with the skins of an animal, which died in their place to cover their shame. He exiled them from paradise, lest they eat of the tree of life and live forever in their fallen state. Adam then gave his wife her proper name, Eve, for she was to be the mother of all the living. Together they waited for the promised Seed until their own deaths: "For as in Adam all die, so also in Christ shall all be made alive" (1 Corinthians 15:22).

Lord God, heavenly Father, You created Adam in Your image and gave him Eve as his helpmate, and after their fall into sin, You promised them a Savior who would crush the devil's might. By Your mercy, number us among those who have come out of the great tribulation with the seal of the living God on our foreheads and whose robes have been made white in the blood of the Lamb; through Jesus Christ, our Lord.

20
DECEMBER

Today, we remember and give thanks to God for the beloved wife of Martin Luther, **Katharina von Bora Luther.**

Katharina von Bora (born in 1499) was placed as a five-year-old child into the keeping of the Benedictines for education. When she was nine, she moved to a Cistercian foundation where her mother's sister also was cloistered. Like many other nuns at the time, Katharina heard of and grew quite interested in the spreading reform movement in Germany. In 1523, she conspired with several of her sister nuns, wrote to Luther, and begged his assistance in obtaining their release.

Easter of that year, Luther arranged with a fish merchant (who made deliveries at the monastery) to hide the sisters among his empty barrels. Thus the nuns made their escape and arrived in Wittenberg. Luther tried to restore them to their families, but most declined to take them back. Over the next two years, Luther arranged marriages for all of them, except for Katharina. A number of men were interested in her, but she had declined them all. She finally disclosed to Nicholas von Amsdorf that she'd only marry him or Luther.

Luther, still believing that he would likely be martyred, had never seriously contemplated marriage. Yet, Katharina's persistence finally paid off: in June of 1525, they were married. He was forty-one and she was twenty-six. Since married clergy had not existed in the West for centuries, Luther and his wife set the pattern for what would become the Protestant parsonage.

Together they lived in what was the former monastery of the Augustinians in Wittenberg, a gift to the Luthers from Elector John. Katharina proved to be a wise household manager and quite industrious in her own right.

Oh, blest the house, whate'er befall,
Where Jesus Christ is all in all!
A home that is not wholly His—
How sad and poor and dark it is!
Oh, blest that house where faith is found
And all in hope and love abound;
They trust their God and serve Him still
And do in all His holy will! (LSB 862:1–2)

The Lord blessed them with six live births. They sadly lost two children, one at but eight months and another at age thirteen. Their family circle, however, also included four orphans whom they adopted. Throughout their marriage, they demonstrated a respectful and playful relationship with each other. Katharina always called Martin "Herr Doktor." She worried about her husband's poor health, and he teased her on that account, inviting her to trust instead in the Lord. When Luther died, she experienced a great deal of financial hardship. During the Smalcaldic War, her property was laid waste. She did receive some support from those who gratefully remembered her husband's service to the Church. Katharina died 1552, having fled to Torgau due to plague in Wittenberg. Her final words were reportedly, "I'll stick to Christ like a burr to a cloth."

O God, our refuge and our strength, You raised up Your servant Katharina to support her husband in the task to reform and renew Your Church in the light of Your Word. Defend and purify the Church today and grant that, through faith, we may boldly support and encourage our pastors and teachers of the faith as they proclaim and administer the riches of Your grace made known in Jesus Christ, our Lord, who lives and reigns with You and the Holy Spirit, one God, now and forever. Amen.

21
DECEMBER

Today, the Holy Church celebrates the
Festival of **St. Thomas, Apostle**.

Thomas, named also Didymus (that is, the twin),
was one of the Lord's twelve chosen apostles. Only
St. John's Gospel records any words from him. When
Lazarus died and Jesus proclaimed that He was going
to Judea to awaken him, Thomas said to the other
disciples, "Let us also go, that we may die with Him"
(John 11:16). Thus Thomas shows that he had heard and
heeded the Lord Jesus' predictions of His own Passion.

During the Lord's farewell discourse, Jesus announced that He was
going to prepare a place for the disciples and would come again to take them
to Himself. He told the disciples that they knew the way to the place He is
going. But Thomas replied, "Lord, we do not know where You are going.
How can we know the way?" Jesus responded to Thomas, "I am the way, and
the truth, and the life. No one comes to the Father except through Me. If you
had known Me, you would have known My Father also" (see John 14:1–7).

Most famously, Thomas is remembered for doubting the words of his
fellow disciples when they told him that Christ had indeed been raised
from the dead. He had not been with them in the Upper Room on Easter
evening when the Lord had appeared. He announced his stubborn doubt:
"Unless I see in His hands the mark of the nails, and place my finger into the
mark of the nails, and place my hand into His side, I will never believe." In
great mercy, Christ appeared again a week later, and this time Thomas was
with them. He bid Thomas do exactly what he proposed. "Put your finger
here, and see My hands; and put out your hand, and place it in My side.
Do not disbelieve, but believe." Thomas then confessed, "My Lord and my
God!" Jesus asked if he had believed because of what he saw and proclaimed

All praise, O Lord, for Thomas,
*   Whose short-lived doubtings prove*
Your perfect twofold nature,
*   The fullness of Your love.*
To all who live with questions
*   A steadfast faith afford;*
And grant us grace to know You,
*   True man, yet God and Lord. (LSB 517:6)*

---

blessed those who do not see and yet believe (John 20:24–29). Thomas also was with the disciples when Christ revealed Himself alive in Galilee and granted them a miraculous catch of fish (see John 21:1–14).

After Pentecost and the dispersion of the apostles, Thomas reportedly traveled as far east as India. To this day, a group of Christians in India still refers to themselves as "Christians of St. Thomas." It is believed he was martyred for Christ by being killed with a spear, and thus his symbol is a spear with a builder's square (for he was one of the architects by whom Christ built His Church). His feast day in the West has been observed on December 21 at least since the ninth century.

Almighty and ever-living God, You strengthened Your apostle Thomas with firm and certain faith in the resurrection of Your Son. Grant us such faith in Jesus Christ, our Lord and our God, that we may never be found wanting in Your sight; through the same Jesus Christ, who lives and reigns with You and the Holy Spirit, one God, now and forever. Amen.

READINGS
JUDGES 6:36–40 / EPHESIANS 4:7, 11–16 / JOHN 20:24–29

24/25
DECEMBER

Today, the Holy Church celebrates with greatest joy **the Nativity of Our Lord**, God, and Savior, Jesus Christ.

Terrified, the shepherds stared into the light that bathed the night and listened to a voice of mirth, ringing with heaven's laughter. "Fear not," cried the angel, "for behold, I bring you good news of great joy that will be for all the people. For to you is born this day in the city of David a Savior, who is Christ the Lord" (Luke 2:10–11).

That baby is the great joy Himself come down to earth. There, wrapped up like any other human child, the shepherds (and you with them) found the world's Creator. The very flesh He assumed from His holy mother remains the irrefutable proof that your God does not hate you. He loves every one of us, and that is why He gave His great joy, His beloved Son.

Behold the measure of His great love: our Savior came, a child of man by nature, to make the fallen and lost the children of God by grace! And what He once put on, He will never take off. From the moment of His incarnation He will always be not only the eternal Word of the Father but also your brother, flesh of your flesh and bone of your bone. Even to this day, exalted at the right hand of His Father, He bears the body that He took for Himself in Mary's womb.

This is the mystery that led the angels to exult in their Christmas Glorias. Their Master! How great His love! Who ever would have conceived it? dreamed it? For the lost race of men, He becomes a man. When humanity could not come to Him, He came to us. This is the mystery that sent the shepherds running to Bethlehem. In faith, you journey with them. With them you bend your knees in silent adoration. With them you gaze in

From east to west, from shore to shore
Let ev'ry heart awake and sing
The holy child whom Mary bore,
The Christ, the everlasting king.
Behold, the world's creator wears
The form and fashion of a slave;
Our very flesh our maker shares,
His fallen creatures all to save. (LSB 385:1–2)

---

wonder and awe upon Jesus, the great joy, who now lives and breathes in our human flesh and will forever.

And there in the manger's lowly wood, you may see prefigured already the cross on which those little limbs, grown to manhood, would be so cruelly stretched and torn. The same love that brought Him to you will bring Him to that. He will embrace His Passion to wipe out your every sin, destroy your death, and bring you home to His Father. That's why He came, after all.

As you kneel to receive His Eucharist, He gives all this to you, and you taste anew the great joy. You have been loved with a love eternal, vast, divine.

Most merciful God, You gave Your eternal Word to become incarnate of the pure Virgin. Grant Your people grace to put away fleshly lusts, that they may be ready for Your visitation; through Jesus Christ, our Lord, who lives and reigns with You and the Holy Spirit, one God, now and forever. Amen.

READINGS
MICAH 5:2–5A / TITUS 3:4–7 / LUKE 2:(1–14) 15–20

26
DECEMBER

Today, the Holy Church celebrates the
Festival of **St. Stephen, Martyr**.

The observance of St. Stephen, the first martyr of
Christ, upon the day after Christmas always comes
as a bit of a shock to contemporary sensitivities. Still
ready to dwell upon shepherds and mangers, angels
and a newborn wrapped in swaddling clothes, the
Church invites our attention instead to this truth: "He
came to His own, and His own people did not receive Him.
But to all who did receive Him, who believed in His name, He
gave the right to become children of God" (John 1:11–12).

Stephen was one of the first seven deacons. He had been put forward
by the early congregation in Jerusalem as a man "of good repute, full of the
Spirit and of wisdom" and the apostles prayed and laid hands on him and
the other six, putting them into office.

Stephen himself was "full of grace and power" and did "great wonders
and signs among the people." He bore persuasive and eloquent witness in
the synagogue of the Freedman that the Lord Jesus was indeed the promised
Messiah. When they could not win their debate with him, they decided to
conspire against him. So began Stephen's passion, which in many details
mirror that of our Lord's. Stephen was charged by false witnesses before
the Sanhedrin (the Jewish ruling council) of speaking blasphemous words
against Moses and the temple. The high priest asked him if the accusations
were true. Stephen then preached a powerful sermon that indicted the
people of Israel for always resisting the Holy Spirit, killing the prophets,
and now having killed the Righteous One, the Lord Jesus.

As the enraged council and crowd rose in anger against him, Stephen
was given a heavenly vision of the Son of Man standing at the right hand

Praise for the first of martyrs
Who saw You ready stand
To help in time of torment,
To plead at God's right hand.
Like You, our suff'ring Savior,
His enemies he blessed,
With "Lord, receive my spirit,"
His faith, by death, confessed. (LSB 517:7)

---

of God. They literally stopped their ears, ran at Stephen, dragged him from the city, and stoned him to death. As he was dying, he prayed, "Lord Jesus, receive my spirit." He begged with his dying breath, "Lord, do not hold this sin against them."

A man named Saul (later, of course, our great St. Paul) guarded the coats of the men who killed Stephen. After the death of this first martyr for Christ, Saul led the first great persecution against the followers of Christ. The disciples were dispersed, but everywhere they went they proclaimed the Gospel. Indeed, "the blood of the martyrs is the seed of the Church" (Tertullian).

Curiously, Stephen's name means "crown" and so recalls words of Jesus in Revelation 2:10: "Be faithful unto death, and I will give you the crown of life." In such confidence, Stephen became the first of the noble army of martyrs and was welcomed home by his Lord.

Heavenly Father, in the midst of our sufferings for the sake of Christ grant us grace to follow the example of the first martyr, Stephen, that we also may look to the One who suffered and was crucified on our behalf and pray for those who do us wrong; through Jesus Christ, our Lord, who lives and reigns with You and the Holy Spirit, one God, now and forever. Amen.

READINGS
2 CHRONICLES 24:17–22 / ACTS 6:8—7:2A, 51–60 / MATTHEW 23:34–39

27
DECEMBER

Today, the Holy Church celebrates the Festival of **St. John, Apostle and Evangelist**.

St. John was brother of James (whose festival falls July 25) and son of Zebedee and Salome. Like his brother and father, he was a fisherman by trade. John was among the first whom Christ called to be an apostle. In his Gospel, he often refers to himself as "the disciple whom Jesus loved," indicating a particularly close friendship between himself and His Master. This is evident at the final Supper, where John reclined on his Lord's breast and relayed to him questions from the others. John is also the only one of the Twelve not to abandon Jesus during the time of His Passion. Together with the Mother of God, he stood vigil at the foot of the cross. It was there that Christ gave His mother into John's keeping and gave John to her as her own son. According to the Church's tradition, Mary lived with St. John until the day of her death. After Pentecost, he lived for a time in Jerusalem and finally settled in Ephesus. It was there that John reportedly wrote his three letters, Revelation, and the Gospel that bears his name.

His sign as an evangelist is that of the eagle, for his Gospel soars high above the other three in its witness to the eternal Word, who was before time began and who was made flesh for us, full of grace and truth, and whose hour of exaltation upon the cross draws all people to Himself. Especially beloved from his Gospel are the conversation with Nicodemus (which contains the Gospel in a nutshell, John 3:16); the bread of life discourse (John 6); the sayings of Jesus about being the Good Shepherd (John 10); the raising of Lazarus (John 11); and the great farewell discourse (John 14–16) with its comforting promises.

For Your belov'd disciple
Exiled to Patmos' shore,
And for his faithful record,
We praise You evermore.
Praise for the mystic vision
Through him to us revealed;
May we, in patience waiting,
With Your elect be sealed. (LSB 517:8)

According to Early Church tradition, John was the only one of the Twelve who did not die a martyr's death. Hence, he is the only apostle observed with white upon the altar instead of the usual red (red recalls the blood of the witnesses of Christ). He suffered a time of exile upon the island of Patmos during which the great revelation was granted to him.

As a very old man, John was carried to church, where he never tired of encouraging the disciples, "Little children, love one another." It was the belief of some that John would not die before the Lord Jesus appeared in glory. Yet, the Revelation to John makes perfectly clear that Jesus never made such a promise to His beloved apostle. John's death brought to an end the apostolic era, but his Spirit-inspired writings continue to be a bright light shining in the Church.

Merciful Lord, cast the bright beams of Your light upon Your Church that we, being instructed by the doctrine of Your blessed apostle and evangelist John, may come to the light of everlasting life; for You live and reign with the Father and the Holy Spirit, one God, now and forever. Amen.

READINGS
REVELATION 1:1–6 / 1 JOHN 1:1–2:2 / JOHN 21:20–25

28
DECEMBER

Today, the Holy Church celebrates the Festival of **the Holy Innocents, Martyrs**.

Contemplating the three festivals after Christmas, the Church has long noted a curious fact: St. Stephen was a martyr for Christ in both will and deed. St. John was His martyr in will, but not in deed. The Holy Innocents were His martyrs not in will, but in deed.

Matthew relates how after Jesus was born in Bethlehem of Judea, Magi arrived from the East in the capital city of the Jews, Jerusalem. They were searching for the newborn King of the Jews. A star had announced the birth of this King to them, and now they had come to worship Him.

Herod the Great, vicious and jealous, suffered no rivals. He had already murdered members of his own family whom he believed to be conspiring against him. He sought the counsel of the scribes, the Jewish experts in the sacred writings, to discover exactly where the promised Christ was to be born. He then sent the Magi to find him, asking only that when they did, they bring him back word so that he could offer his homage as well.

Not suspecting the king's malicious intent, the Magi began the trip to Bethlehem. The star that had appeared in the East reappeared and shone over the place where the child was. Entering that house, the Magi beheld the child in the arms of Mary, His mother. They fell down and worshiped Him, offering Him gifts of gold, frankincense, and myrrh. After being warned in a dream not to go back to Herod, they left for their own country by a different route.

Then, Joseph was warned in a dream to leave quickly because Herod was seeking to kill the child. The holy family fled to the relative safety of Egypt. Upon realizing the Magi had deceived him, Herod took a shotgun approach. He ordered his soldiers to go into Bethlehem and kill every male

All praise for infant martyrs,
Whom Your mysterious love
Called early from their warfare
To share Your home above.
O Rachel, cease your weeping;
They rest from earthly cares!
Lord, grant us crowns as brilliant
And faith as sure as theirs. (LSB 517:9)

---

child they found there, two years old and under. So much, he thought, for this so-called newborn King.

The soldiers ruthlessly carried out their orders. The evangelist in Matthew proclaimed in the infant blood spilled in Bethlehem a fulfillment of the words of Jeremiah 31. The prophet had foretold that Rachel (whose tomb was near Bethlehem) would weep for her children, refusing consolation, because they were no more. In the face of such sad slaughter, and the rivers of blood mad men have spilled ever since, the Church finds comfort in the words of the newborn King grown to manhood: "The thief comes only to steal and kill and destroy. I came that they might have life and have it abundantly" (John 10:10).

Almighty God, the martyred innocents of Bethlehem showed forth Your praise not by speaking but by dying. Put to death in us all that is in conflict with Your will that our lives may bear witness to the faith we profess with our lips; through Jesus Christ, our Lord, who lives and reigns with You and the Holy Spirit, one God, now and forever. Amen.

READINGS
JEREMIAH 31:15–17 / REVELATION 14:1–5 / MATTHEW 2:13–18

29
DECEMBER

Today, we remember **David**,
prophet and king.

David, ancestor of the Lord Jesus, was the greatest
of ancient Israel's kings. He ruled from about 1010
BC to 970 BC. When his predecessor on the throne,
King Saul, disobeyed God, God rejected Saul as king.
The Lord sent the prophet Samuel to a man named
Jesse in Bethlehem to anoint a new king. From Jesse's
children, Samuel anointed the most unlikely—his youngest
boy, David.

David was a shepherd and musically gifted. His experience in defending
his sheep from predators and his firm trust in the God of Israel gave him
courage to confront and strike down the gigantic Goliath of Gath. He
entered the service of Saul, the king, and became fast friends with Jonathan,
the king's son. David's gift of music soothed Saul's frequent foul moods.
Saul soon became jealous of David's popularity with the people and sought
numerous times to kill him, eventually driving David into exile and hiding.
Though he had several opportunities to do Saul harm, David refused to lift
a finger against "the Lord's anointed."

After Saul's death in battle, David assumed first the kingship of Judah
and finally of all Israel. He transferred his capital to Jerusalem. His greatness
grew and his fame spread. When he wished to build God a house, God
forbade him and told him that instead God would build him an everlasting
house. A son from his body would build the house for the Lord, and God
would establish that son's kingdom forever.

Ironically, shortly after receiving this promise, David fell into grave sin.
He committed adultery, impregnated another man's wife, and subsequently

Hail to the Lord's anointed,
Great David's greater Son!
Hail, in the time appointed,
His reign on earth begun!
He comes to break oppression,
To set the captive free,
To take away transgression
And rule in equity. (**LSB 398:1**)

---

arranged the murder of her husband. He then took the woman, Bathsheba, as his own wife. The prophet Nathan confronted him with his sin. David gave no excuses but simply confessed and repented.

God brought temporal punishment on David and his house because of his disobedience, and yet in grace He established David's kingdom through a son whom Bathsheba later bore to him, King Solomon. Chastened, David remained faithful to God through the difficult times that surrounded his final years of life.

David is the prime example in the Old Testament of a man who was both simultaneously justified and sinner. His great and lasting gift to the Church of all ages is his Book of Psalms (called the Psalter or the Psalms of David). The people of God have delighted to sing these inspired words in all ages. They find in them words to address God in every conceivable circumstance.

God of majesty, whom saints and angels delight to worship in heaven, we give You thanks for David who, through the Psalter, gave Your people hymns to sing with joy in our worship on earth so that we may glimpse Your beauty. Bring us to the fulfillment of that hope of perfection that will be ours as we stand before Your unveiled glory; through Jesus Christ, our Lord, who lives and reigns with You and the Holy Spirit, one God, now and forever. Amen.

THE MOVABLE DAYS AND SEASONS OF THE CHRISTIAN CHURCH YEAR

As Christians gather for worship, they do so with a strong sense of time and history. Early Christians recalled the historic time-related events that were important to their faith, especially events in the life of Jesus. Over time, the Church has added her own unique celebrations and adapted others to trinitarian understandings. Easter is the principal feast day of the Church. It is the Son's Day of Days as the Church celebrates the Resurrection of Our Lord; it is also an event by which Christians identify themselves as distinctly new creations. The Nativity of Our Lord, celebrated on December 25, is the second great Christian feast and is most clearly the Father's Day. On this day, God gives His most precious gift of life to the world in the person of His Son, Jesus. Finally, Pentecost is celebrated with a specific focus on the Holy Spirit's presence, power, and purpose. Thus Pentecost is the Spirit's Day. Celebrations of the Epiphany and the Transfiguration of Our Lord also recall Jesus' ministry in power and glory. Holy Trinity Sunday reminds us of the great controversies and struggles in the first three centuries of Christianity as the Church sought to clarify and articulate the biblical revelation of God's unity in three distinct persons. As time passed, notable Church leaders were remembered on their death day, underscoring the fact that death is actually an entrance or birth into the new life with Christ in heaven.

This yearly cycle of the Church Year is helpful to keep the remembrances before us. Just as God commanded the Jewish people to recall how He had delivered them in the past (e.g., the Passover), so, too, early Christians recalled the historic time-related events that were important to their faith, as Jesus had encouraged His disciples to do in Luke 22:19. Second, following their Jewish predecessors, Christians consider the regularity of the holidays as teaching moments, with the celebration of the events of Christ's life used to tell and retell the Good News. Finally, Christians recognize that this life is

not an end in itself. Christ's victory over death means that daily life focuses beyond the mundane to eternity. A calendar of Christian events unites present-day believers with those of the past as well as the future.

THE TIME
OF CHRISTMAS

Wolcum, Wolcum,
Wolcum be thou hevenè king,
Wolcum Yole!
Wolcum, born in one morning,
Wolcum for who we shall sing!
Wolcum be ye, Stevene and Jon,
Wolcum, Innocentes every one,
Wolcum, Thomas marter one,
Wolcum be ye, good Newe yere,
Wolcum, Twelfthe Day both in fere,
Wolcum, seintes lefe and dere
Wolcum Yole, Wolcum Yole, Wolcum!
(Anonymous, English, fourteenth century)

The Savior's birth is second in importance only to His resurrection on Easter Sunday. During Christmas and its season, Christians take time to reflect on God's great and gracious gift of Himself.

ADVENT SEASON

Advent means "coming." In this little season of approximately four weeks, we prepare for our Lord's threefold arrival. Advent begins always the Sunday nearest to St. Andrew's Day. Like Lent, Advent is a season of penitence.

During these days, first we seek from our Lord renewal in His gifts of repentance and faith so that we may greet Him with a joyful, clear conscience when He appears as Judge on the Last Day. Only humble, repentant, Spirit-wrought faith can make us ready to lift up our heads with joyful confidence on that day because our redemption is drawing near.

Second, we seek from Him renewal in His gifts of repentance and faith so that we welcome Him as He comes to us even now in His Means of Grace. The Church tends to offer more opportunities to worship during these days. This allows the light of Christ's Word to shine even more on our hearts and minds. Families may also use an Advent wreath to mark the light of Christ that no darkness can overcome as they gather daily in the home for Bible reading, prayers, and hymn singing.

Third, we seek from Him renewal in His gifts of repentance and faith so that we may welcome our Lord with joy at the great Feast of His Nativity. Through hearing the Word and receiving the Sacrament, we will go in heart and spirit to Bethlehem. In faith, we will behold the baby wrapped in swaddling clothes lying in the manger, hear the song of angels with the shepherds, and fall down before Him with the Magi.

Advent is a yearly gift when Christians discover anew the truth: "In returning and rest you shall be saved; in quietness and in trust shall be your strength" (Isaiah 30:15).

CHRISTMAS SEASON

American culture tends to begin its holiday celebration sometime after Halloween, kicks it into high gear between Thanksgiving and Christmas, and promptly wraps it up on Christmas Day, or certainly by New Year's. In the Church, our experience of these days is markedly different.

The quiet days of fasting and penitential reflection that mark Advent gradually give way on the evening of December 24 to a twelve-day season of intense joy. Christmas, for us, is not only a day. The Feast of the Nativity inaugurates a celebration that stretches for almost two weeks.

Our liturgy provides for three distinct services to begin the feast: a midnight service (often observed with candlelight and focusing upon Luke 2:1–14); a dawn service (rarely observed in our times, but finishing Luke's account with the visit of the shepherds and their joyful return to the fields); and the third and historically chief Divine Service for Christmas Day with its solemn reading from John 1, "And the Word became flesh and dwelt among us."

The days following Christmas celebrate St. Stephen, the first martyr; St. John, the apostle and evangelist; and the Holy Innocents, martyrs. We commemorate the Lord's circumcision and His receiving the name "Jesus" on January 1. The Sundays (there can be one or two) after Christmas commemorate other events early in our Lord's life.

Throughout this season—whenever a saint's day doesn't direct otherwise—the solemn Christmas preface is prayed with its focus upon the Word made flesh. The numerous hymns of Christmas continue to sound in the Church services. The world may be tired of and finished with the feast, but for us there is simply too much to squeeze into a single celebration. Christmas joy spills over and fills these days with praise to the incarnate Lord.

EPIPHANY
SEASON

The Feast of Epiphany (January 6) inaugurates a season of varying length that concludes with the Feast of the Transfiguration of Our Lord. Although most other Christian traditions observe this event on August 6, the Lutheran tradition from the century of the Reformation has seen it as the crowning Feast of Epiphany. The number of Sundays following Epiphany varies by the year, depending on when Lent begins.

Epiphany means "manifestation" or "shining forth." The readings appointed in the Church's lectionary in this season focus on the truth that in our Lord's incarnation, God Himself has come to visit us. If Christmas is the season to celebrate that the Word became *flesh*, Epiphany celebrates that it is the *Word* that became flesh, and we beheld *His glory*.

"In Him all the fullness of God was pleased to dwell," St. Paul proclaimed in Colossians 1:19. These days proclaim this truth by many events. We see it in the miraculous light of Bethlehem's star, in the Father's own voice and the Spirit's descent as a dove at our Lord's Baptism, in the water becoming wine at Jesus' word, in His many miracles of healing, and finally in His Transfiguration, where Jesus' own flesh glitters with the light of His eternal Godhead.

The Epiphany season has another emphasis as well. It is the season when the Church remembers that Christ came *for all*. Epiphany is the preeminent season for missions. By tradition, the Magi were thought to be the firstfruits of the Gentiles to be brought to faith and give Christ their worship. If they were the first, however, they were not the last. "Nations shall come to your light, and kings to the brightness of your rising" (Isaiah 60:3).

THE BAPTISM OF OUR LORD

On this Sunday after the Epiphany, the Holy Church celebrates with great joy the Feast of the **Baptism of Our Lord**.

The Feast of Epiphany originally had gathered into itself the many ways our Lord's glory shone forth in human flesh. It celebrated His birth, the visit of the Magi, His Baptism, and even His changing the water into wine at Cana. Through the years in the Western Churches, each of these spun off to its own day, leaving the Feast of Epiphany solely to celebrate the manifestation of the star to the Magi. Eastern Christians still celebrate the Feast of Epiphany primarily as the feast of our Lord's Baptism. Originally, Western Christians observed the Baptism of Our Lord on the octave of Epiphany. In recent years, it has become customary simply to celebrate it on the Sunday following Epiphany.

Dr. Luther wrote in his House Postils regarding this feast:

Therefore, learn to esteem this festival highly. The star given to the wise men was a manifestation, too, but this was much more wonderful. For here the three preeminent Kings—God the Father, God the Son, God the Holy Spirit— are present as Christ was baptized. And how wondrous that this glorious manifestation occurred at Christ's baptism at the Jordan! Had God so willed, it might have been in the wilderness or in the temple. But it happened at the baptism, in order that we might esteem baptism highly and regard ourselves as nothing other than newly created, holy people by our baptism. (House Postils 1:220)

Matthew's Gospel is literally framed by Baptism. Following the infancy narrative, it starts with Jesus' receiving a sinner's Baptism at the reluctant hands of John "to fulfill all righteousness." It then ends with the command to bring the gift of Baptism to all nations.

In this way, Matthew shows how the Baptism Jesus commands delivers

From God the Father, virgin-born
To us the only Son came down;
By death the font to consecrate,
The faithful to regenerate.
Beginning from His home on high,
In human flesh He came to die;
Creation by His death restored,
And shed new joys of life abroad. (LSB 401:1–2)

---

to poor sinners exactly what happened to Jesus in His Baptism. Baptism in the triune name truly opens heaven, makes you a coheir with the Son as the Father declares the baptized to be His own beloved, and gives the gift of the Holy Spirit. Jesus, of course, needed none of that. He was eternally the Father's beloved Son and the Spirit proceeded eternally from Him. Yet, He came into the flesh to give these gifts to fallen human beings. And He chooses to do so precisely in the waters of Holy Baptism. Additionally, His accepting a Baptism for sinners shows His commitment to embrace His cross, where He who had no sin would become sin for us.

Father in heaven, at the Baptism of Jesus in the Jordan River You proclaimed Him Your beloved Son and anointed Him with the Holy Spirit. Make all who are baptized in His name faithful in their calling as Your children and inheritors with Him of everlasting life; through the same Jesus Christ, our Lord, who lives and reigns with You and the Holy Spirit, one God, now and forever. Amen.

READINGS (ONE-YEAR LECTIONARY)

JOSHUA 3:1–3, 7–8, 13–17 OR ISAIAH 42:1–7 / 1 CORINTHIANS 1:26–31 / MATTHEW 3:13–17

THE TRANSFIGURATION OF OUR LORD

On this last Sunday after the Epiphany, we celebrate with great joy the Feast of **the Transfiguration of our Lord**, God, and Savior, Jesus Christ.

When we think of the Transfiguration, we must above all consider what experiencing this miracle meant to the three men who were there to witness it. That is the clue to what it means to us. You see, this miracle didn't end simply with Jesus saying, "Don't tell anyone." He added, "Don't tell anyone until the Son of Man has been raised from the dead."

Peter, James, and John saw Jesus shine on the mountain not for His own sake, but for theirs and yours. Grasp this and you will love Jesus forever for what He did on the Mount of Transfiguration. The glory that lit up the sky that night is a glimpse of the glory He came to impart to you. The glory that shone from His body is the glory He came to give to you, to your very body, at the Resurrection! The glory of His body that day will be your own when He raises you from death.

In order for that to transpire, Jesus came down one mountain and began to walk toward another, from Tabor to Golgotha. From "this is My beloved Son, with whom I am well pleased" to "My God, My God, why have You forsaken Me?" Because this is how Jesus would bring glory to your body, rescuing you from death and the steely grip of sin—by trading places with you, by owning your shame, by dying lost and alone. He dies your death to give you His life. He bears your shame to give you His glory. That's how much He loves you!

The three that witnessed the Transfiguration no doubt needed that vision just to get them through the horror of Good Friday. Imagine, though, their joy on Easter! They see Jesus, glorified, never again to be touched by death. Imagine how their hearts burst as they saw Him as He was at the

O wondrous type! O vision fair
Of glory that the Church may share,
Which Christ upon the mountain shows,
Where brighter than the sun He glows!
With Moses and Elijah nigh
The incarnate Lord holds converse high;
And from the cloud the Holy One
Bears record to the only Son. (LSB 413:1–2)

Transfiguration, but that way forever, and when He said, "Because I live, you too shall live!"

That changes how you will face your own suffering and death. Baptism makes your final destiny to be a coheir with Christ of His glory. In the water, He says, "You are now My family. You are My sister, My brother. You will share My glory with Me. You will see. The day I raise you from the grave your body will shine like My own!"

O God, in the glorious transfiguration of Your beloved Son, You confirmed the mysteries of the faith by the testimony of Moses and Elijah. In the voice that came from the bright cloud You wonderfully foreshowed our adoption by grace. Mercifully make us coheirs with our King in His glory and bring us to the fullness of our inheritance in heaven; through the same Jesus Christ, our Lord, who lives and reigns with You and the Holy Spirit, one God, now and forever. Amen.

READINGS
EXODUS 24:29–35 *OR* EXODUS 3:1–14 / 2 PETER 1:16–21 / MATTHEW 17:1–9

THE TIME OF EASTER

Christians, to the Paschal Victim
Offer your thankful praises!
The Lamb the sheep has ransomed:
Christ, who only is sinless,
Reconciling sinners to the Father.
Death and life have contended
In that combat stupendous:
The Prince of life, who died,
Reigns immortal. (LSB 460:1)

Easter celebrates the chief event in the life of Christ and was the major celebration among early Christians. Given that Easter is both a movable date and also a principle celebration of the Church Year, the date of Easter determines much of the rest of the Church Year. Generally speaking, Easter is observed on the first Sunday after the first full moon on or after the vernal equinox. The date of Easter will influence the date of Ash Wednesday, the fortieth day (not counting Sundays) before Easter; the date of the Transfiguration, the Sunday before Ash Wednesday; and the number of Sundays in Epiphany and after Pentecost.

LENTEN
SEASON

For forty days, exclusive of the Sundays (which remain celebrations of the Resurrection), the Church observes the season of Lent.

But by Babylon's sad waters
Mourning exiles now are we. (LSB 417:2)

Lent begins with this realization. We are a people in exile. We are wandering far from our true home. And thus the beginning of repentance isn't merely the terror that one finds in wandering in a strange land. The beginning of repentance is always homesickness—something the Holy Spirit stirs up inside us to make us long for home. At Church, we sometimes glimpse that homeland in a way that we experience nowhere else, as the Spirit stirs up the hunger for it within. We ache for home; we long for it. Home is communion with the blessed Trinity in the company of the holy angels and all His redeemed. Lent teaches us to confess how often we've settled down in the land of our exile as though it were our true home. It confronts us with how we have attempted to still the yearning the Spirit has created by losing ourselves in physical or psychological pleasure. It never works. Everything about the Church's existence stirs this homesickness in us. Through her hymns, her liturgy, her readings, her disciplines, she seeks to help us ache and long for that which can never be wholly satisfied this side of heaven. Even the Supper causes the ache to grow more in us, as we realize that this *is* what we long for: not for only the moment on our knees at the rail, but forever to become one with Christ; His life our life; His joy our joy; His peace our peace. Yet the brief taste is enough to assure us that we *have* a home and make us determined to settle for nothing less.

ASH
WEDNESDAY

The Holy Church begins the season of Lent with the observance of **Ash Wednesday**.

Two words for today: Remember. Return.

Remember. That is the word that goes with the ashes for which this day is named: "Remember, O man, that you are dust, and to dust you shall return." Sad words from the saddest day of human history. The day Adam and Eve opened the door and invited in death to their bodies, to this world, to their children's lives. From that day to this, the grave has been our common destiny. Too often we have helped each other to it. As Luther put it in is his hymn: "In the very midst of life snares of death surround us!" (*LSB* 755:1). Accidents, disease, malice, murder—it's all around. So, remember, O man, that you are dust, and to dust you shall return. Ashes to ashes. Dust to dust. The ashes of this day have nothing to do with fasting. Our Lord warned against making a public show of your fasting with disfiguring your face. Instead the ashes of this day simply announce, "You're looking at a dying man living in the midst of dying men. We don't know *when*, but we do know *that* the grave is where we're headed. Remember."

But remember this too: the ashes will go onto your head in the form of a cross. The cross of Him who became dust and ashes that He might lift from our race the sin that is the cause of our death and bear it Himself to destroy it and so wipe out death's power. Remember that He will raise our bodies by His life-giving Spirit on the Last Day. Remember that too!

Remember all this, and remembering, return! "Return to the LORD Your God, for He is gracious and merciful, slow to anger, and abounding in steadfast love." Return because you remember that you are dying and why you are dying. Return to Him who has more life to give you than you've got death, more forgiveness than you've got sin. Return to Him who eagerly

Savior, when in dust to Thee
Low we bow the adoring knee;
*   When, repentant, to the skies*
*   Scarce we lift our weeping eyes;*
O, by all Thy pains and woe
Suffered once for us below,
*   Bending from Thy throne on high,*
*   Hear our penitential cry!* **(LSB 419:1)**

---

waits for you to come to Him. Him who never says, "What? You here *again* for forgiveness?" Rather, Him whose steadfast love always throws His arms around you and welcomes you home.

Let this whole season of Lent be for you a time of returning to Him, each and every day coming to Him who delights to welcome you home. Remember. Return.

Almighty and everlasting God, You despise nothing You have made and forgive the sins of all who are penitent. Create in us new and contrite hearts that lamenting our sins and acknowledging our wretchedness we may receive from You full pardon and forgiveness; through Jesus Christ, our Lord, who lives and reigns with You and the Holy Spirit, one God, now and forever. Amen.

READINGS

JOEL 2:12–19 OR JONAH 3:1–10 / 2 PETER 1:2–11 / MATTHEW 6:(1–6) 16–21

Holy
Week

During the final week of the Lenten season, the Holy Church remembers the events surrounding the Passion of Our Lord.

This Holy Week begins with the Lord's triumphant and joyful entry to Jerusalem. In many congregations, palms are distributed and the people process into the Divine Service, singing, "All glory, laud and honor to You, Redeemer King!" Then crosses and statues may be veiled, as the service moves in a somber direction. Matthew's account of the Passion is read and the Divine Service celebrated. Holy Monday's service traditionally features an extended reading from John 12 ("the hour has come for the Son of Man to be glorified"). Holy Tuesday provides opportunity to hear the account of the Passion from Mark, and Holy Wednesday from Luke.

Holy Thursday, Good Friday, and Holy Saturday form a unit called *Triduum* (Latin for "three days"). Triduum is a single service that continues (with interruptions) from Thursday to Saturday evening. In the evening of Holy Thursday, we especially remember the institution of the Holy Eucharist and the "new command" Jesus gave regarding His love. The altar is stripped as the congregation prays Psalm 22, then leaves in silence. The congregation gathers again on Good Friday for the chief service. The liturgy this day is severely simple, featuring St. John's Passion account, the ancient Bidding Prayer, and the adoration of the crucified. Communion sometimes is celebrated. Many churches also observe Tenebrae, a service where psalms are prayed during growing darkness, symbolizing the extinguishing of our Lord's breath upon the cross. The conclusion of the three-day service, the observance of the great vigil of Easter, constitutes the longest piece of the three-day service. It begins in the darkness where Tenebrae left us and then brings us to the shining light that broke forth in resurrection, celebrating our Passover with Christ from death to life in Holy Baptism and the Eucharist.

PALM
SUNDAY

Today, the Holy Church celebrates with solemn joy **Palm Sunday**, also known as *Palmarum* (one-year lectionary) or the Sunday of the Passion (three-year lectionary).

God rarely seems to act the way we expect He ought to. So when God comes to save the world, we can expect something different. Think Bethlehem or Calvary. He shows Himself to be a God singularly unconcerned about His own dignity. He is a God whose single-minded goal is that we should not die but come to share in His own life—no matter the cost to Himself.

And so, should we really be surprised? How else would such a King make His grand entrance? Remember He was born in a borrowed stable and cradled in a feeding trough. He was destined to be enthroned on a cross and crowned with thorns. So when He makes His grand and glorious entrance into His Holy City, of course He comes astride a borrowed burro, a dinky donkey.

Yet, how fitting that it would be a donkey for *this* King! Had He not come to lift off from our shoulders the burdens that were crushing us and that we could not bear—the burden of our sin, our shame, our death, God's wrath? He is, after all, not entering Jerusalem to fix all the things the crowd (or we!) might think is wrong with the world. He wasn't riding into town to receive their list of grievances and repair the world according to their specifications. He wasn't riding into town to work their will. It was inevitable that they'd end up dismayed with Him, even demanding His death.

He doesn't come to make your life in this world better. Rather, He comes to you because He knows that your life in this world is literally a dead end. He comes to give you the hope of a brand-new life altogether. It's true that He promises the healing of all sorrow, the wiping of every tear, even a joy

Ride on, ride on in majesty!
Thy last and fiercest strife is nigh.
The Father on His sapphire throne
Awaits His own anointed Son. (LSB 441:4)

---

that overflows for eternity. Yet, He promises none of that for *this* age. These are things He promises you in the age to come.

He does have gifts for you now though. He rides to Jerusalem and to Calvary to give you peace, peace that His spilled blood alone can give. He gives you the peace of knowing with certainty that your every sin has been forgiven, covered, atoned for. He rides to Jerusalem to bring you deliverance from fear, both the fear of death and the fear of what others think about you. He comes to bring you the confident freedom of being a beloved child of the heavenly Father, blessed with an inheritance that can never be taken from you.

Almighty and everlasting God, You sent Your Son, our Savior Jesus Christ, to take upon Him our flesh and to suffer death upon the cross. Mercifully grant that we may follow the example of His great humility and patience and be made partakers of His resurrection; through the same, Jesus Christ, our Lord, who lives and reigns with You and the Holy Spirit, one God, now and forever. Amen.

READINGS (ONE-YEAR LECTIONARY)
MATTHEW 21:1–9 OR JOHN 12:12–19 / ZECHARIAH 9:9–12 /
PHILIPPIANS 2:5–11 / MATTHEW 26:1–27:66 OR MATTHEW 27:11–54

Holy (Maundy) Thursday

Today, the Holy Church celebrates **Holy (Maundy) Thursday**.

Having loved His own who were in the world, He loved them to the end. Such is His life, a life that loves to the end. And so a life that serves. He wanted them to understand this. He showed His almighty power with a bowl of water and a towel. He showed them that this is who God is: the One who came not to be served, but to serve.

It was to fill the water with life-giving power that He was preparing to go to His cross. There His love would reach out to the end, loving all—even His enemies, especially His enemies. Thus He would destroy the power of Satan. Love is His power, His indestructible weapon, and His might. His love can never be conquered by bitterness, hatred, or anger. His love triumphs over all. His love dies in the place of all, bearing the sins of all in His own body, pouring out His blood to blot out forever the accusations that were against our race.

Tonight we think of how Love in our flesh loved us so much as to establish a memorial that would be ours for all our days. Yet, this memorial would not have us remember an *absent* Lord, but taste and see the goodness of a *present* one.

By His gift of love He would change us, set us free from the chains of our sinful fears, worries, hatreds, and angers. By His gift of the Eucharist, Love Himself would live in us, would heal us with His peace, would honor us with His life, and would transform us with His joy.

And whenever we say, "But I can't. I can't stop with this sin. I can't overcome this bitterness. I can't give up this worry. I can't, I can't, I can't,"

He blotted out with His own blood
The judgment that against us stood;
For us He full atonement made,
And all our debt He fully paid.
That this forever true shall be
He gives a solemn guarantee:
In this His holy Supper here
We taste His love so sweet, so near. (LSB 634:2–3)

He comes to us in such gentleness. He says, "I know you can't. That's why you need Me. Because I have, I can, and I will. And if you let Me, I will do so also in you. I will be in you a love that loves to the end. I will be in you forgiveness for your sin and healing for your hurts. I will be in you strength in your temptations and hope stronger than all your despair. I will come to you anew as I have always come: to serve you. Out of my great love for you I choose to walk the way of sorrows, shouldering your sin, bearing your curse, loving you all the while without fail, love that reaches to the end and goes on forever. That's who I am. That's who I would be in you. Take, eat, drink, My body, My blood, for you, for forgiveness. Remember."

O Lord, in this wondrous Sacrament You have left us a remembrance of Your Passion. Grant that we may so receive the sacred mystery of Your body and blood that the fruits of Your redemption may continually be manifest in us; for You live and reign with the Father and the Holy Spirit, one God, now and forever. Amen.

READINGS
EXODUS 12:1–14 *OR* EXODUS 24:3–11 / 1 CORINTHIANS 11:23–32 / JOHN 13:1–15 (34–35)

GOOD FRIDAY

Today, the Holy Church honors the death of our Lord and Savior as we celebrate **Good Friday**.

Tetelesthai. One word in Greek. Three in English: "It is finished." More literally, "Fulfilled, completed, accomplished, done." Strange words to hear from the mouth of a man who is preparing to give Himself up to death. They are the words one expects to hear when the artist has finished the masterpiece, or when the poet lays down her pen after writing the perfect poem, or when the craftsman runs his hand along the table he's been laboring over and at last is satisfied that it's all he intended it to be. "It is finished."

The craftsman of the first creation, through whom "all things were made . . . and without whom nothing was made that has been made," is today finishing up a new project as He hangs upon the cross. It's like creation all over again. He now restores a creation that had fallen from its perfection, from its "good" and "very good," by the deceit of the devil and the sin of humanity.

Here is a good and a very good Friday. Here we meet not only the carpenter through whom the world was made, but we meet Him as a man, the carpenter from Nazareth. As the new Adam born of the Virgin soil of Mary, He stands in the place of the First Adam. God had entrusted dominion over this world to Adam, and yet he surrendered it all to the devil. He let sin and death in and thus placed this world out of joint with God, under wrath and judgment. But today we meet the new Adam. Unlike the old, this one has no truck with the devil. This one has come to destroy the works of the devil, to expose his lies, to deliver humanity from his clutches, and to hand our race back to His Father.

Sing, my tongue, the glorious battle;
Sing the ending of the fray.
Now above the cross, the trophy,
Sound the loud triumphant lay;
Tell how Christ, the world's redeemer,
As a victim won the day. (LSB 454:1)

Satan implied that God was holding out on Adam and Eve and so they'd best look out for themselves. We've been doing it ever since. Yet, here for once stood a man, true man, our very brother, who refused that lie. He knew His Father was not holding *out* on us, but holding out *to* us more hope and life than we could ever dream or desire. He is that gift in our flesh.

On this day in our flesh He completes the task given: flawless human obedience. He accomplishes an unbroken "yes" in our flesh. His obedience reached even to death upon a cross. He, the Creator Himself, came into our flesh to offer that perfect obedience to His Father, that He might give it to you as your very own. A perfect righteousness, now complete and completely yours.

Almighty God, graciously behold this Your family for whom our Lord Jesus Christ was willing to be betrayed and delivered into the hands of sinful men to suffer death upon the cross; through the same Jesus Christ, Your Son, our Lord, who lives and reigns with You and the Holy Spirit, one God, now and forever. Amen.

READINGS
ISAIAH 52:13–53:12 / 2 CORINTHIANS 5:14–21 / JOHN 18:1–19:42

HOLY
SATURDAY

Today, the Holy Church celebrates **Holy Saturday**.

It was a Friday in the account of creation when God finished His work. It was a Saturday when He rested from all His labors. He instituted a weekly reminder of this in the Old Testament by establishing the Sabbath. Once a week, God's people were reminded of God's rest and summoned to enter into that rest, to have a day to simply enjoy His good creation without toil and to give thanks to Him.

It was a Friday in the account of redemption when our Savior finished His work. He cried out before His death, as we observed yesterday: "It is finished." The One through whom all things were once made had come into the flesh to restore His creation, to set it back to rights. Having wrought redemption by His suffering on the cross, He announced His work complete and finished. He then slept in death.

His body was quickly taken by Joseph and Nicodemus to Joseph's tomb, and before the sun set His body was laid to rest. As the sun set that Friday, Sabbath began. Even as God had rested from creating and blessed and hallowed the Sabbath rest, so God in our flesh rested from His labors of salvation. He rested in a tomb.

It was, of course, to be a temporary rest. The eternal Son of the Father was sanctifying our graves, our burial sites. He was preparing to make every one of them as temporary as His own. As He laid down and slept in death, but then arose to a life that was forever beyond the grave, so He would teach us to go to our graves as to a little rest, a little Sabbath. Our bodies sleep there for a time, but at the last He will stand on the earth and call with the sound of trumpet. We shall rise and be glorified in our bodies forever.

In life no house, no home
 My Lord on earth might have;
In death no friendly tomb
 But what a stranger gave.
What may I say?
 Heav'n was His home
 But mine the tomb
Wherein He lay. (LSB 430:6)

His burial attests not only to the fact that He did truly die and needed burial. His temporary rest in the tomb opens up to us a new way for His baptized children to look at that hole in the ground. It has been made holy by His presence there. There is nothing we go through that He does not know, even the darkness of the grave closing us in. Yet, as it did not and could not hold Him, neither shall it hold us. We know that beyond our own holy Saturdays there will come the Easter feast that never ends.

O God, creator of heaven and earth, grant that as the crucified body of Your dear Son was laid in the tomb and rested on this holy Sabbath, so we may await with Him the coming of the third day, and rise with Him to newness of life, who lives and reigns with You and the Holy Spirit, one God, now and forever. Amen.

READINGS
DANIEL 6:1–24 / 1 PETER 3:17–22 / MATTHEW 27:57–66

EASTER SEASON

"Alleluia! Christ is risen!" cries the pastor. The people shout back in joy, "He is risen indeed. Alleluia!"

This greeting, by tradition, is not used merely on the Feast Day of the Resurrection of Our Lord. It marks the entire season of Easter as a time for celebrating the Resurrection and the new life our Lord has given us to live in Him.

In the mind of the ancient Church, Easter was not so much a single day as a season of fifty days. The celebration stretched from the Feast of the Resurrection until the arrival of the Day of Pentecost, some fifty days later. Thus, Easter was the fulfillment of which the ancient Israeli jubilee was but a picture. The fifty days of Easter signaled a time of grace, a time for people to return to their true home, freed from every bondage and slavery. In the ancient Church, there was no kneeling during these days in the public service and no fasting. They were days of overflowing joy.

During them all, the joy of resurrection is unpacked. On Easter, of course, we hear the Easter Gospel, with the rest of the feast days during Easter week reveling in the various experiences of the apostles with the Risen One. The Second Sunday of Easter is always dedicated to St. Thomas being summoned from doubt to faith and the beatitude "Blessed are those who have not seen and yet have believed." A beloved Sunday (third in the one-year lectionary, fourth in the three-year) celebrates Christ as the Good Shepherd. Ascension falls on the Thursday after the Sixth Sunday of Easter. The seventh and final Sunday of Easter celebrates Christ seated in majesty at the Father's right hand, interceding for His Church and preparing to pour out His Spirit.

THE RESURRECTION OF OUR LORD (EASTER SUNDAY)

Today, the Holy Church celebrates with overflowing joy her feast of feasts: **the Resurrection of Our Lord (Easter Sunday).**

Once upon a time (a real time, mind you, not an imagined one), there was a wolf. He was a fat old thing. You see, he had it pretty easy. Whenever he wanted to eat, he only had to walk the door of his cave and look at the sheep that fed right outside. He'd eye this one or that one. Then he'd go after it, and with a pretty minimal struggle he'd bring the sheep down and eat away. And the more that he ate, the bigger he grew, and the bigger he grew, the hungrier he got. He was a wicked old thing; sometimes he'd just poke his head out the door and howl. All the sheep began to shiver at the very sound of him. He'd chuckle to himself, "Yes, you better be afraid, you stupid sheep, because one of these days I am going to eat you, and it won't be pleasant. Oh no, it won't. Ha! Ha!" This big, bad wolf had a name that the sheep feared. They had only to think of his name and they'd get wobbly on their knees and some would faint outright. His name, you see, was Death. And Death was always hungry and never satisfied. He was always eating sheep and always wanting more. And he stank. The very smell of him was worse than his name or his howl. He was altogether dreadful, let me tell you! He was in charge, and all the sheep knew it.

There came a day when he was feeling hungrier than usual. He poked his head out the cave door to roar and he couldn't believe his eyes. Why, right there in front of his door, on his very doorstep almost, was the fattest, juiciest sheep he'd ever laid his eyes on. The effrontery of it! He drew in the air to fill his vast lungs and then he let out a stone-splitting howl. All the other sheep in the vicinity turned tail and ran. They were afraid—all but the sheep that still grazed just outside his cave. That sheep paid him no heed at

So let us keep the festival
To which the Lord invites us;
Christ is Himself the joy of all,
The sun that warms and lights us.
Now His grace to us imparts
Eternal sunshine to our hearts;
The night of sin is ended.
Alleluia!
Then let us feast this Easter Day
On Christ, the bread of heaven;
The Word of grace has purged away
The old and evil leaven.
Christ alone our souls will feed;
He is our meat and drink indeed;
Faith lives upon no other!
Alleluia! (LSB 458:6–7)

---

all. Kept on eating, just like it hadn't even heard him. The wolf was getting mad now. He came bounding out the door and right up to that impertinent animal. Again he sucked the air into his lungs, and this time he breathed out right in the sheep's face. The sheep looked up and blinked as the hideous odor of decay was blasted in its face. Totally unconcerned, the sheep blinked and then stared.

Now the wolf was getting himself into quite a tizzy. "Don't you know who I am?" he snarled. The sheep looked at him and said, "Yes. I know." Calm, at peace even. The other sheep began to creep back at a distance to watch. They couldn't believe what they were witnessing. "Well," snarled the wolf, "aren't you afraid?" The sheep looked Death, that old wolf, right in the eyes and said, "Of you? You have got to be kidding!" Now the wolf was so livid with anger that he spoke low and menacing, "You're in for it, lamb chops. You are not going to have it easy. I'm going to take you out slow and painfully." There was a moment of silence and then the sheep said, "I know."

The other sheep had all been watching because they'd never heard anything like this before. But the moment that the wolf pounced, they turned away. A great sadness filled them. They had thought—well, they had scarcely dared to hope—but it was just possible that, this once, the wolf wasn't going to get his way. But their hopes were dashed. It was an awful and ugly sight. The wolf chowed down. It was slow and it was painful, just like he said. And in the end, there was nothing left. He turned his rude face, red with blood, to the other sheep, and he belched. They turned tail and ran, knowing that he'd be back for them one day soon.

As the wolf went back to his cave, he took out a toothpick and cleaned his teeth and he thought that he'd never tasted a sheep that was quite so good before. Nothing tough about that meat. It was tender and rich and really altogether satisfying. The thought hit him with surprise. It was almost as though his insatiable hunger had actually been quenched for once. The thought was a little disturbing. Well, no matter, he thought. And off he went to bed.

When the morning came, the wolf wasn't feeling quite himself. It was almost as though he were getting a bit of stomachache. Such a thing never happened. He always woke up ravenous and went off to start eating first thing in the morning, at least a dozen or so sheep before the dew was off the grass. But not this morning. His stomach *was* grumbling. By noon, he was feeling more than discomfort. He was feeling positively ill. He who had brought such pain on those poor sheep was getting a taste of pain himself—and it was most unpleasant. He kept thinking back to that impertinent sheep he had eaten yesterday afternoon, the one that had tasted so strangely good. Could it actually have been poisoned or something? It wasn't long before he stopped thinking altogether. The pain was just too great. He rolled around on the floor of his den and howled and yammered.

The sheep heard the sound and didn't quite know what to make of it all. They crept cautiously nearer and nearer to the door of his house and turned their heads listening. What could it mean?

It was sometime in the dark of the night that the wolf let out a shuddering howl. Something was alive and moving inside his own gullet. Something that pushed and poked and prodded until with a sudden burst, the gullet was punctured and a hole ripped open. And something, rather, someone stepped right out through the hole, right out of the massive stinking stomach. The wolf felt like he was dying. And I suppose in a way he was.

The figure that stepped out of the wolf's belly was totally unknown to the wolf. Why, it looked like a shepherd. He'd heard of such a critter but had never actually met one. With a staff in His hand, He walked around and stood facing the wolf. And He began to laugh. He laughed, and His laugher burst open the door of the wolf's house. He laughed, and the sheep were filled with bewilderment, wondering what was going on in there. He laughed, and He looked the wolf right in the eye.

"So, you don't recognize Me, old foe? It was I who ate outside your house three days ago. 'Twas I that you promised would die horribly, and how you kept your promise. But what do you propose to do about Me now?"

"You?" The wolf gasped. The voice was the same; he recognized it. This shepherd was indeed the sheep whom he had swallowed down. "You. But how? Oh, the pain!" The shepherd smiled and said, "Well, I think you're pretty harmless now, My friend. Go on and try to eat some of My sheep. I promise you that as fast as you swallow them down I will lead them right out through the hole I made in your stomach. And then you'll never be able to touch them again! Ha!"

The wolf howled in fear and anger and rage, but there was nothing he could do. The Shepherd had tricked him, fooled him good! And the shepherd then stepped outside the door and called the sheep together. They knew His voice too. They'd heard it before. They stood before the Lamb who had become the Shepherd, and they listened as He told them what would happen to them. "You'll die too. He'll come out in a few days and be hungrier than ever. He'll swallow you down. But don't worry. I punched a hole right through his belly and I promise you I'll bring you out again."

Once upon a time, and the time was about two thousand years ago, but the promise still holds: "My sheep hear My voice, and I know them, and they follow Me. I give them eternal life, and they will never perish, and no one will snatch them out of My hand." Let the old wolf howl and snarl all he will. We know about the hole in his stomach. We know about the Sheep who is the Shepherd—our risen and reigning Lord, our Good Shepherd.

O God, for our redemption You gave Your only-begotten Son to the death of the cross and by His glorious resurrection delivered us from the power of the enemy. Grant that all our sin may be drowned through daily repentance and that day by day we may arise to live before You in righteousness and purity forever; through Jesus Christ, our Lord, who lives and reigns with You and the Holy Spirit, one God, now and forever. Amen.

READINGS

JOB 19:23–27 / 1 CORINTHIANS 5:6–8 / MARK 16:1–8

THE ASCENSION OF OUR LORD

Today, forty days after Easter, the Holy Church celebrates with great joy the feast of **the Ascension of Our Lord**.

The Book of Acts relates that after our Lord Jesus rose from the dead, He appeared to His disciples at various times across a period of some forty days. He spoke to them about the Kingdom and the promised coming of the Spirit. They asked Him if it was then that He would restore the Kingdom to Israel. They still didn't understand the full scope of what had happened in His death and resurrection. Jesus told them that it was not for them to know times and seasons that the Father has established. Instead, He had work for them to do. He promised that He would pour out on them His Holy Spirit and in the Spirit's power they shall be His witnesses in Jerusalem, Judea, and to the ends of the earth.

Then, as they looked on, He was lifted up until a cloud hid Him from their sight. As they stared into the sky, perhaps with tears, two angels appeared to them clad in white. "Men of Galilee, why do you stand looking into heaven? This Jesus, who was taken up from you into heaven, will come in the same way as you saw Him go into heaven" (Acts 1:11).

Thus began the Church's long wait. The disciples would die before this promise was fulfilled. Generation after generation would arise in the Church and be succeeded by the next, and still the people of Christ wait. We wait because we know that He who has kept His every other promise to us will not fail to keep the promise of His final appearing. Meanwhile, we live as a community of faith in what is not seen, but what we know to be true. Jesus sits enthroned at the Father's right hand, filling all things with Himself and waiting with us for the Father to signal the moment of His joyous appearing. It is true that He has withdrawn His visible presence

He has raised our human nature
On the clouds to God's right hand;
There we sit in heav'nly places,
There with Him in glory stand.
Jesus reigns, adored by angels;
Man with God is on the throne.
By our mighty Lord's ascension
*We by faith behold our own. (**LSB** 494:5)*

---

from us, but He is nevertheless truly with His Church to the end of the age. Hidden beneath His Means of Grace, He still comes to us. His Ascension did not take Him far; rather it brought heaven near. "Behold, I am with you always," He promised.

In the Church, the paschal candle has stood beside the altar since Easter. In today's liturgy, it is extinguished and moved back to its usual spot by the baptismal font. Even so, the visible presence of Christ has withdrawn into His invisible presence in Word and Sacraments. We join the ages in the long wait for Jesus' final appearing, yet are comforted by His constant nearness.

Almighty God, as Your only-begotten Son, our Lord Jesus Christ, ascended into the heavens, so may we also ascend in heart and mind and continually dwell there with Him, who lives and reigns with You and the Holy Spirit, one God, now and forever. Amen.

READINGS
2 KINGS 2:5–15 / ACTS 1:1–11 / MARK 16:14–20 OR LUKE 24:44–53

PENTECOST

Today, the Holy Church celebrates with greatest joy the Feast of **Pentecost**.

Make no mistake about it: it had all been for this. To pour out the Spirit, He first by that same Spirit had taken flesh from the holy Virgin. To pour out the Spirit, He had lived that life of love, suffered and died, descended to hell, and rose in victory on the third day. To pour out the Spirit, He had ascended into heaven and was seated at the right hand of the Father. It was this day, fifty days after He rose from the dead, that He kept His promise. Jesus poured out His Spirit, and the Spirit rushed into human history like never before. He came with a startling suddenness that was impossible to miss.

He came that morning in wind and flame and the miracle of the apostles proclaiming God's mighty works in languages they'd never learned. But as Peter preached, he invited the people not to wait around for a similar miracle. Rather, he pointed them to where they (and every generation since) may receive the Holy Spirit no less powerfully than the apostles had: "Repent and be baptized every one of you in the name of Jesus Christ for the forgiveness of your sins, and you will receive the gift of the Holy Spirit. For the promise is for you and for your children and for all who are far off, everyone whom the Lord our God calls to Himself."

No less than three thousand people took the plunge that day. Adults and children got into the baptismal water. There they received the exact same Spirit that had fallen on the disciples earlier. "I baptize you in the name of the Father and of the Son and of the Holy Spirit." And He came bringing joy abounding.

276

Come, Holy Ghost, God and Lord,
With all Your graces now outpoured
On each believer's mind and heart;
Your fervent love to them impart.
Lord, by the brightness of Your light
In holy faith Your Church unite;
From ev'ry land and ev'ry tongue
This to Your praise, O Lord, our God, be sung:
Alleluia, alleluia! (LSB 497:1)

Your Baptism is not only your personal Easter, joining you to Christ's death and resurrection; it is also your personal Pentecost. Baptism is where Peter tells you to go to receive in Jesus' name forgiveness for all your sins and a share in the promised Spirit.

And how we need the Holy Spirit! We cannot by our own reason or strength believe in Christ or even come to Him. Faith is always the work and gift of the Holy Spirit. St. Paul declares in 1 Corinthians 2:12: "Now we have received not the spirit of the world, but the Spirit who is from God, *that we might understand the things freely given us by God*" (emphasis added). So we constantly pray with the Church, "Come, Holy Spirit!"

O God, on this day You once taught the hearts of Your faithful people by sending them the light of Your Holy Spirit. Grant us in our day by the same Spirit to have a right understanding in all things and evermore to rejoice in His holy consolation; through Jesus Christ, Your Son, our Lord, who lives and reigns with You and the Holy Spirit, one God, now and forever. Amen.

READINGS
GENESIS 11:1–9 / ACTS 2:1–21 / JOHN 14:23–31

THE
HOLY TRINITY

On this day, the Holy Church celebrates with great joy the Feast of **the Holy Trinity**.

In the first edition of his *Loci Communes*, Philipp Melanchthon begins with the warning that the mysteries of God are to be adored, not investigated. The Feast of the Holy Trinity is not a day for explaining and investigating the unfathomable mystery of God's triune being; it is a day for adoration. Thus, the Athanasian Creed (widely used in Lutheran churches on this day) confesses, "And the catholic faith is this, that we *worship* one God in Trinity and Trinity in Unity, neither confusing the persons nor dividing the substance" (emphasis added).

The worship of the three divine persons who are but one God runs from start to finish in the Church's liturgy. The service begins with the invocation, "In the name of the Father and of the Son and of the Holy Spirit." Note *name*, singular! Three persons yet only one God. Forgiveness is proclaimed in the triune name in the Absolution. We join in singing "Glory be to the Father and to the Son and to the Holy Spirit." We speak to each of the three divine persons in the Kyrie: "Lord, have mercy upon us. Christ, have mercy upon us. Lord, have mercy upon us." We proclaim in the Gloria in Excelsis that Jesus Christ is most high with the Holy Spirit in the Father's glory. There are three alleluias. The Creed has three articles. The "holy, holy, holy" of the Sanctus adores the Trinity with the hosts of heaven. The Aaronic Benediction hints at the Trinity with its threefold repetition of "the Lord." The prayers are offered "through Jesus Christ, our Lord, who lives and reigns with You and the Holy Spirit, one God, now and forever."

Thus, every time the historic liturgy is used, the Trinity is worshiped, confessed, adored. Yet, the Church sets aside the Sunday following Pentecost

Glory be to God the Father,
  Glory be to God the Son,
Glory be to God the Spirit:
  Great Jehovah, Three in One!
    Glory, glory
  While eternal ages run! (**LSB 506:1**)

---

to meditate specifically on the mystery of this true and living God around whom we can never wrap our minds. This day the Church teaches us not to confuse the divine persons, for the Father is not the Son, nor the Son the Holy Spirit. She also teaches us not to divide the Unity, for the Father is God, the Son is God, and the Holy Spirit is God, yet not three gods, but only one. The Proper Preface best captures the joys into which the Church summons us on this day: "It is truly good, right, and salutary that we should at all times and in all places give thanks to You, holy Lord, almighty Father, everlasting God, who with Your only-begotten Son and the Holy Spirit are one God, one Lord. In the confession of the only true God, we worship the Trinity in Person and the Unity in substance of majesty coequal."

Almighty and everlasting God, You have given us grace to acknowledge the glory of the eternal Trinity by the confession of a true faith and to worship the Unity in the power of the Divine Majesty. Keep us steadfast in this faith and defend us from all adversities; for You, O Father, Son, and Holy Spirit, live and reign, one God, now and forever. Amen.

READINGS
Isaiah 6:1–9 / Romans 11:33–36 / John 3:1–15 (16–27)

THE SUNDAYS AFTER PENTECOST

The Sundays after Pentecost (called in the one-year series the Sundays after Trinity) bring us to the *Semester Ecclesiae*, the half-year of the Church. The Time of Christmas and the Time of Easter together constitute the *Semester Domini*, or the half-year of our Lord. The *Semester Domini* focuses upon the events of the Lord's life: His conception and birth, His fasting and temptation, His suffering and death, His resurrection and Ascension, His session at the right hand of the Father, and His pouring out of the Spirit. The *Semester Ecclesiae*, in contrast, focuses much more upon the teachings of the Lord. What exactly does it mean to live by faith in Jesus? How may we love Him in His people? How do we shine the hope that God has given us into this sad world?

For most of these Sundays (unless a major feast or festival interrupts), green is upon the altar. Green bespeaks growth. The words of Psalm 1:3 ring in: "He is like a tree planted by streams of water that yields its fruit in its season, and its leaf does not wither." As the Christian congregation and each member of it lives rooted next to the living waters of God's Word, God constantly gives us His Spirit. The Spirit nourishes our faith, strengthens our love, and helps us be shining witnesses to the everlasting hope our Lord's resurrection brings.

Toward the end of the *Semester Ecclesiae* (around the month of November), the Church invites us to focus primarily upon the last things: the resurrection of the body, the Day of Judgment, eternal life. We do so that we might be a people ready and prepared to welcome Christ when He appears in clouds of light on the Last Day.

Acknowledgments

Introduction

The quotation from Martin Luther is from Luther's Works. Vol. 40. Edited by Conrad Bergendoff. Copyright © 1958 Fortress Press. Used by permission.

The quotation from Urbanus Rhegius is from *Preaching the Reformation. The Homiletical Handbook of Urbanus Rhegius*. Edited, translated, and introduced by Scott Hendrix. Copyright © 2003 Marquette University Press. Excerpted and reprinted by permission of the publisher. All rights reserved. www.marquette.edu/mupress/

The quotations from Berthold von Schenk are from *The Presence*. Copyright © 2010 The American Lutheran Publicity Bureau. Used by permission.

2 January

The prayer is from Wilhelm Loehe, *Agende*, in *Gesammelte Werke*, ed. Klaus Ganzert, vol. 7/1 (Neuendettelsau: Freimund, 1986), 12–15. Translated by David Ratke.

10 January

The quotation from St. Basil is from *De Spiritu Sancto*. Translated by Blomfield Jackson. From *Nicene and Post-Nicene Fathers*, second series. Vol. 8. Edited by Philip Schaff and Henry Wace. New York: The Christian Literature Series, 1898. Revised and edited for New Advent by Kevin Knight. http://www.newadvent.org/fathers/3203.htm.

The quotation from Gregory of Nyssa is from "On the Holy Trinity." Translated by H. A. Wilson. From *Nicene and Post-Nicene Fathers of the Christian Church*, second series. Vol. 5. Edited by Philip Schaff and Henry Wace. New York: The Christian Literature Series, 1886–90.

27 January

The quotation from John Chrysostom is from "Homily 33 on the Acts of the Apostles." Translated by J. Walker, J. Sheppard, and H. Browne, and revised by George B. Stevens. From *Nicene and Post-Nicene Fathers*, first series. Vol 11. Edited by Philip Schaff. New York: The Christian Literature Series, 1889. Revised and edited for New Advent by Kevin Knight. http://www.newadvent.org/fathers/210133.htm.

The quotation from John Chrysostom is the author's translation of the Anaphora of John Chrysostom; Part 1: Prayer to God the Father.

15 February

The quotation from Martin Luther is from *Christian Freedom: Faith Working through Love*. Copyright © 2011 Concordia Publishing House. Used by permission.

23 February

Hymn 667 © Stephen Starke; admin. by Concordia Publishing House.

The quotation from Polycarp is from "Epistle of Polycarp to the Philippians." Translated by Alexander Roberts and James Donaldson. From *Ante-Nicene Fathers*. Vol. 1. Edited by Alexander Roberts, James Donaldson, and A. Cleveland Coxe. New York: The Christian Literature Series, 1885. Revised and edited for New Advent by Kevin Knight. http://www.newadvent.org/fathers/0136.htm.

The quotation from Polycarp is from "The Martyrdom of Polycarp." Translated by Alexander Roberts and James Donaldson. From *Ante-Nicene Fathers*. Vol. 1. Edited by Alexander Roberts, James Donaldson, and A. Cleveland Coxe. New York: The Christian Literature Series, 1885. Revised and edited for New Advent by Kevin Knight. http://www.newadvent.org/fathers/0102.htm.

19 March

Hymn 517, stanza 14 © Gregory J. Wismar. Used by permission.

6 April

The quotation from *Christian Dogmatics* is from Francis Pieper, *Christian Dogmatics*. Vol. 3. Copyright © 1953 Concordia Publishing House.

24 April

The quotation from Martin Luther is from Luther's Works. Vol. 53. Edited by Ulrich S. Leupold. Copyright © 1965 Fortress Press. Used by permission.

2 May

The quotation from Athanasius is from "On the Incarnation of the Word." Translated by Archibald Robertson. From *Nicene and Post-Nicene Fathers*, second series. Vol. 4. Edited by Philip Schaff and Henry Wace. New York: The Christian Literature Series, 1892. Revised and edited for New Advent by Kevin Knight. http://www.newadvent.org/fathers/2802.htm.

The quotation from Athanasius is from "Letter XXXIX." From *Nicene and Post-Nicene Fathers*, second series. Vol. 4. Edited by Philip Schaff and Henry Wace. New York: The Christian Literature Series, 1892.

28 June

The quotation from Irenaeus is from "Against Heresies." From *Ante-Nicene Fathers*. Vol. 1. Edited by Alexander Roberts, James Donaldson, and A. Cleveland Coxe. New York: The Christian Literature Series, 1885. Revised and edited for New Advent by Kevin Knight. http://www.newadvent.org/fathers/0103418.htm.

31 July

The quotation from Martin Luther is from "Preface to Robert Barnes *Confessio Fidei* (1540)." Translated by Mark DeGarmeaux. From pp. 449–51 of vol. 51 of *D. Martin Luthers Werke: Kritische Gesamtausgabe* (Weimar: Hermann Böhlau, 1883–).

24 August

Hymn 518, stanza 23 © Gregory J. Wismar. Used by permission.

29 August

Hymn 518, stanza 24 © Gregory J. Wismar. Used by permission.

23 October

Hymn 518, stanza 27 © Gregory J. Wismar. Used by permission.

31 October

The quotation from Martin Luther is from *Luther's Works*. Vol. 32. Edited by George W. Forell. Copyright © 1958 Fortress Press. Used by permission.

23 November

The quotation from Clement of Rome is from "Clement's First Letter." From *Early Christian Fathers*. Translated and edited by Cyril C. Richardson. Vol. 1 of *The Library of Christian Classics*. Philadelphia: The Westminster Press, 1953.

The Baptism of Our Lord

The quotation from Martin Luther is from *Sermons of Martin Luther*. Vol. 1, *Sermons on Gospel Texts for Advent, Christmas, New Year's Day, Epiphany, Lent, Holy Week and Other Occasions*. Copyright © 1996 Baker Publishing.

INDEX OF SAINTS

IMAGE SOURCES